Contents

◦ fakultativ

◦ fakultativ [ ] nicht in allen Bundesländern obligatorisch

Dein Englischbuch enthält folgende Teile:

UNITS	die sieben Kapitel des Buches
TOPICS	zwei spezielle Themen (*English songs* und *Doing a project*)
REVISION	Grammatik- und Wortschatzübungen zum Selbermachen
INTERPRETING	Dolmetschübungen
UK MAG	Geschichten, Berichte, Lieder usw. in Form einer Jugendzeitschrift
LANGUAGE SUMMARY (S)	eine Zusammenfassung der Grammatik jeder Unit
VOCABULARY (V)	das Wörterverzeichnis zum Lernen der neuen Wörter
DICTIONARY (D)	das alphabetische Wörterverzeichnis zum Nachschlagen
LISTS	Listen: *Names, Countries and Continents, Grammatical terms, Irregular verbs, Classroom phrases*

Jede Unit besteht aus vier Teilen:

'LEAD IN'	die erste (Doppel-)Seite einer Unit; Einstieg in das neue Thema
▶ A: A-SECTION	der neue Lernstoff mit ersten Übungen
▶ P: PRACTICE	Übungen, Sprachspiele und Aktivitäten
▶ T: TEXT	eine interessante, spannende oder lustige Geschichte

In den Units findest du diese Überschriften und Symbole:

ACTIVITY	Aufgaben, bei denen du etwas tust – z.B. malen oder basteln.
GAME	Spiele für zwei, für eine Gruppe oder für die ganze Klasse.
PROJECT	Allein, zu zweit oder in der Gruppe kannst du hier Nachforschungen anstellen, Fotos und Bilder sammeln, malen usw., um dann ein Poster oder etwas anderes zu machen.
▶▶▶ NOW YOU	Hier kannst du über dich selbst sprechen oder schreiben.
FOCUS ON GRAMMAR	Hier machst du Bekanntschaft mit neuen Grammatikstrukturen.
FOCUS ON WORDS	Hier lernst du mit Wörtern umzugehen.
LISTENING	Hier gibt es Hörtexte auf Cassette/CD und dazu Aufgaben im Buch.
REVISION	Hier wird wiederholt – damit du nichts vergisst.
WORD WATCH	Unter dieser Überschrift geht es immer um Wortübungen.
WORKING WITH THE TEXT	Unter dieser Überschrift gibt es Aufgaben zum Text.
HOW TO ...	Hier kannst du die Fertigkeiten *reading, writing, listening, speaking* gezielt trainieren.
◆◆	Partnerarbeit
❖	Gruppenarbeit
1	schwierigere Übung
◆	parallele Übung auf zwei Niveaus

OUR HEROES

We're looking for everyday heroes. Has someone from your town, your street, your school or your family done something special, for example, something brave or kind? Do you have an everyday hero? Write to us and tell us about him or her. Who knows? Perhaps you and your hero will be on the BBC's 'Our Heroes Special'. Send your story now. All letters must be with us by 31st May.

Or come and see us – there's a BBC office near you.

BBC SPECIAL BBC SPECIAL BBC SPECIAL

ACTIVITY

Now start an English album. Stick a photo of one of your heroes in your album.
What makes him or her special?

How many times can you find this poster – or part of it – in the book?

LONDO
Bangor
Anglesey
DUBLIN
WALES
SNOWDONIA NATIONAL PARK
Bus routes in Camden Tow
Camden Town bus timetable
Camden Town
Kentish Town
Hampstead
Jack Straw's Castle
London Transport Buses
CD 7111
Child
Child Rate
London Transport issued subject to conditions – see over
168
Hampstead Heath – Camden Town – Elephan
68
Euston – Camberwell – West Nor
73
Stamford Hill – Eus
74
4
Archway – Finsbury Park – Waterloo
10
Tufnell Park – King's Cross – Hammersmith
Baker Street – Aldwych

Find out as much as you can about Megan Owen from these two pages. Make notes like this:

old home: Wales	*– new home: ...*
old school: Bangor High	*– new school: ...*
old school journey: ...	*– new school journey: ...*
family: ...	
hobbies: ...	

▶▶▶ NOW YOU and a partner

Make notes like this:

my family	*my hobbies*	*my school journey*
mother	*chess*	*by bike*
...	...	

Swap notes with your partner. Then tell your class about your partner.

▶ 1

Until she was thirteen, Megan Owen lived in a village near Bangor, a town in North Wales. Two years ago – when she was eleven years old – her mother died. For a long time Megan was very miserable.
After a year and a half her father found a new job in London. He sold the house in Wales and bought a small flat in London.

▶ 2

In July Mr Owen and Megan moved to the big city.
'New places, new faces! It's better this way,' he said.
Six weeks later Megan wasn't so sure. She hated the noise of the traffic in London and she missed the country. She was lonely without her friends.
'Tomorrow is the first day of term,' she thought, 'and I don't know anyone at Tufnell Park.'

→ P 1, 2, D 1 ■ (p. 115)

▶ 3

It's 8.15 on Tuesday, 10th September.
'Megan, have you packed your rucksack yet?' asks her dad.
'Yes, I have,' she answers. 'But I'm really scared about the new school, Dad!'
'Poor Meg! Oh, have I given you money for your lunch yet?'
'Yes, you have,' Megan laughs. 'Are you nervous about my first day too, Dad?'
'I suppose I am, Meg. Well, good luck!'
'Thanks, Dad.'

? *How did Megan feel*
– when her mother died?
– when she moved to London?
– about her new school?

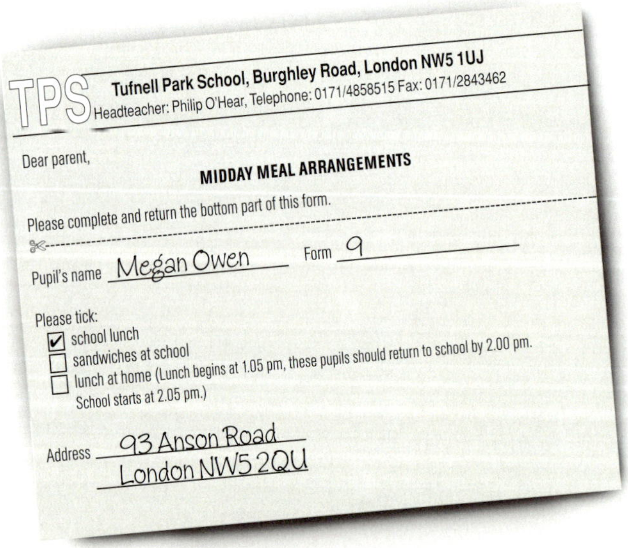

TPS **Tufnell Park School, Burghley Road, London NW5 1UJ**
Headteacher: Philip O'Hear, Telephone: 0171/4858515 Fax: 0171/2843462

Dear parent,

MIDDAY MEAL ARRANGEMENTS

Please complete and return the bottom part of this form.

Pupil's name Megan Owen Form 9

Please tick:
☑ school lunch
☐ sandwiches at school
☐ lunch at home (Lunch begins at 1.05 pm, these pupils should return to school by 2.00 pm. School starts at 2.05 pm.)

Address 93 Anson Road
London NW5 2QU

▶ 4

SECRETARY Next ... and what's your name?
MEGAN I'm Megan Owen.
SECRETARY Ah, yes, Megan. Hello. Have you brought your medical certificate?
MEGAN Yes, I have.
SECRETARY And has your father filled in the midday meal form?
MEGAN Yes, here it is.
SECRETARY Good. Then you can go to your classroom now ... room 103. Good luck, dear.

→ P 3 (D 2 ◆, p. 115), P 4, 5

▶ 5

MEGAN Excuse me, please, where's room 103?

TEACHER Go down the corridor – and then left, up the stairs.

MEGAN Thank you.

MEGAN I'm looking for room 103.

GIRL It's on the left, opposite the library.

MEGAN Thanks.

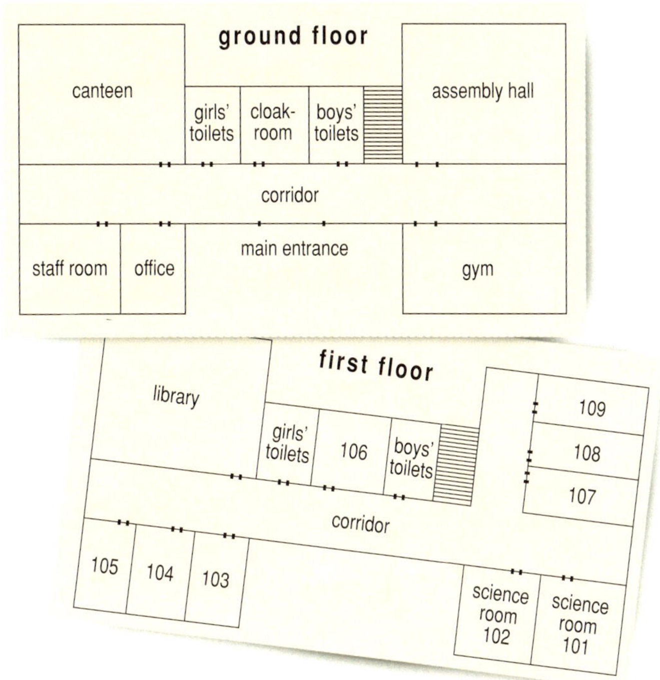

FOCUS ON WORDS

Collect 'school' words. You can make a plan of your school like the plan in A5. Or you can make a network like this:

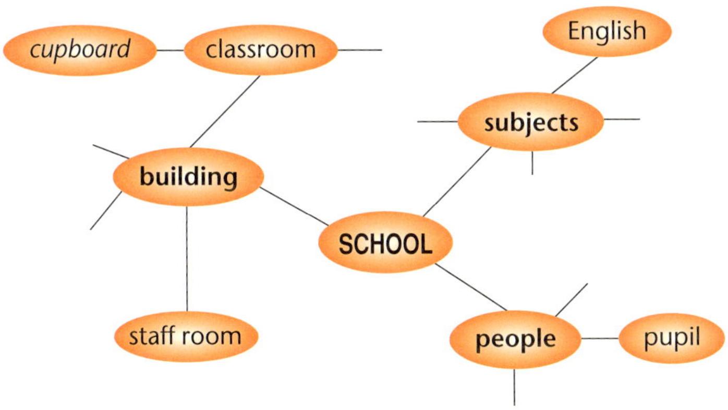

GAME Guess the room

One of you explains the way from your classroom to another room in your school. But don't say the name of the room. The others have to guess. Example:

Go out of the classroom, turn right/left. Go straight down the corridor and then up/down the stairs. The room is next to/opposite the main entrance/... .

– Oh, I think the room is the gym/the ... .

▶ 6

It was almost 9 o'clock when Megan found room 103. There were lots of kids and she felt very nervous. One friendly girl came to talk to her.

'Hi!' she said. 'Are you new?'

'Yes, I'm Megan Owen. Hello.'

'I'm Hannah Grant. Where do you live, Megan?'

'I live in Anson Road,' said Megan.

▶ 7

HANNAH Have you just moved to London, Megan?
MEGAN Yes, I have.
HANNAH When did you move here?
MEGAN We came in July.
HANNAH Have you ever been to London before?
MEGAN No, I haven't.
HANNAH And where are you from?
MEGAN I'm from Wales.
HANNAH Oh, I've been to Wales. I went there for a day last year when I stayed with my cousins Nick and Debbie in Chester. Have you ever been to Chester?
MEGAN No, I've never been there.
HANNAH Pssst. There's Herby – Miss Herbert, our new form teacher, with the timetables.

FOCUS ON GRAMMAR Revision

– *Collect examples of the present perfect and the simple past in A7.*

present perfect: Have you just moved to London?
simple past: When did you move?

– *In some examples, a word or words tell you that you must use the present perfect or the simple past. Make a list:*

present perfect	*simple past*
just	...

– *When do you use the present perfect and when do you use the simple past?*

→ S 1 (p. 121)
→ P 6, 7, D 3■ (p. 115)

▶ 8

TIMETABLE – YEAR 9

	Monday	Tuesday	Wednesday	Thursday	Friday
9.10	Maths	French	RE	Geography	Spanish
9.55	Science	Design & Technology	History	Maths	Science
10.35	Science		English	PE	Science
Break 11.20 – 11.40					
11.40	Art	Geography	Maths	English	RE
12.20	Art	English	French	Spanish	English
Lunch 13.05 – 14.05 and Assembly 14.05 – 14.15					
14.15	History	PE	Science	Design & Technology	Maths
14.55	English	Drama	Dance		Music

HANNAH Yuck! Maths first lesson on Monday. I hate Maths!
MEGAN Oh, I like Maths – I'm good at it. But my favourite subject is Music. What's yours?
HANNAH Mine is English.

▶▶▶ **NOW YOU** and a partner

a *Write your own timetable in English.*

b *Find the differences between Megan's timetable and yours.*

YOU We haven't got Dance, …
YOUR PARTNER Megan hasn't got Biology, but she has got … .

	Monday	Tuesday
8.00-8.45	German	Musi…
8.50-9.35	English	PE
Break		
9.55-10.40	PE	Socia…
10.45-11.30	Chemistry	En…
Break		
11.45-12.30	Social Studies	
Lunch		
13.30-14.15	Maths	
14.20-15.05	Clubs	
15.10-15.55	Clubs	

FOCUS ON WORDS

Have you made a school network? (see p.11) Then you can add new words to it.

Or you can write sentences about the subjects.

+	–
I love Maths/… .	*I hate Geography/… .*
I'm good at Science/… .	*I'm bad at Art/… .*
English/… is easy.	*German/… is hard.*

▶ 9

I met some of Hannah's friends in the canteen at lunch-time – Tony, Marie, Ali and Leroy. We talked about school clubs. There's a choir, a jazz club and an orchestra – great! I was really happy for the first time today. Hannah left the table, and then Tony asked me, 'Have you written your name on the cloakroom wall yet? All new kids have to write their names on the cloakroom wall.' Leroy gave me his felt-tips. And so I went to the cloakroom.

▶ 10

The teacher shouted at me when she came into the cloakroom. She wanted to know my name. I was very frightened and couldn't answer. At that moment Hannah arrived. 'This isn't Megan's fault, Miss Picken,' she said. 'She's new and some kids have played a stupid trick on her.'

▶ 11

Then the teacher smiled. She said something about 'New Kids' Trick Number 25' and she made me clean the wall at once. Hannah is great: she saved me from Miss Picken and she helped me to clean the wall. She's my hero! She has invited me to the market at Camden Lock on Saturday. I'm really excited!

?
- *Look at the picture on the top left. Which boy is Leroy? How do you know?*
- *Hannah said, 'This isn't Megan's fault.' Whose fault was it? Why?*

FOCUS ON WORDS

Lots of adjectives in this unit tell you how people feel. Collect them and make two lists (good feelings and bad feelings). Can you remember more words from books 1 and 2? Add them to your two lists.

+	–
happy	*scared*
…	…

▶▶▶ NOW YOU

a *Look at this poem about feelings.*

Long, long afternoons
One person
No friends
Evening comes
Look – no one – just
You

b *Now can you put this poem in the right order?*

Empty places
Alone in the
Snakes
Room
Danger
Cold nights

c *Write a poem about your feelings. Use one of these adjectives:*
happy, angry, sad, fine

Hours of good feelings
A good …
P …
P
Y

→ P 8, 9, 10
→ UK Mag, pp. 94–96

REVISION

◆◆ 1 ▶ **They moved, too**

a *Not all the other kids in Megan's form are from London. Work with a partner. Partner B: look at the information on page 110. Partner A: look at this information. Ask about Mark, Sandra and Thomas. Write down the missing information in your exercise book.*

	Mark	Sandra	Thomas
Where did … live before?	?	?	In Liverpool.
When … his/her family move?	In 1998.	?	Three years ago.
Why … move?	?	Her dad lost his job.	?
… worry about the new school?	?	No, she didn't.	Only a little.

A Where did Mark live before? B In Cardiff. When did his family …?

b *Complete the text about Mark. Then write about one of the other children.*
Mark lived in Cardiff before he came to London. His family moved to London in … . They moved because his mum … . He worried … .

2 ▶ **What did you do?**

a *Use these phrases in sentences about your holidays/birthday/weekend.*

… in the summer holidays • … on my last birthday
… last weekend

I went to Austria in the summer holidays.

Some ideas
ate / gave
made / drank / flew
was/were in / bought

❖ b *Walk around the classroom. Who did the same things? Find one person for each sentence.*
I went to Austria in the summer holidays. What did you do?

c *Tell your class: I went to Austria in the summer holidays. Christian went there, too.* → D 1 ■ (p. 115)

◆ 3 ▶ **Megan and her father have moved in** → D 2 ◆ (p. 115)
Look at the pictures and say what Megan and her father have done and haven't done.

1

hurt

2

not close

3

not open

4

not put

5

buy

6

cook

1 *Megan's dad has hurt his hand.* 2 *Megan hasn't …*

❖ 4 **LISTENING** What has happened?

a *Make groups of 3 or 4. Listen to the cassette/CD. Talk about what has just happened. The words in the box can help you. Then write one sentence about each situation in your exercise book.*

break • drink • eat
have a shower • see
talk on the phone
wake up

1 *Two people have just talked on the phone.* 2 *A boy has ...*

b *Now compare your group's ideas with other groups' ideas. Check again with the cassette/CD.*

5 ▶ **The evening before Megan's first day at her new school**

a *It's 7 o'clock. Complete these sentences. Add* just *or* yet.

1 Megan (wash) her rucksack.
Megan has just washed her rucksack.
2 Megan (not clean) her shoes.
Megan hasn't cleaned her shoes yet.
3 Megan (not pack) all her things in her rucksack.
4 She (find) her ruler.
5 Megan (check) the bus timetable.
6 But she (not write) to her grandpa.

b *It's 7.15. Complete Mr Owen's questions and give Megan's answers. Add* yet.

1 Meg, have you washed your rucksack *yet?*
Yes Dad, I have.
2 And have you ... your shoes ...?
No, I haven't.
3 And ... all your things in your rucksack ...?
4 And have ... your ruler ...?
5 And ... the bus timetable ...?
6 And ... a letter to Grandpa ...?

6 ▶ Where have they been? When were they there?

1
Italy / last summer

Liz

2
~~Italy~~ / Scotland / a week ago

Eddie

3
~~Scotland~~ / Germany / when he was in Year 10

Charlie

4
~~Germany~~ / the USA, in Chicago / three years ago

Diana

5
~~Chicago~~ / New York / last month

Sarah

6
~~New York~~ / Cardiff / for a week last year

Andy

1 *Liz has been to Italy. She was there last summer.* 2 *Eddie hasn't been to Italy, but he has ...*

7 ▶ What are they doing? Have you ever done it?

a *What are they doing? Choose phrases from the box and make sentences.*

play beach volleyball • sing in a choir
eat Indian food • watch a play
cook a meal

1 *They're playing ...*

◆◆ **b** *Has your partner ever done these things? Did he/she like them? Ask questions.*

A Have you ever played beach volleyball?
B Yes, I have.
A Did you like it?
B Yes, I did./No, I didn't. Have you ever cooked a meal?
A No, I haven't. Have you ever ...?

c *Think of more questions. They can be funny.*

→ D 3 ■ (p. 115)

1

2

3

4

5

WORD WATCH

8 ▶ A funny person, a stupid animal, an exciting book

a *Which adjectives in the box go with:*

a person	*an animal*	*a thing*

beautiful • big • black • blue • boring • brave • brown • busy
cheap • clean • dangerous • dirty • divorced • excited • exciting
expensive • fast • funny • great • green • grey • long • loud • lucky
married • nervous • new • old • quiet • red • sad • short • silly • slow
small • stupid • tall • white • wild • yellow • young

b *Now write three sentences:*
- *one about a person in your family,*
- *one about your pet (or a friend's pet) and*
- *one about something in your room at home.*

1 *My mum is a funny person.*
2 *My friend's dog is a stupid animal.*
3 *'Moby Dick' is an exciting book.*

❖ 9 ▶ A person can have ...

Work in five groups. Each group will work on one of these five groups of words:

clothes, a mouth | a family, a nose | hair, legs | eyes, a voice | hands, teeth

People have got all of these things. Look at the adjectives in P8.
Now each group makes two charts like this:

A person can have	*beautiful*	*clothes.*
	big	
	...	

A person can have a	*beautiful*	*mouth.*
	...	

10 ACTIVITY

Find a picture of a TV, film, sports or music star. Write 3–5 sentences about him/her. Use words from P8 and P9. Example:

This person is a TV star. He's a funny man with a silly face. He has got dark hair. His real name is Rowan Atkinson.

Bring the picture and your text to your next lesson. Make a collage of all the pictures.
Collect all the texts in a box. Each pupil has to take one text out of the box and match it to the right picture on the collage.

1 T

The Boy with Green Hair

Before you read the text, think about this question: You're at a place for the first time. A stranger talks to you. What do you do?

Breakfasts at the weekend were always special for Megan and her dad – no work, no school. Mr Owen made bacon and eggs, Megan made lots of toast and then they sat and talked – sometimes until 11.00 or 11.30. This Saturday Megan talked a lot about her new school and about Hannah.
'I need a hero like Hannah at my new office!' laughed her dad. 'Oh, there's someone at the door.'

'That will be Hannah,' said Megan.
'Meg, how big is the market at Camden Lock?'
'I don't know, Dad.'
'Well, be careful! And don't talk to strangers. And don't ... '

When Hannah and Megan got to the market, it was already very noisy and full. 'People come here from all over London,' Hannah told Megan.
Just then they heard two kids: 'Das ist ja total billig!' – 'Ja, irre!'
'And from all over the world!' laughed Megan.
They met Hannah's friends at a clothes stall. 'Hi, everyone!' said Hannah.
'Oh, these blouses are beautiful!' said Megan. 'My mum made blouses like these.' She looked very sad.
'Well, meet Sue. She made these.'
'Hi!' said the girl behind the stall.
The group walked to the next stall. Then Marie said: 'Let's go to *Scoobidoo*.'
'Good idea!' said Hannah. 'Megan, you wanted to ... Oh no! Where's Megan?!'

Just a minute away from all the people and the noise, Megan sat on a bench by the canal. She looked into the dark water. Then she saw a little bird on the path. It looked up at Megan. She smiled. The bird found a piece of bread and flew away.

Then Megan heard music. She looked around and saw a busker. He looked a bit scary – he was very tall and he had green hair, black clothes and big black shoes. Megan looked away again. 'Maybe I should go back and look for the others,' she thought.

The music came nearer ... *call – and I'll be there, – you've got a friend ...* Suddenly the busker stood in front of her.

Back in the market Hannah was getting nervous.

'"Don't worry!" I said to her dad. "I know Megan is from the country, but I'm a real Londoner: I'll look after her." What will he say? Oh, what has happened to her?'

'Megan comes from the country but she isn't stupid!' said Tony. 'We talked about our favourite café at school. She won't forget a name like *Scoobidoo* – she'll meet us there, you'll see!'

But Hannah was still very worried.

'Sue, have you seen Megan?' she asked.

'She went down to the canal – about five minutes ago. She looked a bit sad.'

'Thanks, Sue,' said Hannah. 'Quick, Tony, let's go!'

The two of them ran through the market. Soon they came to the path by the canal. They looked left, they looked right: no Megan.

'Come on, this way!' Hannah said.

'Oh Hannah, must we?'

'Yes, Tony, we must,' said Hannah. 'Maybe Megan needs our help.'

About half a mile along the canal, the path went through London Zoo. On the other side of the canal you could see the giraffes, and on this side you could see the aviary.

'They're beautiful, Bert!' said Megan as she stood with the busker and watched the birds. 'I can't believe it: you love music *and* birds – like me!' She looked at her watch. 'Oh no! Look at the time! I really must go and meet my friends now ... maybe you would like to come, too.'

'Thank you, Megan ...'

'Megan! Megan!'

They turned around. It was Hannah.

'Megan, is everything all right?' She looked at the boy with green hair.

'Oh, yes!' said Megan. 'I thought London was a terrible, dirty, noisy place. But now I've found this lovely path and the birds in the aviary and ...'

'Well, panic over!' said Tony. 'Come on, everyone, let's go to *Scoobidoo*.'

'I have to go and sing,' said Bert. 'No songs, no money! But I'm down here every Saturday. Maybe I'll see you next week?'

'Maybe,' said Hannah. 'Come on, Megan!'

'Goodbye, Bert!' said Megan.

'Goodbye, Megan. And remember ... *You've got a friend!*'

WORKING WITH THE TEXT

1 ▶ What did you think?

How did you answer the question at the top of page 18? Did Megan do the same?

2 ▶ Right or wrong?

a *Are these statements right or wrong? What do you think?*

1 Megan's father was very happy when Megan left after breakfast.
2 When Hannah and Megan got to the market, it was quiet.
3 Sue said, 'Megan went to the bus stop.'
4 Bert and Megan are friends now.

◆◆ **b** *Make two more statements and show them to your partner. He/She must decide: are they right or wrong? Now it's your partner's turn.*

3 ▶ Hannah's story

Hannah is telling her mum about the morning at Camden Lock. Finish her story.

I went to Megan's house at about 10.30, and I met her dad. He's very nice, but he was a bit nervous. Then Megan and I went to ..., and we met ... . When Megan met Sue, she ... . Suddenly ... . I was getting ... . I asked Sue about Megan and she ... . Tony and I ... . Then we ... . She was with ...

→ TOPIC English Songs, p.32

HOW TO ... say what people feel

1 LISTENING People at Camden Lock

a *Before you listen, imagine how people sound when they are angry. Or excited. Or worried.*
Try to say this sentence 'Where are we going?' with those feelings.

◆◆ **b** *Now listen to three scenes at Camden Lock. How do these people feel?*
- *Eddie*
- *the man behind the stall*
- *Rebecca and Laura*

Choose from:
angry
excited
worried

Check with your partner. Do you agree?

c *Listen again. Try to answer the following questions:*
What's Eddie's problem? What has just happened at the stall? Who is Marvin?

2 SPEAKING How do people feel?

a *First look at these photos and* think *about how the people feel. (You can look at your lists of feelings from page 13.) Why do you think they feel like this?*

1

2

3

4

5

6

◆◆ **b** *Now talk about the photos with your partner.*

A I think the boy in the first photo is scared. That's a very big dog!
B I 'm not sure he's really scared. Maybe he's only ... .

3 WRITING My best friend

Stick two pictures of people into your English album: one of you and one of another person. Write three or more sentences under each picture like this:

This is a picture of my best friend. She has got beautiful, long hair. She is a happy person, and she laughs a lot. But here she is very nervous. I took this photo before the school play.

REMEMBER

- When you listen to people, don't listen only to what they say, but also to how they say things. That helps you to understand the situation better.
- When you describe people, imagine how they feel, too. Try to say why they feel like that.

ARE YOU a Sports Freak – or a Couch Potato?

Write down your answers to these questions. For your score, look at p. 110.

1 How many hours of sport do you do in a week?

A Only the PE lessons at school.
B 1 to 3 hours after school.
C More than 3 hours after school.

2 How many different sports do you do?

A None.
B 1 sport.
C 2 or more sports.

3 What would you most like to do on a sunny winter day?

A Go ice skating or skiing.
B Go ice skating *and* skiing.
C Drink a cup of hot chocolate and watch TV.

4 What would you most like to do on a nice spring or autumn day?

A Go cycling or inline skating.
B Watch TV.
C Go walking.

5 Imagine: You're going to school, and the bus is coming. You're 100 metres from the bus stop. What do you do?

A Run to the bus stop and take the bus to school.
B Walk to the bus stop and wait for the next bus.
C Go back home and go to bed.

6 What do you know about sport?

a The 1996 Summer Olympic Games were in:
A Atlanta.
B Berlin.
C Sydney.

b Match the sports to the pictures:

A riding
B rugby
C cricket
D golf
E badminton
F table tennis

ACTIVITY Fitness for couch potatoes
Listen and move to the music.

▶ 1

'Rubbish!' said David as he threw the magazine away. 'I like sport, but I'm not a freak!' 'Yes, you are, David,' said his friend Colin. 'Everyone in Aberaeron[1] knows you're only interested in rugby and bike racing.' 'Let's go,' said Steve, the team captain. 'I don't want to be late for training.'

[1] Aberaeron [ˌæbər'aɪrən]

▶ 2

There were two really good rugby teams in the county of Dyfed[1] in Wales – the one from Aberaeron and the one from Llandysul[2]. But only one team could play for Dyfed in the Welsh championships. Everyone was excited and the big question at both schools was: 'Will we be the lucky ones?'

→ S 2:1 (p. 122)
→ P 1

[1] Dyfed ['dʌvɪd] [2] Llandysul [læn'dɪsɪl]

▶ 3

THE RULES OF RUGBY

- A rugby ball is oval, not round.
- There are 15 players in a team.
- Players can kick, carry, or throw the ball (but they mustn't throw the ball forward).

- Players can tackle the player with the ball. Then that player has to give up the ball.

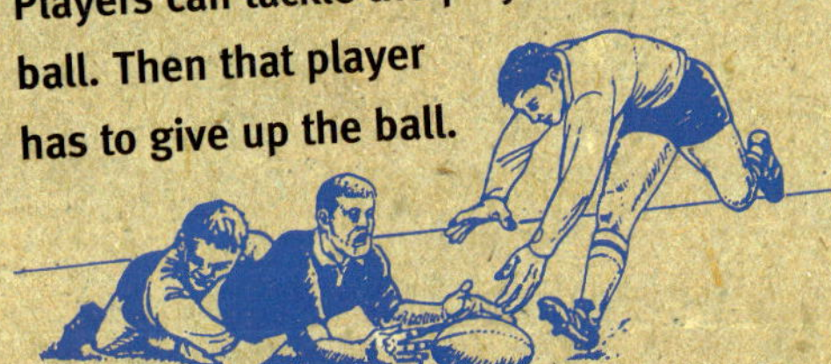

- When a player puts the ball on the ground behind the other team's goal-line, it's a 'try' (5 points).
- After a team gets a try, a player from that team can kick the ball over the other team's goalposts for a 'goal' (2 points).

- A player can also kick the ball over the other team's goalposts when he's running with it (3 points).

▶▶▶ **NOW YOU**

Look at the rules of rugby again. What's different from football? Find three things.

In rugby the ball is oval. In football ... .

Now try and write two or three rules for your favourite game or sport. (You can put them in your album.)

→ P 2, 3, 10, 11, 12

▶ 4

Chwaraeon mwyaf poblogaidd yngh Nghymru

Merched	Bechgyn
1 nofio	pêl droed
2 aerobi…	rygbi
	beicio
	nofio
	loncian
	golff
	tenis
	pêl fasged

Most popular sports in Wales

Girls	Boys
1 swimming	football
2 aerobics	rugby
3 jogging	cycling
4 cycling	swimming
5 badminton	jogging
6 tennis	golf
7 athletics	tennis
8 riding	basketball

? *Look at the two tables.*
In Wales, lots of people speak two languages, Welsh and English.
Can you find the Welsh words for 'girls' and 'boys'? And the word for 'ball'?

FOCUS ON WORDS

Different sports have different verbs.
For example:

Let's do ...	*Let's go ...*	*Let's play ...*
aerobics	*swimming*	*badminton*
athletics	...	...

Can you put the names of the sports in A4 in the right place in the chart?

▶▶▶ NOW YOU and your class

What are the eight most popular sports for boys and girls in your class? Make two groups: girls and boys.
One pupil in each group asks questions: 'Who goes swimming/does aerobics/plays ...?'
Make a table. Are the sports in your class very different from the ones in Wales? → P 9, D 1 ■ (p. 116)

▶ 5

MR JONES So, Tim, do you think our boys will beat Llandysul on Saturday?
MR EVANS I hope they win. They're the better team.
MR JONES So is your David in good form?
MR EVANS He's in top form. The rugby match isn't the problem. He has got a bike race the next day – so he may be a bit tired.
MR PRICE David may be the best athlete in the area, but isn't that too much sport for one weekend?
MR EVANS I don't know ... you might be right. Now let's have another beer.

Star light, star bright

Star light, star bright,
First star I see tonight.
Wish I may, wish I might,
Have the wish I wish tonight:
I hope we win the match on Saturday!

▶▶▶ NOW YOU

Have you got a wish?
Say the poem, close your eyes and make your wish.

▶ 6

When the Aberaeron coach is angry, he shouts. And three days before the big match against Llandysul, he shouted a lot:
'I don't think you want to win!' he said. 'Everyone, run to the goalpost and back. Twenty seconds, no more. Go!!'

The boys ran to the goalpost – again and again and again.
'Now let's see some *real* rugby!' the coach shouted.
That evening David worked very hard until 7.00. He was very tired. When he got home every part of his body hurt.

▶ 7

DAVID Hi, Dad. I'm home.
MR EVANS Hi, David. How was training?
DAVID Terrible! – Where's Mum?
MR EVANS Oh, she phoned an hour ago. She has to work till 9.00 this evening.
DAVID Have you already made something to eat?
MR EVANS Yes, I have. But can you make the salad, please?
DAVID Oh, Dad ...
MR EVANS Look, if you want to eat, make the salad. I've only got two hands, you know.
DAVID Oh, all right.
MR EVANS If we finish quickly, we can watch *Champions' League* after dinner.
DAVID But if we watch *Champions' League*, we can't watch *Wednesday Night Football*.
MR EVANS Life is hard, David.

BBC 1 Wales		HTV Wales		S4C	
6.00	Six O'Clock News	6.00	Home and Away	6.00	Newyddion
6.30	Wales Today	6.25	Wales Tonight	6.15	Heno
7.00	Small Talk	6.50	Coronation Street	7.00	Pobol y Cwm
7.30	Wednesday Night Football: Manchester United v Parma	7.20	Champions' League	7.25	Eisteddfod Yr Urdd Bro Maelor
		10.00	News at Ten		
		10.30	Local News, Weather	8.00	American Football: London Monarchs v Amsterdam Admirals
9.00	Nine O'Clock News	10.40	Football Weekend Countdown		
9.30	Formula One Racing				
11.45	Bad Boys	11.10	Something Strange	10.15	NBA Basketball

Look at the list of TV programmes and make sentences like this:

If they watch ..., they can't watch ... .

→ P 4, D 2■ (p. 116)

▶▶▶ NOW YOU

Are your favourite programmes sometimes on TV at the same time? Talk about the problem like this:

If I watch ..., I can't watch ... .

▶ 8

On Friday evening, David was at his girlfriend's house. He and Emma wanted to plan a bike trip. They had some guidebooks and a brochure – *Cycle Wales* – open in front of them.

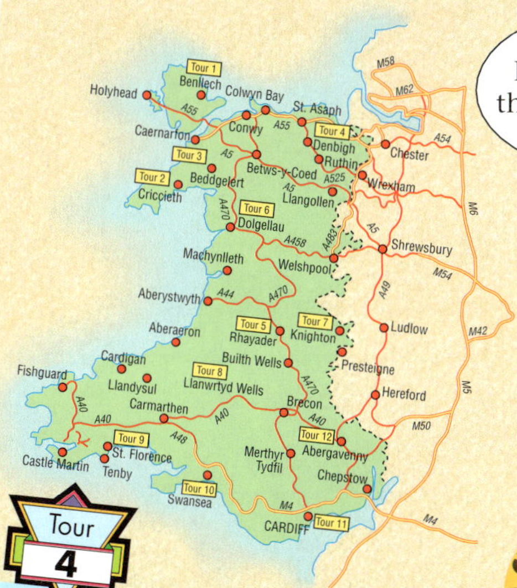

Look, David. If we do this tour, we'll see Snowdonia.

Tour 2

On the road, on cycle tracks; some hills. Look east and you'll see the mountains of Snowdonia. And if you look west, you'll see the coast and the sea.

A word to tourists

CYCLE WALES BEICIO CYMRU

About 550,000 of the 3 million Welsh people speak Welsh. Most Welsh speakers live in the north and west of the country (Tours 1–4 and 6). But don't worry! Most signs are in English and Welsh. And everyone speaks English, too. But why don't you try to learn a little Welsh? Croeso i Gymru! – Welcome to Wales!

Tour 4

Lots of hills, some off-road cyling. On this tour you'll ride through one of the most beautiful valleys in North Wales. See Denbigh with its famous castle and town walls.

If we do this tour, we won't be far from Chester. I've never been there.

Tour 11

All cycle tracks. A tour of South Wales. You can visit Brecon Beacons National Park, ride on the Mountain Railway and spend a day in Cardiff, the exciting Welsh capital.

We'll see lots of new things if we go to the south.

? *What have you learned about Wales?*
Look again at pp. 22–25 and find five facts. Make questions and test your partner.

FOCUS ON GRAMMAR

Copy the table on the right. Look for sentences with 'if' in A7 and A8. Now write the subject and verb forms from the if-clause and the main clause in the table.

Can you say what verb forms appear in the two clauses?

if-clause	*main clause*
you want to eat	*make*
we finish	*we ...*
...	...

→ S 2 : 2 (p. 122)
→ P 5, 6, 7, (D 3 ◆, p. 116), D 4 ■ (p. 116), P 8, 13
→ TOPIC Doing a Project, p. 33 → UK Mag, pp. 97–98

◆◆ 1 ▶ **Excuse me, I've lost my helmet**
Work with a partner. Say what you have lost at school. Swap after each dialogue.

A Excuse me, I've lost my helmet.
B Can you see it here?
A Yes, the green one.

B Excuse me, I've lost my shorts.
A Can you see them here?
B Yes, the black ones.

2 **REVISION** Guess the game
Read the rules of the games and put in the modal verbs. Then try and guess the games. (The answers are on page 110.)

a

can • have to

Two to six people *can* play. You … move your counter[1] around a board[2]. You … buy streets, stations, houses and hotels, but of course you … have lots of money first. Other players … pay you money when they are on your street.

b

can • have to
mustn't • needn't

Two teams of six usually play. (Of course you … have twelve people; smaller groups … play, too.)
They … hit a ball over a net. The ball … fall on the ground, and the players … kick it. They … hit it with their hands, arms – or their heads.

3 **REVISION** I have to, but you don't

a *What sorts of jobs do you have to do at home? What don't you have to do? Make two lists with five things each.*

I have to do the dishes.	*I don't have to … .*
I have to … .	

◆◆ b *Make a window like this:*

	My partner has to …	*My partner doesn't have to …*
I have to …	*do the dishes*	
I don't have to …	*clean the kitchen*	

Now talk to your partner and fill in the window:

A I have to do the dishes. What about you?
B I have to do the dishes, too. / No, I … .
A I don't have to clean the kitchen. What about you?
B I have to clean the kitchen. / I don't … either.

c *Now tell your class. Example: Elke and I have to … . I have to …, but she doesn't … .*

[1]counter Spielstein [2]board (Spiel-)Brett

4 ▶ If or when?

Put in if *or* when.

a

DAVID Can I get you anything from the shop, Dad?
MR EVANS … they have nice tomatoes, please buy some.
DAVID OK, Dad. Is that all?
MR EVANS Oh, … you're there, ask Mr Williams how he is. And … his wife is there, say 'Happy birthday'. It's her birthday tomorrow.

b

COLIN The coach will be angry … I'm late for training again.
DAVID Don't worry. … I've been late, he has never said anything.
COLIN That's because you're the star. But … I'm late, he'll shout at me.
DAVID Well, then let's go together. … he wants to shout, he'll have to shout at both of us.

5 ▶ Snowdonia National Park

Match the sentence halves.

1 If Emma and David go to the north-west,
2 If they go to Snowdonia National Park,
3 'If it isn't too expensive,' said Emma,
4 'If you want to see the mine,' said David,
5 If they have time,
6 If they're late,

they'll have a great day.
they'll finish the day with a trip on a mountain railway.
'you'll have to go without me. I hate dark places.'
they'll be near Snowdonia National Park.
they'll phone their parents so they won't worry.
'we can go on the mine tour.'

♦♦ 6 ▶ A trip around 'Nameshire'

Partner B: look at p. 111.
Partner A: here is a map for a trip around the county of Nameshire. Some of the information about activities in Nameshire is missing. Ask your partner.

A What can I do if I go to Peterpool?
B If you go to Peterpool, you can spend the night in a castle. What can I do if …?

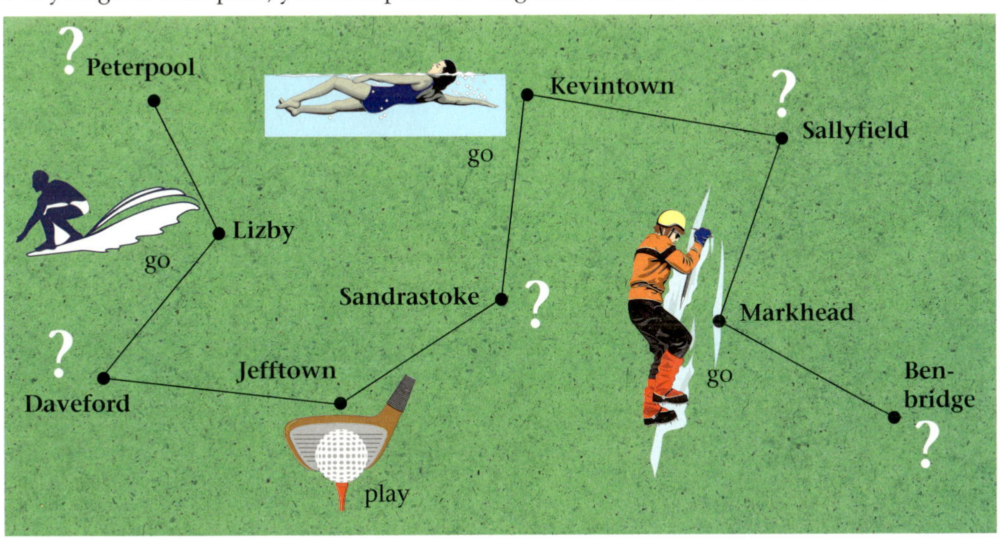

7 ▶ David is thinking ...

→ D 3 ◆ (p. 116)

Fill in the right forms of the verbs.

1 If we *don't play* (not play) well on Saturday, we won't be in the championships.
2 If I'm in bad form, the coach (be) angry.
3 If I'm hurt, I (not go) to the match.
4 If we (lose), mum and dad won't be sad.
5 If Emma doesn't want to do a bike tour with me this summer, I (not go).
6 If we (not do) a bike tour, it'll be a boring holiday.
7 And if it (rain), I won't go out much.

→ D 4 ■ (p. 116)

◆◆ 8 ▶ What if ...?

Partner A: tell your partner what you want to do and when. (Use the information below.) Then answer his or her questions.
Partner B: ask questions about your partner's plans.
Swap after number 4.

1 A ... play tennis next Saturday.
B it – rain?
A do – homework

Example:
A *I want to play tennis next Saturday.*
B *But what will you do if it rains?*
A *Then I'll do my homework.*

2 A ... go sailing at the weekend.
B there – be – no wind?
A visit – friends

3 A ... go on a bike tour with my friends in the holidays.
B they – not want to come?
A go – alone

4 A ... visit my friend David this evening.
B he – not be – at home?
A visit – Julie

5 B ... go to a pop concert on Saturday.
A there – be – no tickets?
B watch – it – on TV

6 B ... buy a new CD player tomorrow.
A it – be – too expensive?
B buy – it – when I have the money

7 B ... go windsurfing on the coast this summer.
A parents – say – no?
B not go – windsurfing

9 LISTENING Radio commentaries

1 *Have you ever listened to sports on the radio? Listen to these sports reporters and try to guess what sports they're talking about. Choose from:*

athletics (running) • basketball
cricket • football • ice-hockey
riding • tennis • volleyball

2 *What words and phrases helped you to guess the sports? As you listen again, write down the words or phrases.*

3 *Here are the words to the song. Do you know it? When and where do people usually sing it? Have you ever sung it? When?*

We are the Champions Words and music by Queen

We are the champions, my friend.
And we'll keep on fighting till[1] the end.
We are the champions. We are the champions.
No time for losers 'cause we are the champions of the world.

[1] (to) keep on fighting till ... ['faɪtɪŋ] *weiterkämpfen bis ...*

WORD WATCH

10 WORD BUILDING

You can sometimes add endings like -er *to the end of words and make new words. In the 'Word building' exercises in this book, you'll learn some of the most important endings. Then you'll understand lots of new words when you hear or read them.*

a *You already know a few nouns like:*

driver • player • teacher • winner

What verbs do they come from?
What are the spelling rules for nouns with an -er *ending? (Think of the spelling rules for an* -ing *ending.)*

b *Make nouns with an* -er *ending from these verbs. Use them in the sentences below.*

listen • lose • run • sing • write

1 Radio Chester is giving away prizes. ...s can win £1,000.
2 Stephen King is a famous ... .
3 Last year 500 ...s ran in this race.
4 My friend has got a beautiful voice. She wants to be a ... .
5 Paul was angry when the other team won the match. He's a very bad ... .

◆◆ **c** *Choose two verbs and make nouns with an* -er *ending. Write sentences for the new nouns. Can your partner guess your words?*

dance • kill • plan • ride
speak • spell • work

Example:
A I don't want to go to the disco because I'm not a good ... .
B Oh, I know. Your word is 'dancer'.

11 WORD LINK

Look at the verbs in the box and say which ones fit in the sentences below.

break • carry • change • cheer
drop • hit • know • lose • make
play • scream • shout
sing • throw • watch • win

1 You can *carry, drop,* ... a ball.
2 You can *break,* ... a rule.
3 A team can ... .
4 Fans at a match can ... .

12 TROUBLE SPOT

Which word is right?

1 It's warm, so I'm not going to (carry/wear) a jacket. But it could be cold later, so I'm going to (carry/wear) a pullover over my arm.
2 You can (bring/take) my CDs home with you, but don't forget to (bring/take) them back tomorrow.
3 You never (hear/listen to) me! Did you (hear/listen to) what I said?
4 Sandra sent me a (card/map) with her address, but I can't find the street on the (card/map).

13 WORD FIELD In the country

a *Look back at* *p. 25* *and collect words for things in the country. Can you add more?*
Draw pictures like the one on the right and label them with your country words.

b *Which words describe the area where you live? You can use them for your project* *(p. 33)**.*

2 T

The Race

Look quickly at the two texts and answer these questions:

- Where can you find texts like these?
- What is the first article about? And the second one?
- What do the two have in common?

Aberaeron will go to championships!

Aberaeron beats Llandysul 24 : 17

by Barry Masters

After their big win against Llandysul at Aberaeron stadium on Saturday, our boys are on their way to the Welsh championships. Aberaeron got the first try after only 17 minutes of play. Aberaeron's team

captain Steve Phillips ran for the try after David Evans threw him the ball. 'It was brilliant,' said Phillips. 'The players from the other team were really surprised. David usually goes for the try, but today he threw me the ball. I just ran with it.'

Local boy 3rd in cycle race

by Will Roberts

Aberaeron's own David Evans, 16, took third place in the Junior Welsh Cycling Championships over 60 kilometres yesterday. He came in after Tom Porter, 18, from Cilcain, and Nathan Rosser, 17, from Cardiff.

The favourites in the race were Evans and 16-year-old Aled Jones, from Bangor. For a long time the two boys were ahead of the others. They were together at the 55-kilometre checkpoint, but Jones fell and was hurt only three kilometres before the finish. An ambulance took him to hospital with a broken leg.

No one knows why Evans did not win after his rival fell. This reporter could not reach him at the weekend for an interview.

Aberaeron Monitor
Monday, 17 September

WORKING WITH THE TEXT

1 ▶ What the newspaper says

Match the two sentence halves.

1 Aberaeron got the first try	Steve could run for the try.
2 David threw the ball to Steve so	David didn't win after his rival fell.
3 The Llandysul players were surprised because	after 17 minutes of play.
4 David Evans and Aled Jones were	Aled fell and broke his leg.
5 Late in the race,	David usually goes for the try.
6 The reporter was surprised that	the favourites in the race.

2 ▶ All about David

Use what you have learned about David in this unit and correct the following text:

David is very interested in sport, but he isn't very good at it. He isn't in any school teams. He and his girlfriend Sarah want to do a bike tour of England in the summer. David cycles a lot, and sometimes he rides in races. In September he won the Junior Welsh Biking Championships. Everyone knows why he won: his rival, Tom Porter, fell and broke his arm.

HOW TO ... listen and find out

1 LISTENING What do you want to find out?

You're going to listen to an interview with Aled Jones.
You know David didn't win the race.
Why not? Here are four different ideas. Match them to the pictures.
Which one do you think is correct?

1 David was so tired after his rugby match on Saturday that he almost fell before he reached the finish.
2 After Aled fell, David looked back and fell, too.
3 David went back and helped Aled, so he lost a lot of time.
4 Without his rival, David wasn't interested in the race, so he didn't ride very fast.

a

b

c

d

2 LISTENING Listen and find out
Now listen to the radio interview with Aled Jones. Which picture shows what happened?

3 LISTENING Listen for details
Read the questions below and make notes like the ones on the right. Then listen and write down your answers.

1 What's the name of the programme on Radio Dyfed?
2 Why did Aled fall after the 55-kilometre checkpoint?
3 How far in front of David was Aled when he fell?
4 What were Aled's first words to David after the accident?
5 Did David wait until the ambulance came?

1. programme
2. why Aled fell
3. how far in front was A
4. A's first words
5. did D wait

REMEMBER
- **Before you listen,** think: What do you already know? What do you want to find out?
- **Then** listen just for what you want to know. Don't worry about other details.
- **If you need more details,** make short notes: first your questions and then – while you are listening – your answers.

◦ English Songs

You can hear English songs everywhere. But how can you understand them better and talk about them? Here are some ideas.

1 *You all know some English songs. What is your favourite one at the moment? How could you describe it? Think about:*
- *the sort of music it is*
- *how slow/fast it is*
- *who the singer/group is*
- *where the singer/group is from*
- *what the song is about*
- *why you like it*

You can use these expressions

It's a pop/rock/folk/rap/jazz/… song.
It's fast, very slow, … / It changes a lot.
It's by a singer/group called …
He's/She's/They're from …
It's a love song. / It's about life in … / …
I like this song because …
it's beautiful.
the singer has got a great voice.
it makes me feel sad/happy/…
it's great for dancing.

2 *Look at the parts of the song below – they are in the wrong order. Try and write the letters in the correct order in your exercise book. Now listen to the song. Did you get it right?*

A You just call out my name,
and you know wherever[1] I am,
I'll come running[2] to see you again.

B When you're down and troubled[3]
and you need some loving care[4],
and nothing, nothing is going right,

C Keep your head together[5],
and call my name out loud.
Soon you'll hear me
knocking at your door[6].

D Close your eyes and think of me
and soon I will be there
to brighten up[7] even[8] your darkest
night.

E If the sky above[9] you
grows[10] dark and full of clouds
and that old north wind begins to
blow,

F Winter, spring[11], summer or fall[12],
all you have to do is call,
and I'll be there.
You've got a friend.

❖ **3** *Here is part of another song. The last word of every line is missing. Try and complete the lines. Check with your group. Give the song a title.*

I miss ☆
but I haven't met you ☆ .
So ☆ –
but it hasn't happened ☆ .
You are ☆
but I haven't met you ☆ .
I ☆
but it hasn't happened ☆ .

And if you believe in ☆
or, what is more ☆ ,
that a dream can come ☆ ,
I will meet ☆ .

Then listen to the song and check.
Is 'your' song or the real song better?

4 *Bring some English songs to school and listen to some of them. How can you describe the songs? Look at* **1** *for help. What are the songs about? Say why you like or don't like the song.*

[1] wherever [weər'evə] *wo auch immer* [2] (to) come running *angelaufen kommen* [3] down and troubled *völlig am Ende* [4] loving care etwa: *liebevolle Zuwendung* [5] Keep your head together. *Versuche, ruhig zu bleiben.* [6] (to) knock at sb.'s door [nɒk] *bei jm. anklopfen* [7] (to) brighten up [ˌbraɪtn‿'ʌp] *erhellen* [8] even ['iːvn] *sogar* [9] above [ə'bʌv] *über* [10] (to) grow [grəʊ] *werden* [11] spring ['sprɪŋ] *Frühling* [12] fall [fɔːl] *(American English) Herbst*

Doing a Project

Imagine your school has invited a group of schoolchildren from Britain to your town or village. Work in groups and plan a tour around your area for them.

1 *First collect ideas in your group.*

You can tell the others your ideas like this:

- ✦ Let's go to (the swimming-pool/zoo/...).
- ✦ What about (the old church/'Pony Ranch'/...)?
- ✦ The (castle/museum/...) is always nice/good/ interesting/... .

2 *You will need lots of information about your area. Where can you get the information?*

3 *Decide how you want to present your tour.*

You can suggest things like this:

- ✦ Let's (make a poster/...).
- ✦ Why don't we make (a map/ brochure/...)?
- ✦ We could do it on my computer.
- ✦ I think we should (make a cassette).
- ✦ I'd like to (make a video).

4 *What words and phrases will you need for your project? Write them down. Then put your project together and check your English. In P13 on page 29 you collected words to describe your area. You can use the dictionary (pp. 166–185) and the language summary (pp. 121–134) to check your English.*

5 *Who will present the different parts of your project? Practise your presentation before you present the tour to your form.*

First we want to show them ... . Then ...

We decided on a tour to ... .

The tour starts at ...

If you look here, you'll see ...

3 UNIT 3 Great Ideas

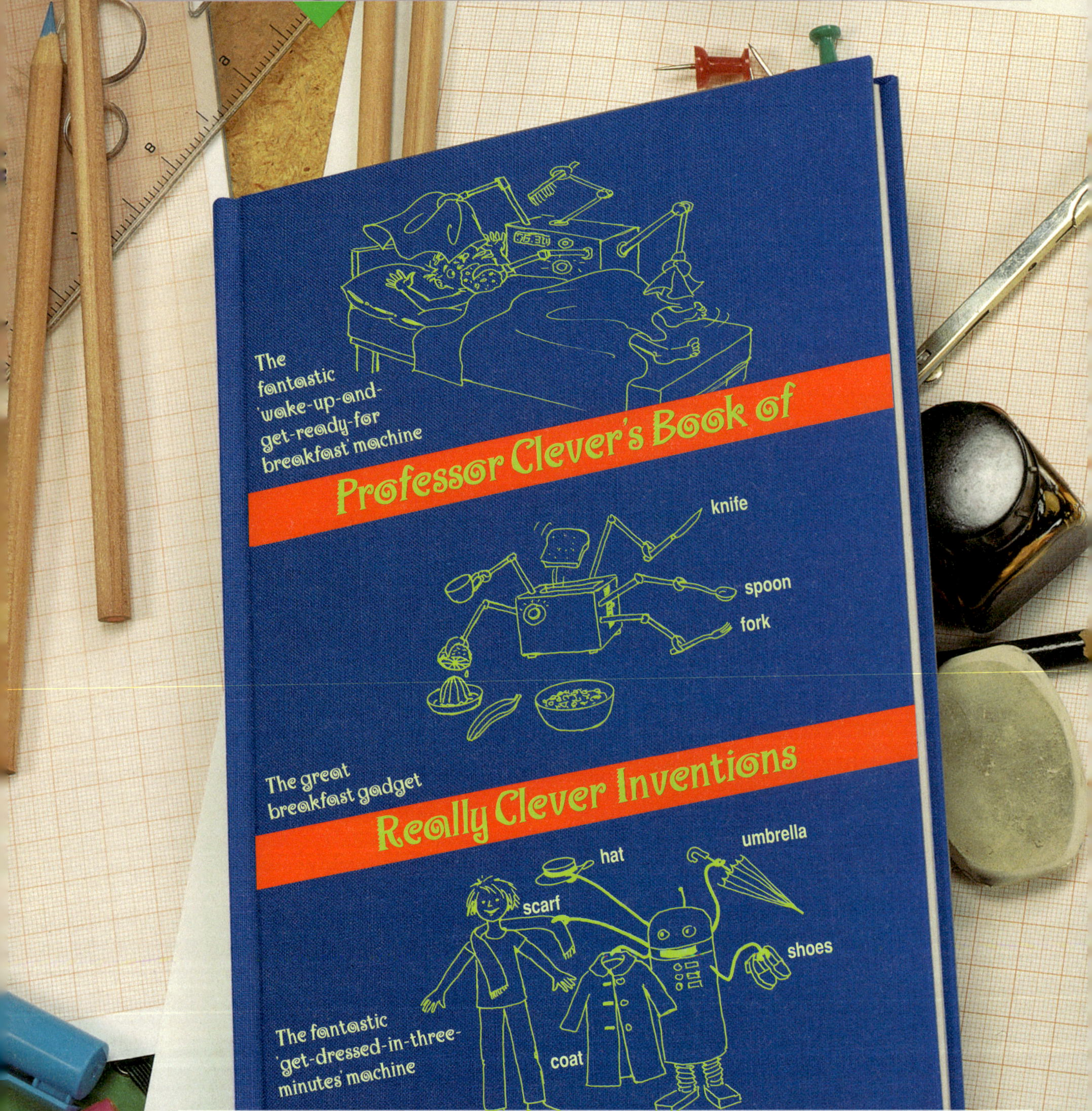

?

- *What do all these fantastic inventions do?*
- *Imagine you can have one of them as a present from Professor Clever. You choose. Explain your choice.*

▶▶▶ NOW YOU

What sort of thing would you like to invent? A 'tidy-up-my-room-in-one-minute' machine perhaps? Or a 'take-the-dog-for-a-walk' machine? What does your invention look like? Draw it and put the picture in your English album. Give it a name and write down what it does.

They all come from Scotland!

Scotland is a small country, but a lot of important inventions and discoveries have come from there. Here are just a few.

The fridge

This keeps food cold. A great Scottish invention by James Thomson.

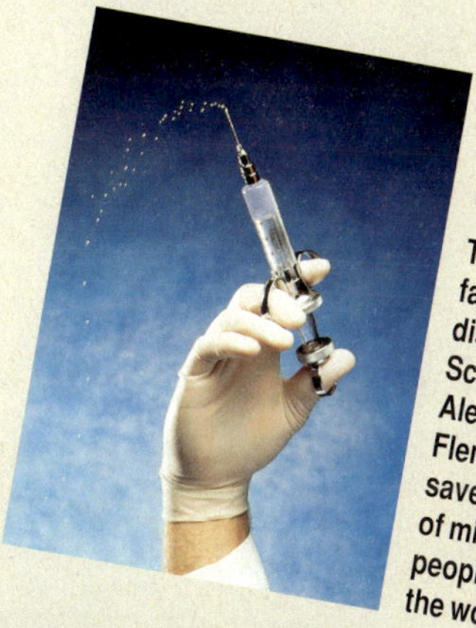

Penicillin

This was a fantastic discovery by Scotsman Alexander Fleming. It has saved the lives of millions of people all over the world.

Television

Think of life without your favourite programme! Difficult? Well, say thank you to Scotsman John Logie Baird.

Radar

This helps planes to land safely. Scottish inventor: Sir James Watson-Watt.

FOCUS ON WORDS

What things, like a cooker or a CD player, do you use at home? Make a table like this:

in the kitchen	*in my room*	*in other rooms*
cooker	*CD player*	*TV (living-room)*
...	...	...

CD player • computer • cooker • fridge
microwave • radio • stereo • TV
telephone • video recorder

▶▶▶ **NOW YOU** and a partner
What things can you live without? What can't you live without? Why not?

I can live without a microwave.
But I can't live without a fridge because I don't like warm milk.

→ P 1

▶ 1

Sheena Stewart looked up from her homework. 'All these fantastic inventions!' she thought. 'But they aren't giving me any ideas for my project! *What* am I going to do?' She looked again at her project instructions.

▶ 2

INVERNESS HIGH SCHOOL – YEAR 9
DESIGN & TECHNOLOGY PROJECT

Instructions

1. This project will be all your own work – your ideas and your designs.
2. Your project must be the answer to a real problem. So first find an interesting problem.
3. What's the best answer to the problem? Why? Make notes.
4. Your project report is very important. So think. How can you explain your ideas best? Don't just write about them. Pictures and photos will help you to get better marks.

▶ 3

ALL THEIR OWN WORK

Jason Barnes and Lucy Rice

This week we're looking at 'Design and Technology'. It isn't an easy subject, and not everyone chooses it.
The pupils who do it have to work very hard. They have to make something that is really all their own work. First they learn skills that will help them with their work. Then they design and make their own gadget.
We talked to lots of young people who are all working on interesting projects. Here are just some of their many gadgets.

JENNY ALSFORD
CHILTERN EDGE SCHOOL

In my family we're all people who are always very busy.
So I'm designing a sort of message box that will help us all. We can leave messages on a cassette. And the box also helps us to plan our everyday lives.

22

LISA McKENNA
INVERNESS HIGH SCHOOL

You don't just make things. You invent things. That means you have to think and plan really carefully before you start. I'm designing an automatic cat feeder. It's a gadget that feeds the cat automatically every day. I can use it when we go away.

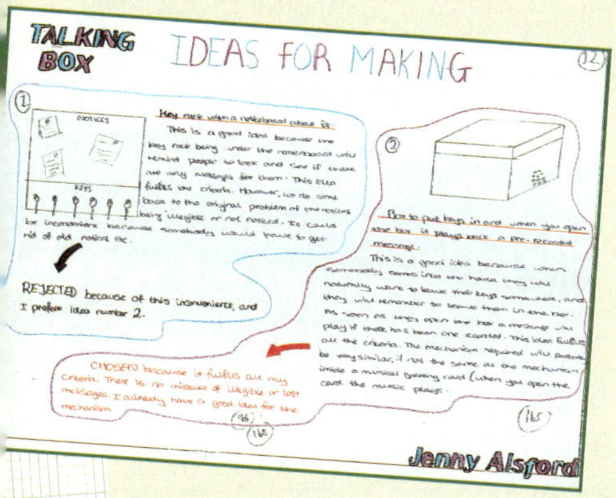

ANDREW MITCHELL
PORTSMOUTH HIGH SCHOOL

I've got no left hand, but I love windsurfing. So I've made a gadget that helps me to stay on my board. I've tried it and it works. That feels great. Maybe I'll be an engineer when I leave school.

FOCUS ON GRAMMAR

a *Look at A3. Find sentences like the ones below and write them in your exercise book. Underline* who *and* that.

The pupils <u>who</u> do it have to work very hard.
They have to make something <u>that</u> is really all their own work.

b *Look at the arrows.*

The pupils who ...
They have to make something that ...
What words do the arrows point back to? Draw arrows like these over the sentences in your exercise book.

c *Look again. When do you use* who *and when do you use* that*? Think about people and things.* → S 3: 1a, b (p. 123)
→ P 2, 3
→ (D 1 ◆, p. 117)
→ D 2 ■ (p. 117)
→ P 8

GAME Who are they?

Think of a famous person. Think of important things about this person. Then say, for example:

She's the woman	*who*	*won at Wimbledon last year.*
He's the man		*flew the first plane.*
		...

The others have to say the name.

▶ **4**

Sheena looked at some old postcards on the wall. They were all from her grandad. He was an engineer whose work took him all over Scotland. But then he had an accident on an oil rig. 'Hey!' she thought. 'Grandad knows *everything* about technology. Maybe he can help!'

→ S 3: 1c (p. 123)
→ P 4

1

2

3

? *Look at grandad's cards (1–3). Then match them to what he wrote (A–C).*

A

Dear Sheena,
Here's a card from the Highland Games at Braemar. I'm working on a new power station in the mountains quite near Braemar, so I went to the Games last Saturday. They were fun, and the music and dancing was great, too. I might go again next year!

Love, Grandad

B

Well, I've just moved to Edinburgh. It's good to be back in good old Scotland after that job down south. London is all right, but there are just too many English people there! Edinburgh is a much better capital city, I think. It's not too big, and it's much friendlier. And there's the wonderful castle on the hill. I love this place!

Love, Grandad

C

Hi Sheena,
I'm now part of the great Scottish oil industry! And this is a picture of my new home – an oil rig. It's an hour by helicopter across the North Sea to land and the city of Aberdeen. And a kilometre under my feet is the 'black gold'. We work very hard when we're on the rig, but then we have long holidays, too.

Love, Grandad

Mis
Sheen
45 Carlt
Inverness

? *Read again and answer these questions.*
- *What did grandad do at Braemar?*
- *Why does grandad like Edinburgh?*
- *What is 'black gold'? Explain the phrase.*

ACTIVITY
Look at an atlas. Can you find Braemar, Aberdeen, Edinburgh, the North Sea and Loch Ness?

→ P5

▶ 6

Sheena got to her grandad's house at one o' clock. It was raining. At first no one came to the door. 'Grandad,' she shouted. Nothing. 'He can't hear me,' she thought. Suddenly the door opened. 'Ah, Sheena! Hello!' Grandad said. 'Sorry I was so slow.'
'That's OK, Grandad. And look, here's your post. Your postbox was full.'
'Oh, thank you! I can't get down there very easily when the weather is bad. These old legs are really useless!'

→ S 3 : 2a (p. 124)
→ P 6

▶ 7

Sheena and her grandad were talking about Sheena's project when she asked about his accident. 'Grandad, what were you doing when you had your accident on that oil rig?'
'Oh, I was pulling a man out of a fire when something heavy fell on me.'
On the bus home Sheena thought about her grandad. She really wanted to help him. But how?
She was looking out of the bus window when she noticed the ski-lifts of Aviemore – and she suddenly had a fantastic idea …

FOCUS ON GRAMMAR

Look at this sentence.

Sheena and her grandad were talking … →
↑ *when she asked about his accident.*

What was going on? (→ past progressive)
What happened? (↑ simple past)

Look at A7. Find more sentences with the past progressive. Write them in your exercise book with → and ↑ .

→ S 3: 2b (p.124)
→ P 7 (D 3 ◆, p. 117)

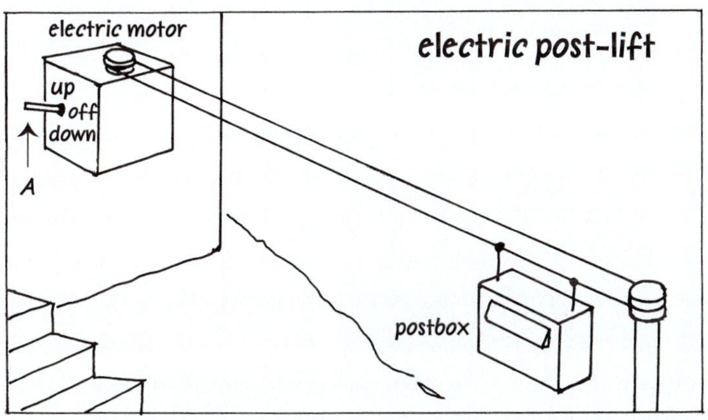

? *How does Sheena's electric post-lift work? Start like this.*

Grandad moves A to UP. This starts the …, and the … comes up. Grandad moves A to OFF and the … stops. He takes his post out of the box. Then he moves A to …

→ P 9, 10
→ UK Mag, pp. 99–101

1 LISTENING How things work

a *Listen to the first part of the cassette/CD. Where can you hear noises like these? What do people do there?*

b *Listen to the second part. What are the people talking about? Choose from:*

bike • CD player • computer • cooker
fitness machine • fridge • microwave
radio • stereo • TV

c *What words or phrases helped you to guess? As you listen again, write them down.*

2 ▶ Who is who at the race?

Read the sentences and find the names of boys 1–5.

- Tom is one of the boys who are wearing red and yellow shirts.
- Gareth and Steve are the boys who are wearing blue shorts.
- Steve is also one of the boys who are wearing red and green shirts.
- Peter is the other boy who is wearing a red and green shirt.
- Peter is also the boy who is standing between Tom and Rod.
- Rod is the only boy who is wearing grey shorts.

3 ▶ What is it? Who is it? → D 1 ◆ (p. 117)

Make sentences about the pictures. Use who *or* that.

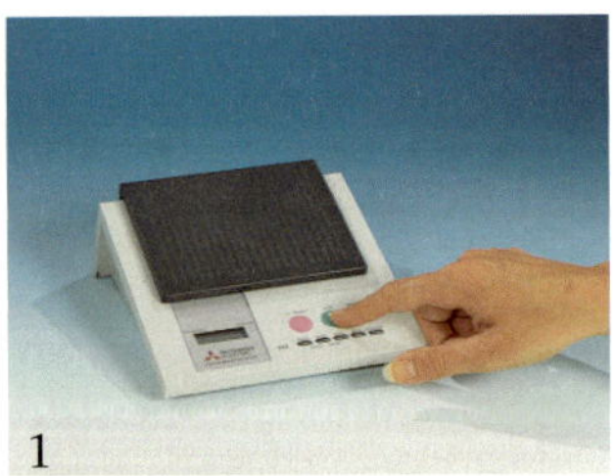
1

2

3

4

5

6

1 It's a machine … answers the phone.
2 She's a person … never has time to talk.
3 It's a gadget … opens tins.
4 He's someone … loves to read.
5 They're children … shout a lot.
6 It's a film … everyone loves.

→ D 2 ■ (p. 117)

4 ▶ Problems with the project!

Add who, that *or* whose.

1 Alexander Graham Bell is also a great inventor *who* came from Scotland.
2 He was a Scottish-American ... most famous invention was the telephone in 1876.
3 The telephone is an invention ... has changed the world.
4 There were other inventors ... were also in the race to invent the telephone.
5 But Bell was the man ... machine won the race.
6 Bell had an assistant ... name was Watson.
7 They worked quietly in a house ... was in the country.
8 After three years they made a telephone ... really worked.
9 But the man ... invention helped to make the modern world did not like it much: he never had one in his own home!

5 REVISION Say nice things about your partner

a *Copy the chart into your exercise book (without the ticks) and add ticks for your partner.*

	write	run	sing	talk	work	learn
easy						✔
clear	✔			✔		
beautiful	✔		✔			
quick		✔		✔		✔
good	✔		✔			✔
hard					✔	

◆◆ **b** *Now tell your partner what you think. For example:*

You learn easily.
You write and sing beautifully.
...

6 ▶ It wasn't me!

Sheena's form is on a trip. Their teacher is asking about a broken radio. Look at the pictures and write the kids' answers.

1 SHEENA *I was writing a letter.*
2 SUE AND RORY *We ... playing football in the garden.*
3 LUCY ... a comic.
4 TINA ... my rucksack.
5 TIM AND LIZ ... TV.
6 TIM Maybe it was the dog. I think it ... (run) after a little cat.

◇ 7 ▶ **That little cat again!** → D 3 ◆ (p. 117)

a *What were these people doing when the accident happened? Use the past progressive or the simple past.*

BOY My dog (run) after a cat when I (stop) him.
GIRL I (ride) home when I (see) a cat in the road.
WOMAN I (stand) at the bus-stop when a cat (go) across the road.
CAR DRIVER I (drive) along the road when that stupid cat (run) in front of me.
OTHER DRIVER I (go) along behind the other car when it suddenly (stop) and … CRASH!

b *What happened? Have you got any ideas? Write them down and draw a picture of the situation.*

WORD WATCH

◆◆ 8 ▶ **A person who … and a thing that …**

Partner B: look at page 111.
Partner A: match the clues to the pictures. Then talk about the pictures like this:

A It's a thing that takes photos.
B Is it a …? / It must be a … .
A That's right. / No, sorry. Try again.

person … designs roads and bridges
thing … carries people from station to station
thing … shows you your lesson times
person … takes other people's things
person … helps in a shop
thing … takes photos

9 **WORD BUILDING** -tion and -ation

Copy and complete the table. Then complete the sentences.

verb	*noun*
invent	*?*
?	*correction*
?	*collection*
?	*imagination*
?	*invitation*
pollute	*?*

1 The CD player was a great *invention* of the 1980s.
2 I'm going to … 100 people to my party.
3 Can you … life without TV? It must be terrible.
4 'Mr Schwarz, could you … my English letter, please?'
5 At home we … paper, bottles and tins for recycling.
6 Planes, cars and fires cause … .

10 **TROUBLE SPOT**

Complete the sentences. Choose the right word in the brackets.

1 Sheena and her family (life/lives) in Scotland, and she loves (life/live) there.
2 Every afternoon she (make/does) her homework.
3 She wants to (make/do) a sort of ski-lift for letters.
4 'Are you (sure/safe) your idea will work?'
5 'Don't worry, Mum. It'll be (sure/safe) and grandad will like it.'
6 Sheena wants to get good (marks/notes) for her school project.
7 She was happy when she found her project (marks/notes) again.

What is Loch Ness?
What do you know about it?

A Loch Ness Mystery

It was a beautiful June morning, and the sun was warm on Loch Ness. 'It's a wonderful day for the search,' said Professor Armstrong. On the water 20 boats were waiting – and with them was a mini-submarine.

'What's your plan, professor?' asked one of the reporters.

'We're going to put the boats in a line across the loch and move slowly from this end of the loch to the other end.'

'How far is that?' asked a French reporter.

'Over 40 kilometres. It's the longest lake in Britain. And the deepest. It's more than 300 metres deep.'

'And how will you find the monster then?'

'We're going to use sonar equipment; it's a kind of underwater radar. My assistant and I will be in *Searcher*, our mini-submarine. If we find something, we'll go down and take a look. If we're lucky, we'll get some good pictures.'

An hour later the boats were moving slowly and quietly along the loch. *Searcher* was out there too, with the professor and her assistant, Ian Banks. On every boat people were sitting by their sonar equipment; they were waiting and watching.

For a long time nothing happened. Then two boats near the south side of the loch found something. It was 10 metres long, and it was 100 metres underwater. They sent a radio message to the submarine, and the professor and Ian moved south.

Searcher sank quietly underwater. They went down to 100 metres.

'Ian turn on the outside lights… now!' said the professor. With the lights they could see a few metres into the black water. 'Oh, no,' said Ian. 'It's just a big piece of wood!'

'Oh, well,' the professor smiled, 'we couldn't really be so lucky so soon. Let's go up again. No, wait.' She was looking hard at the sonar again. 'There's something else,' she said. 'It's farther down … and it's moving. It's coming up towards us fast! And it's big! Quick! Where's the camera? This could be *it*!'

Suddenly there was a crash, and the outside lights went out. 'It has pushed us into that old piece of wood!' the professor shouted. 'Hold on!' Then the submarine rolled over. Ian fell back on his head, and everything went black. *Searcher* crashed into the wood a second time. Ian groaned and asked, 'What's happening? Why are we upside-down?'

'I think it's the monster out there, and I think it's playing with us,' the professor shouted back. 'Maybe it thinks we're another monster!'

Again *Searcher* crashed hard. This time the professor fell badly. She groaned. Then, suddenly, she felt … 'Water! It's coming in through the porthole! Quick, Ian! Get to the controls, and start the engine.'

Ian tried the engine, but nothing happened. He looked at the controls. They were at 120 metres, and they were sinking fast.

'Use the radio. Tell the others. And try the engine again.'

Nothing. No radio. No engine. And the water was rising fast.

They were at 180 metres now. 'This looks bad,' said the professor.
Then they heard a loud 'clunk'. 'It's trying to eat us now!' said the professor. But it wasn't. Ian looked at the controls. *Searcher* wasn't sinking now. Slowly they were going up! ... 178 metres ... 176 metres.

'Look!' Ian said. 'It's trying to help us.'
'Well, it'll have to be quick! In a few minutes *Searcher* will be full of water.'
Minutes passed. Inside the water was rising all the time, but outside the water was less black now.
There was another smaller 'clunk' and something moved along under the submarine, pushed it up – and disappeared again. At last they saw blue sky and three waiting boats through the porthole.
'Quick,' the professor said. 'Let's leave the submarine before we sink again!'
Ian and the professor jumped onto a waiting boat. It was fantastic to see the sun again.
The reporters were not pleased.
'You say you found the monster, but you didn't get any pictures?'
'No, we didn't get any pictures – but I *can* show you something,' the professor said. 'Come with me.' Together they went to *Searcher,* now on one of the boats.
'Look! Here!' said the professor and she pointed to two lines of big dents at the back of *Searcher* – one line on top and one line under the little submarine.
'Monster tooth marks?' asked the French reporter.

WORKING WITH THE TEXT

1 ▶ Finish the sentences

1 Two boats ..., so *Searcher* went ... .
2 It was a ... and not ..., but then ... .
3 Suddenly there was a crash and ... .
4 Soon water ..., and *Searcher* was ... .
5 Then they heard ..., and next they ... .
6 At last they saw ..., then the professor ... .

2 ▶ A radio report

Write a radio report on the search. Use your answers to exercise 1. You can start like this:
This morning on Loch Ness, Professor Armstrong started a new ... . There were 20 boats ...

You can record your report on cassette or put it in your album.

3 ▶ Beyond the text

1 *Do you believe there is a monster in Loch Ness? Why/Why not?*
2 *Why do you think people have often tried to find Nessie? Choose a), b) or c) and explain it.*
a) They really believe in monsters.
b) They want to keep Loch Ness interesting for tourists.
c) They want to find out the truth.

HOW TO ... write a story

❖ 1 **WRITING** What happened on the oil rig?

a *Do you remember that Sheena's grandad had an accident on the oil rig? Here is his story. Work in a group. Write one or two sentences in the simple past about each picture. Say* who *is in the picture,* what *happened and* where *it happened.*

b *To make your list of sentences into an interesting story you should say* when *and* why *things happened, too. In your group, add time phrases and linking words now.*
Time phrases: at once, some minutes later, suddenly, the next moment, then, …
Linking words: and, because, before, but, or, so, when, …

Example: There was a fire in the kitchen. The cook shouted for help.
Better: One evening there was a fire in the kitchen, and the cook shouted for help.

2 **WRITING** Can you tell this story?
Write this story for your English album. Start with a list of sentences. Think of who, what, where, when, why. Begin like this: Two children were out on a lake in their boat.

REMEMBER

- First answer the wh-questions *who, what, where, when* and *why*.
- Tell your story. Use linking words and time phrases.
- Check your story. (Are the vocabulary, grammar and spelling correct?)
- OR: Ask your partner to check it.

4 UNIT 4 London

Thames River Tours

★ See the sights from the river!
★ Tours start at Westminster Pier, only two minutes from the Houses of Parliament.

Summer season
(27 May to 1 September)

1100	1130	1200	1225
1300	1325	1400	1430
1455	1530	1600	1630
1700	1730		1830

Prices
Adult
Students/Senic
Citizens
Child 2–15 yr
Family
(Two adults a
two children)

What do you know about London? Talk about the city.
Look at the brochure on the left. Try to find the place where the Thames River Tours begin on the map.

1 **An important building for Britain's kings and queens**

2 **Sir Christopher Wren's most famous building**

3 **You can be Superman or Superwoman for a day**

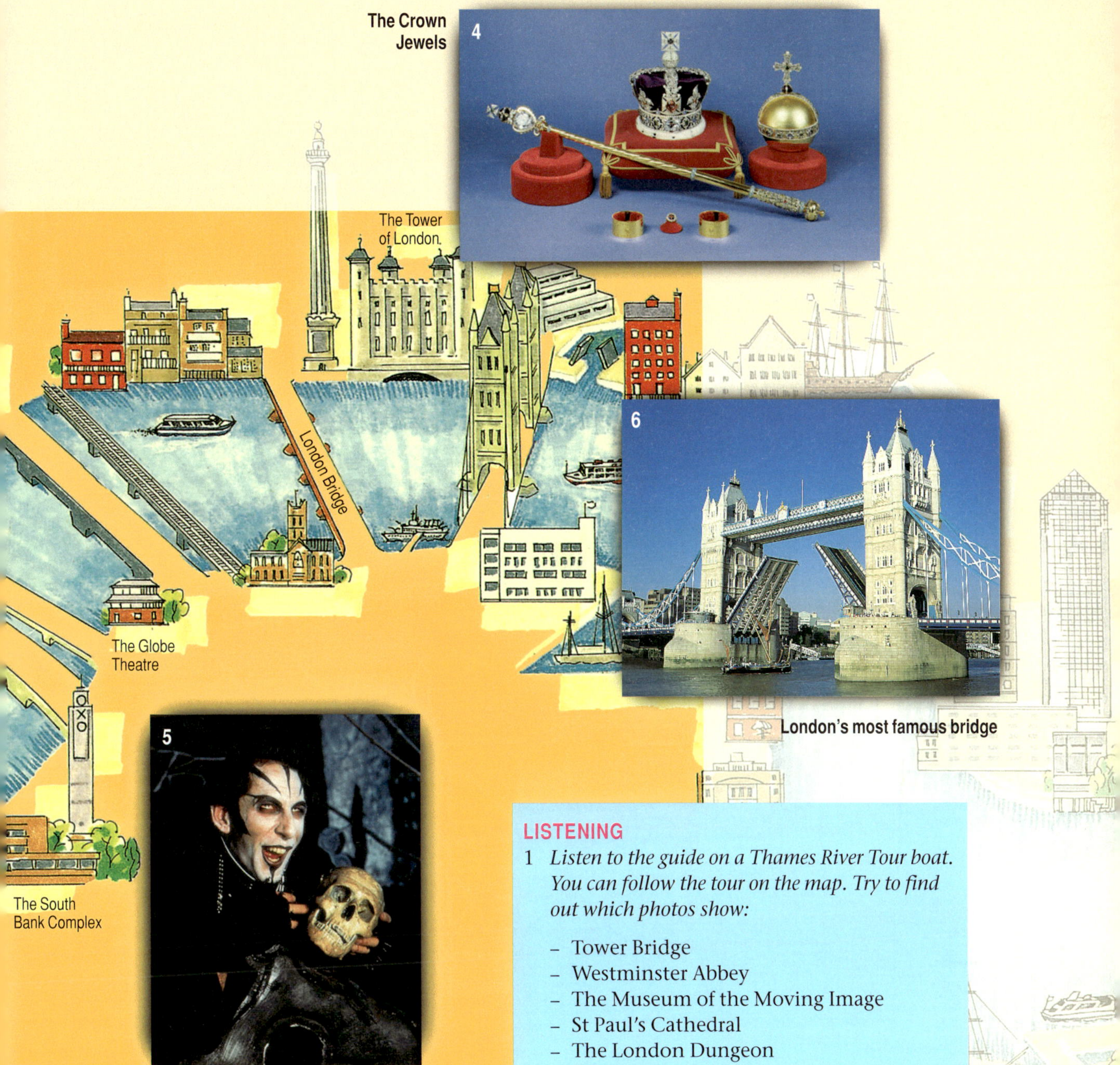

The Crown Jewels

London's most famous bridge

Learn about London's violent history

LISTENING

1 *Listen to the guide on a Thames River Tour boat. You can follow the tour on the map. Try to find out which photos show:*

- Tower Bridge
- Westminster Abbey
- The Museum of the Moving Image
- St Paul's Cathedral
- The London Dungeon
- The Tower of London

2 *Write down the names of two interesting places on the tour. Now listen to the guide again. Write down what you learn about those places.*

3 *Would you like to go to one of these places? Why? Tell your partner.*

... sounds interesting. I'd like to go there because you can ... there.

▶ 1

Some children and teachers from Kingsway High School in Chester have just arrived at Euston Station in London. They are there on a school trip.

MRS MARTIN	OK, everyone. Please stay together. We're going to take the underground to our hotel.
DEBBIE	Can I go and fetch underground maps for everyone, Mrs Martin?
MRS MARTIN	No, Debbie. Please stay with the group. Mr Martin will fetch the maps. – Jeff?
MR MARTIN	I'm on my way, Christine.
MRS MARTIN	Our hotel is near Queensway Station in Bayswater.
MR MARTIN	Yes, Christine, I know. Now, where do they have underground maps ...?
BEN	Over there, Mr Martin, next to the pizza place.

▶ 2

LRT Registered User No 98/2807

? *Where's Euston Station on the underground map?*

It's on the ... Line and the ... Line.

And can you find Queensway?
What's the Kingsway group's best route from Euston Station to Queensway?
They should take the ... line southbound.
They have to change trains at ... .
Then they should take the ... Line westbound to ... and get off there.

GAME

Choose a place in London where you would like to go. Tell your partner. He or she must tell you the best route from Queensway Station. Then swap.

A I'd like to go to ... . What's the best route?

B Well, take the ... Line eastbound / ... . You have to ...

▶ 3

MR MARTIN What would you like to do now?

SITA Well, I've always wanted to see Madame Tussaud's wax museum.

BEN I want to go to the Trocadero. That's the big games arcade at Piccadilly Circus.

NICK You'll need lots of pocket money …

MRS MARTIN Fine. Everyone who wants to go to Madame Tussaud's can go with me. And *Mr* Martin can go with the others to the Trocadero.

MR MARTIN Great!

→ P 1
→ D 1 ■ (p. 118)

▶ 4

Madame Tussaud's is one of the London attractions that you must see.

As a young woman Marie Tussaud learned how to make wax figures. She was soon famous for the masks that she made from dead people's heads in the French Revolution – King Louis XVI of France and his wife Marie-Antoinette are just two of the people who she modelled.

She travelled to Britain with her wax figures in 1802. In 1835 she opened a museum for her figures not far from the one that you can still visit today.

Most of the figures that you can see today are new, but there are still some that Madame Tussaud made before she died in 1850.

Marylebone Road. Baker Street tube. Open 9–5.30. £8.35. Under 16 – £5.25. Family – £21.95.

The man who you see here is Henry VIII. He was king of England from 1509 to 1547. He and his six wives are some of the people who you can meet at Madame Tussaud's.

FOCUS ON GRAMMAR

a *Look at the following. How do you translate* who *in the two examples?*

	object	subject	
The boy		who	is in the magazine …
The boy	who	you	can see in the magazine …

Find the relative clauses in A4. Is the relative pronoun the subject or the object of the relative clause?

→ S 4:1a (p. 125)
→ P 2

b *Now look at A5. Can you find relative clauses there, too? (Here's a clue: there are no relative pronouns.)*

▶ 5

Mr Martin is at the Trocadero with a group of boys and girls from Kingsway.

MR MARTIN Everything is so expensive here!

BEN Not really. Do you remember the skiing holiday you had in Austria?

MR MARTIN Yes, of course.

BEN Was it expensive?

MR MARTIN Yes, very.

BEN Well, you needn't go abroad again! Here's a machine you can use for skiing and it's only £2.

MR MARTIN Virtual skiing, Ben – not the real thing. I like Austria better.

→ S 4:1b (p. 125)
→ P 3, (D 2 ◆, p. 118)
→ P 4, D 3 ■ (p. 118), P 9

GAME I see something you can't see

One pupil must think of something in the classroom. He or she then says, 'I see something you can't see.'
The others ask questions and try to guess:

Is the thing you see red / smaller than a … / …?
Has the thing you see got …?

▶ 6

The next morning, a coach was waiting for the Kingsway group in front of their hotel. It took them everywhere – to all the important sights, and their guide told them everything they wanted to know.

→ P 5

Trafalgar Square with Nelson's Column is a popular place for Londoners and tourists. That's the famous Admiral Lord Nelson on top of the column.

Buckingham Palace is where the king or queen lives. In the summer tourists can visit some of the palace's rooms. Tourists also come to watch the Changing of the Guard ceremony.

THE BIG ISSUE

How much do you know about homelessness? Not many people know about it, but we at *The Big Issue* have all been homeless. We know.

The people who sell *The Big Issue* are homeless. They buy the magazine for 40p and sell it for £1. For a few pence you can help someone to get off the streets. A little money can go a long way.

Please find a little time – talk to us. It's only a few minutes for you, but it means a lot to us. Thank you.

▶ 7

As in most big cities there are a lot of homeless people on the streets of London, like that young woman. She stands there every day and sells *The Big Issue*, a magazine that helps homeless people. She gets 60p for each magazine she sells.

▶▶▶ **NOW YOU**

Think of questions you would like to ask the woman in the photo.

Imagine what her answers might be.

Some ideas ...

name?
how old?
where from?
how long ...?

→ S 4: 2 (p. 126)
→ P 6, 7, 10

▶ 8

The group from Chester liked the London buses. They could see the sights and listen to other passengers' conversations …

WOMAN	Why aren't we moving?
MAN	Traffic.
WOMAN	It gets worse all the time.
MAN	Yeah, it's terrible.
WOMAN	Ah well, late for work again.
MAN	Right: I'm getting off and walking to the office! See you tomorrow.

? *What time of day do you think it is – morning, afternoon or evening? Why?*

→ P 8

FOCUS ON WORDS

Look at pages 46–50 and collect the 'city' words (station, the underground, …). *Add other words you know and put them in groups (for example* transport: bus, tram, …; buildings: cathedral, town hall, …). *How can you arrange them?*
Continue to collect these words for the rest of the unit.

▶ 9

Dear Mum and Dad,
London is great! We've just spent our last afternoon at Covent Garden. It was very exciting! There was a fantastic mime group there.
We were all watching them. Suddenly one of the boys in the group stopped and ran to Mrs Martin. That's when we saw the man – a pickpocket! He was trying to get Mrs Martin's money out of her bag. But Winston – that was the boy's name – chased him away before he could get it. Winston was a real hero!
We're going to the theatre now.
Love,
Debbie and **Nick**

Winston, the boy who saved Mrs Martin's handbag – and everyone's day

▶▶▶ NOW YOU

Think of a city you have visited or a city you would like to visit. Imagine you are there. Write a postcard for your English album. Here's some help:

Dear …,
… is great/fun/ interesting/boring/… .
The weather … . We've just …

▶ 10

On Sunday the Kingsway group wanted to go to the Chinese New Year parade. 'Remember, everyone,' Mr Martin said, 'we have to be on the train at 4.30. So please stay together.'
'The parade is on Gerrard Street. It can't be far,' Mrs Martin said.
Mrs Martin went and asked a police officer, 'Excuse me. Can you tell me the way to Gerrard Street, please?'
'So you're going to the parade?' the woman said. 'Well, go up Shaftesbury Avenue, past the Trocadero, until you come to Wardour Street. Turn right there. The second street on your left is Gerrard Street.'

? *Can you find Gerrard Street on the map? Where did Mr Martin ask the police officer for directions? (Here's a clue: They were at an underground station.)* → P 11, 12

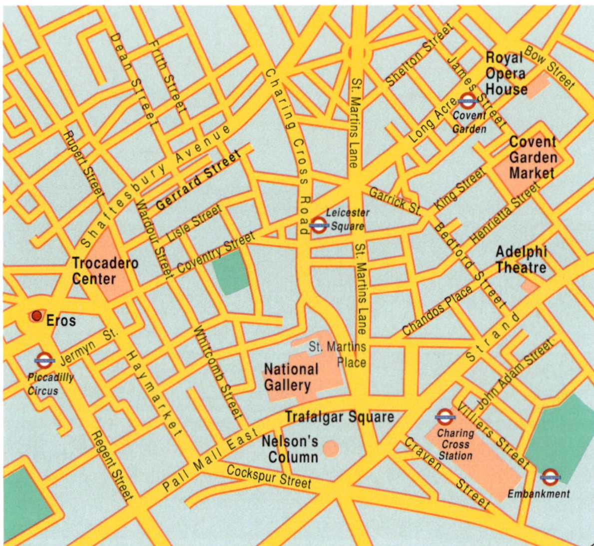

▶ 11

On the train back to Chester on Sunday afternoon, Debbie said, 'Mr Martin, there's one thing I don't understand.'
'What's that, Debbie?'
'Well, I was talking to an old Chinese man at the parade, and he said he was a Londoner. He lives there, but he wasn't born there. *You* say you're a Londoner because you were born there. But you don't live there. What exactly *is* a Londoner?'
Mr Martin looked pleased, but Mrs Martin didn't. 'Oh no,' Mrs Martin said. 'He's going to sing, and it's all your fault ...'

→ UK Mag, pp.102–103

1 **REVISION** I like teachers who …

Choose five words from the box. Say who or what you like, for example:

I like teachers who are funny. I love books that are exciting.

books • boys • cars • clothes • films • games • girls • people • pets • teachers

→ D 1 ■ (p. 118)

2 ▶ **At the Trocadero**

Match the sentence halves and put in the right relative pronoun: that *or* who.

1 The Trocadero is one of the attractions		you see at the Trocadero are tourists.
2 It has got all the newest machines	who	you can ask if you need help.
3 Too many of the video games	that	a lot of young tourists want to see.
4 Most of the people		they have at the Trocadero are very violent.
5 They've got lots of assistants		kids want to try.

3 ▶ **A trip to London** → D 2 ◆ (p. 118)

Match the sentence halves.

1 London is a city	we are going to see tomorrow.'
2 'Look, there is the cathedral	he saw at the Trocadero.
3 St Paul's Cathedral is a beautiful building	I have always wanted to visit
4 Madame Tussaud's is a famous museum	he bought in Chinatown.
5 Ben has got a postcard of Trafalgar Square	you can visit in London.
6 Mr Martin didn't like the skiing machine	Mr Martin loves.

4 ▶ **In London**

Complete the relative clauses.
Where can you leave out who *or* that *?*

1 The girl … is filming in London is Jenny. The sight … she is filming is Nelson's Column.
2 The Chester group wanted maps … show all the London sights. The map … Ben bought was cheap.
3 The group … went to Madame Tussaud's had a great time. The figure … they all loved was Marilyn Monroe.

1

2

3

→ D 3 ■ (p. 118)

5 ▶ **Every…**

Complete Ben's report about the trip to London. Use everyone, everything, everywhere.

In London you can see tourists … . As a tourist you need lots of money. … is expensive in London. When you visit the sights … wants your money! … who visits London goes shopping. In the big shops in Oxford Street and in Harrods you can buy … . And there are markets … . It's great!

6 REVISION London in numbers

Make questions with How much *and* How many. *Then find the correct answers on the right.*

How much …
How many …

water do Londoners use every day?
taxis are there in London?
bread does a Londoner eat every week?
kilometres of streets and roads are there?
people live in London?
money does a tourist spend in London?
trees are there in London's parks and streets?
time do you need for a river tour from Westminster to Greenwich?
restaurants are there in London?

12,381 kilometres.
£310.
45 minutes.
5723.
8,897,000 people.
About 5 million.
18,253.
About 1 kilo.
2000 million litres.

◆◆ 7 ▶ At a party

Partner B: look at *p. 112.*

Partner A: look at the picture with food and drinks at a party. Your partner has got a different picture. Ask about the things in the list below.

Then use the picture and answer your partner's questions with a few / a lot *or* a little / a lot.

A Have you got any apples?
B Yes, I've got a few / a lot.
No, I haven't got any.

A Have you got any bread?
B Yes, I've got a little / a lot.
No, I haven't got any.

8 LISTENING Conversations on a London bus

Copy the chart below. Then listen to three conversations on a London bus.
- *Who is talking?*
- *Do the people live in London, or are they visiting London?*

	Speakers	Londoner/visitor?
1	a man, …	two Londoners, …
2	…	
3	…	

WORD WATCH

◆◆ 9 ▶ How to explain words

a *Partner B: look at p. 112.*
Partner A: try to explain these words to your partner. Can he or she guess the words?

headteacher • penguin • winner

The following expressions will help you
It's someone / a person (who) …
It's an animal (that) …
It's something / a thing (that) …

A It's a person who works at a school and is the boss.
B Do you mean a …?
A Yes, that's right. / No, guess again.

b Relative clauses can be very useful when you want to explain a German word you don't know in English. A really clear explanation will help people to understand you better. Compare:
– A 'Taschenrechner' is something (that) you use for maths.
– A 'Taschenrechner' is a gadget (that) …
– A 'Taschenrechner' is a small gadget (that) …

Now try to explain these German words to your partner. Can he or she guess the words?

Papagei • Schauspielerin
Waschmaschine • Wecker

10 WORD BUILDING

You already know the word homelessness. *What adjective does it come from?*
Now make new nouns with a -ness *ending from these adjectives. Mind the spelling.*
For example:
friendly + -ness   friendliness

dark • friendly • happy • ill
kind • lonely • sad • silly

Then use the nouns in the sentences below.

1 When I go to Britain, I always like the *friendliness* of the people.
2 My aunt always sends me a present on my birthday. Then I send her a card and thank her for her … .
3 The doctors don't know what's wrong with Sandra. She has got a terrible … .
4 Everyone loved the king, so there was great … in the country after he died. The queen died a few months later. People say she died of … .
5 I don't want to be an underground train driver. Just imagine: eight hours of … every day!
6 Nick likes to play the clown at school. His … often gets him into trouble with his teachers.
7 Money is nice, but it can't buy you … .

11 TROUBLE SPOT 'the' or not?

Do we use 'the' with these expressions? (If you aren't sure, look back at the unit.)

two minutes from … Houses of … Parliament (p. 46)
from … Kingsway High School (p. 48)
at … Euston Station (p. 48)
take … underground (p. 48)
at … Piccadilly Circus (p. 49)
to … Trocadero (p. 49)
at … Covent Garden (p. 51)
on … Gerrard Street (p. 52)

12 WORD LINK

Find verbs from the box for the following groups of words:

get • have • take • visit

… a bath, breakfast, lunch, a shower, dinner, time
… friends, a museum, London
… dressed, off a train, on a bus, pocket money, ready, to Trafalgar Square
… off clothes, a photo, a train, the underground

4 T

Save the Crown Jewels

The following text is a maze. Don't try to read it like other texts! Just go where the text tells you. You are in the story: you are Agent 101, and you must save the Crown Jewels. At each step, you and your partner have to agree what you want to do next. Copy the table and write in the numbers of the steps you choose and how long they take. You mustn't go over 300 minutes, or … BOOM!

These phrases and the table will help you

I think the clue means we should … . / Why don't we try …?
That will take too long. / That's too easy. / That isn't hard enough. / I don't think that's the right decision. / No, let's go to … .

Step	Time	Total
1	20 mins	20 mins
2	30 mins	50 mins
	+ ?	?
?	?	?

WORKING WITH THE TEXT

▶ Your story

After you have finished the maze, look at your table, then follow your route through the maze again.

Write about how you tried to save the Crown Jewels: After I found the note at Trafalgar Square, I …

1 You are Agent 101 from the British Secret Service. Your phone rings at 6 o'clock in the morning. It's your boss. 'Come to the office at once.'
Half an hour later you're there. '101,' your boss says, 'Max Gladstone has put a bomb in the Tower of London. He says he'll destroy the Crown Jewels at 12 o'clock.'
'Our people can't stop his bombs,' you say. 'Not without the code. What's the game this time?'
'Here, he left this note for you.'

To my old friend, 101,
I've got another little game for you, 101. If you can find 5 clues – and the answers – by 12 o'clock, you'll find the code for the bomb. If not: BOOM! Here's your first clue:
When he was alive, he wasn't a tall man. Now he's dead, and he's the tallest man in London. Go to him, and he'll give you your next clue.
Yours,
Max G.

'What does it mean?' your boss asks.
'Nelson,' you tell her. 'Admiral Lord Nelson was a small man, but now he stands on top of the column in Trafalgar Square. So now he's the tallest man in London.'
'Brilliant, 101!'
'Yes, I am. … Now, I must get to Trafalgar Square at once.'
'A car and driver are waiting for you, 101. You have five hours – 300 minutes.'

Go to 2, Trafalgar Square. This takes **20 minutes**. Remember: you must add your time at each step!

2 You're at Trafalgar Square. But where's the clue? Then you remember: 'The clue is about Nelson, not Trafalgar Square!'
'Get me a rope,' you say to your driver, and you climb the 44 metres up to the statue. Nelson is holding the next note from Gladstone in his hand: 'That was too easy, 101. Try this one: Everyone knows, "To be or not to be." But do you? Put that in your pipe and smoke it.'
30 minutes have passed. What's next?

a You know that 'To be or not to be' is from a play by William Shakespeare, so you drive to Shakespeare's Globe Theatre on the Thames. **40 minutes**. *Go to 10*.
b Suddenly you see something in the note: 'Everyone knows, "To be or not to be." ' 'One' = 1; 'to' = 2; 'be' = B; 'to' = 2; 'be' = B. 12B2B. 'Of course! The numbers and letters are in the wrong order!' you shout. '2 2 1 B Baker Street! Sherlock Holmes's address.' You drive to Baker Street. **20 minutes**. *Go to 5*.

3 Why are you reading this? *Go back to 2* and follow the directions. Add 10 minutes to your time.

4

The man at the London Dungeon tells you that they *have* got figures of Henry and his wives, that the figures *are* having dinner and that one of them *is* a ghost.

You say you're going to drive there and look at it, but he says you needn't come because they've turned off the power. 'The ghost of Anne Boleyn is a hologram,' he explains. 'She doesn't usually talk. But today she was talking.'

'What was she saying? Can you remember?'

'Yes, of course. She said: "Where did you go to university, you clown?"'

This has taken **10 minutes**. What now?

a You went to university in Oxford, so you take the tube to Paddington Station. The trains to Oxford leave from there. *Go to 7.*

b 'Oxford, you clown!' you think. Then: 'Clown – circus – Oxford Circus!' You take the underground to Oxford Circus. This takes **6 minutes**. *Go to 13.*

5

You're at the Sherlock Holmes Museum, but where's the clue? Then you remember: 'Put that in your pipe and smoke it.' Of course, Holmes's famous pipe! You find Max's note inside the pipe: 'He was married to three Catherines, two Annes and a Jane. Two lost their heads – poor things! Now they're all together for dinner, but one of them is a ghost.'

'He means Henry VIII and his wives,' says your driver.

'But where are they together for dinner?' you ask.

This has taken **10 minutes**. What now?

a You remember that Madame Tussaud's has figures of Henry VIII and his wives. You're very near there, so you decide to send your driver away and walk. This takes **15 minutes**. *Go to 17.*

b You think there are figures of Henry VIII and his wives in the London Dungeon, but you aren't sure. You decide to phone there. *Go to 4.*

6

You quickly find the figures of Henry VIII and his wives and know you've made a mistake. (Look at the picture on page 49.)

This has taken **25 minutes**. If you still have time, you can phone the London Dungeon. *Go to 4.*

7

You arrive at Paddington Station by tube and buy a train ticket. You're waiting on the platform for the train to Oxford when you suddenly hear: 'The next train to Oxford will be 45 minutes late. We are very sorry … .'

35 minutes have passed. Now what?

a You wait for the next train to Oxford. This takes **45 minutes**. *Go to 9.*

b You decide that Oxford Circus wasn't a bad idea and go there. This takes **17 minutes**. *Go to 13.*

8

You run from Tower Hill underground station to the Tower of London, then to the Jewel House. This has taken **10 minutes**. *Go to 11.*

9

You get off the train in Oxford and walk to the taxis outside. Before you get there, you hear your name. You go to the information desk, where they have a message for you: 'A clown like you should be in a circus. Max G.'

55 minutes have passed. What's next?

a You decide that Oxford was a mistake, so you catch the next train back to London. When you arrive at Paddington Station, you take the tube to Oxford Circus. This takes **150 minutes**. *Go to 13.*

b You decide that you must be in the right place because Max has left a message for you. You take a taxi around the university. *Go to 16.*

10

You don't find anything at the Globe. Then you think, 'That was too easy! Max isn't going to make things easy for me.'

45 minutes have passed. What now?

a You remember your other choice and go there. The journey takes **60 minutes**.

b You can't remember your other choice and must *go back to 2* and look again. This takes **50 minutes**.

11

The microchip fits into a hole in the bomb. You put it in, a small door opens and a figure jumps up. It looks like Max Gladstone. Then you hear Max's voice: 'Very good, 101. You're better than I thought. You've saved the Crown Jewels.'

'Yes, I have! That's enough games, Max!'

'Maybe ... but you'll hear from me again, 101. Our little games are really fun!'

12 You take a Central Line train to Liverpool Street, change there to a southbound Circle Line train and get off at Tower Hill.
This takes **29 minutes**. *Go to 8.*

13 You're at the tube station at Oxford Circus, but you can't find the clue. Then you see the sign that usually tells you when the next train will be there. But today it says 'Fish and chips – that great British invention.' This means nothing to you. But then you see a poster for the London Aquarium with a big picture of a fish. You look at it carefully and see that someone has stuck something onto the eye of the fish. It's a microchip – fish and chips! You take the microchip and decide that you have to get to the Tower of London at once.
This has taken **15 minutes**. *Go to 12.*

14 You're looking around Madame Tussaud's when the police come. They take you to the police station and keep you there until your boss phones. The bomb has destroyed the Crown Jewels. You can look for a new job.
This is the end of the story for you.

15 You get into Madame Tussaud's and find the figures of King Henry VIII and his wives. They aren't having dinner. (Look at the picture on page 49.)
This has taken **115 minutes**. If you still have time, you can phone the London Dungeon. *Go to 4.*

16 You drive around the university but find nothing. Oxford was a mistake, so you drive to Oxford Circus in London.
This has taken **60 minutes**, and the drive into London takes **90 minutes**. *Go to 13.*

17 About 500 people are waiting in front of Madame Tussaud's, so you go to the door and tell them you're from the Secret Service. They say you have to wait like everyone else. What do you do now?

a You show them your gun and tell them that you can't wait. You have to see Henry VIII and his wives now. They open the door for you. *Go to 14.*
b You wait like everyone else. *Go to 15.*
c You ask the people at the door to phone their boss. You explain everything; then you can go inside. *Go to 6.*

HOW TO ... scan a text (a reading technique)

1 **▶ Before you scan a text**
Imagine you want to find the words 'Madame Tussaud's' in the text again. How? Close your eyes and try to 'see' the words.

2 **▶ Find the information**

a *Try to find the words 'Madame Tussaud's' in the text on this page. Just move your eyes very quickly along the text. You should still have a picture of the two words in your head. When you move your eyes past the words, they will suddenly be clear. Try it now. – Which steps were the two words in? What information goes with the words? Now try the technique with more words. Write down the numbers of all the steps where you can find:* Oxford Circus, train, boss.
How many times can you find the number 15?

b *Now try different ways to scan: move your finger in wavy lines or move your finger along the edge of the text. Try to find* Henry VIII, Max, station *on p. 57.*

REMEMBER

1 **Before you scan**, imagine the word or words you are looking for.
2 **When you scan**, move your eyes quickly down the text. The word or words will 'jump out at you'.

5 UNIT 5 One Country, Many Cultures

BRADFORD FESTIVAL

The Mela
Lister Park

Saturday & Sunday 6th & 7th July

Europe's biggest Asian festival – over 100,000 people come every year! In India and Pakistan 'mela' is the word for 'bazaar' – come and enjoy yourself at the most exciting bazaar in the country! Everyone is welcome!

LISTENING

a *On the cassette/CD there is a radio interview about the Mela and ethnic minorities in Britain. Before you listen, copy this table into your exercise book.*

b *Listen once. Fill in the correct minority names from this list: Indian, Pakistani, Bangladeshi, Afro-Caribbean.*

c *Listen again and finish the table.*
(Where are the places? Look for them on a world map.)

minority	where from?	numbers in Britain
?	?	895,000
?	?	582,000
?	?	198,000
?	?	500,000

▶ 1

'Hello, Yasmin!' said Mrs Patel. 'I'm sorry, dear, but I have to go. Aunt Nazreen is ill. You know, the one who always eats a lot of cakes.'
Yasmin laughed. 'I remember! But, Mum, what about your Tuesday class?'
'Yes, that's a problem. I can't get through on the phone. Would you be very kind and go there? Tell them I'm very sorry, but I can't teach my class today. OK?'

→ P 1

▶ 2

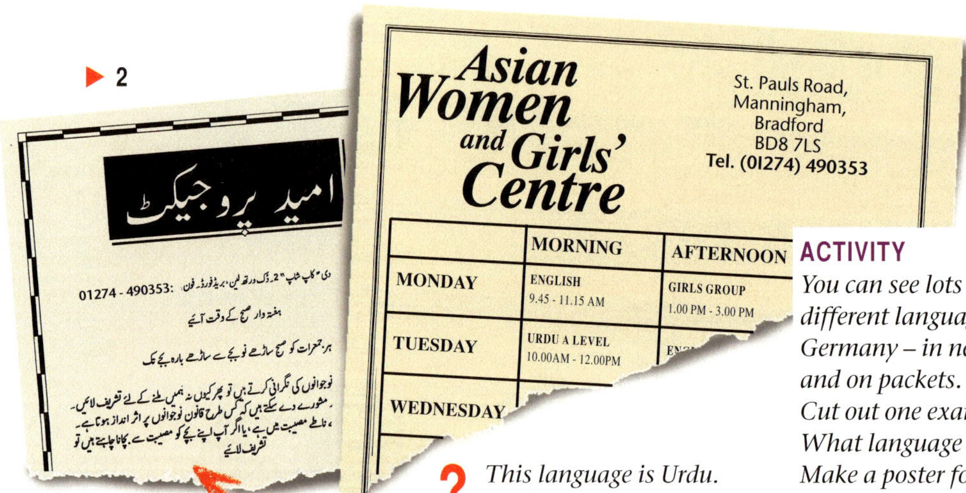

امید پروجیکٹ

01274 - 490353

Asian Women and Girls' Centre

St. Pauls Road, Manningham, Bradford BD8 7LS Tel. (01274) 490353

	MORNING	AFTERNOON
MONDAY	ENGLISH 9.45 - 11.15 AM	GIRLS GROUP 1.00 PM - 3.00 PM
TUESDAY	URDU A LEVEL 10.00AM - 12.00PM	EN…
WEDNESDAY		

? *This language is Urdu. Find out where people speak it.*

ACTIVITY

You can see lots of different languages in Germany – in newspapers and on packets. Cut out one example. What language is it? Make a poster for the classroom.

▶ 3

'Oh dear, I'm late. Will mum's class still be here?' Yasmin asked herself when she arrived at the centre. She went to room 3. Ten Asian women were sitting there. Some of them were recording themselves. Others were trying to correct themselves when they heard their mistakes.
'Hello. I'm Mrs Patel's daughter …'
The women looked up.
'Ah, it's Yasmin!' said one woman. 'Where's your mother, dear? I was teaching myself, but I really need her!'
'Mum can't come because my aunt doesn't feel well. She's sorry, but you'll have to teach yourselves today.'

FOCUS ON GRAMMAR

Look at A3 again and fill in the missing words.

I was teaching … .
You were teaching **yourself**.
Yasmin/She asked … .
He asked **himself**.
We were recording **ourselves**.
You'll have to teach … .
They were recording … .

▶▶▶ NOW YOU

Have you ever recorded yourself on cassette or taught yourself a game? Write one sentence.
I've never recorded myself, but I've taught myself chess / …

→ S 5: 1 a (p. 127)
→ P 2, (D 1 ◆, p. 119), P 3

TOPS SPECIAL – ALL BRITISH

▶ 4

My name is **Leroy Bates** and I'm from Bristol. My grand-parents came to England from Jamaica in 1946. Grandpa worked as a builder and grandma designed and made dresses.
My dad was born here in Bristol. He couldn't get a job when he left school – because he's black, he says – but he's a taxi driver now.

▶ 5

TOPS MAGAZINE
looks at the minorities in some British cities

BRADFORD
Total population: 457,344
Minorities: 68,299

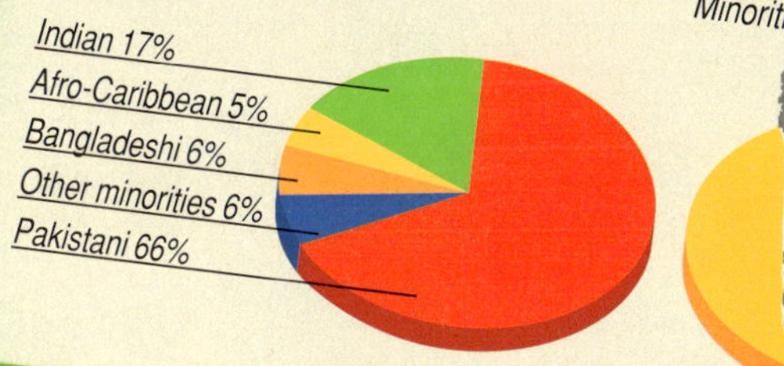

BRIST
Total p
Minorit

? *Explain the chart:*
There are more Pakistanis/ ... than ... in Bradford.
The ... are the largest/smallest ethnic group. → P 11

▶ 6

Hi, I'm **Jenny Lim** from Liverpool. My mum and dad are from Hong Kong. When they arrived in England, they taught themselves English. My mum's English still isn't very good and my Chinese is even worse. So now we're teaching each other: I'm helping her with English and she's helping me with Chinese.
There are a lot of Chinese people in Liverpool, so there's always a big celebration at Chinese New Year. All the people in a family – grandparents, aunts, uncles, cousins – visit each other.

FOCUS ON GRAMMAR

themselves   each other

a *My mum and dad taught my mum and dad.*
How can you say this better?
Look at A6 again and find the right expression: They taught ... .

b *I'm teaching my mum and my mum is teaching me.*
How can you say this better?
Look at A6 again and find the right expression: We're teaching ... .

→ S 5: 1 b (p. 128)
→ P 4, D 2 ■ (p. 119)
→ P 5

▶▶▶ NOW YOU

a *Are you or is anyone you know from a different country? Where do your/her/his parents come from? What languages do you/they speak? Try and find three people. Make a table like this and fill it in.*

name	*where from*	*languages*
Mrs Craxi	*Italy*	*Italian, German*
Ivan	*Russia*	...

b *Find the countries in your table on a map.*

c *Write a few sentences about one person from your table. You can put them in your English album. Example:*
Mrs Craxi is the waitress at our pizzeria. She's from ... and speaks ... . She's very nice.

▶ 7

Bradford's town hall

Mohammed Ajeeb, Lord Mayor of Bradford in 1985, was the first Asian to be a mayor in England. 'I don't think I'll be the last Asian to be a mayor in this country,' he said.

And he wasn't. Of course, there are still racists in Britain – as there are in many countries. But there are also lots of people against racism.

→ S 5: 2 a (p. 128)
→ P 6

▶ 8

As she left the centre, Yasmin met Tim, a boy from her form.
'Yasmin! Perfect! I'm so happy to see you. Now I can ask you.'
'Hello, Tim. Ask me what?'
'It's the Mela on Saturday. I wanted to know more about it, like where to go and what to do.'
'That's easy,' said Yasmin. 'Just go to Lister Park, and have fun!'
They walked along together. When they got to Yasmin's street, she became very nervous.
'I don't know how to say this, Tim,' she began, 'but my dad is so strict, he doesn't let me ...'
Tim understood. 'It's OK,' he smiled. 'See you on Saturday!'
He walked away.

→ S 5: 2 b, c (pp. 128–129)
→ P 7, 8, 13

▶ 9

The day of the Mela came. The Patels arrived at Lister Park at about 11.30.
'I may see Tim here,' thought Yasmin. 'But, of course, he might not come.'
'Hello, Mrs Patel, Mr Patel. Hi, Yasmin!'
Yasmin blushed. 'Oh, Tim, hi!' she said.
'Mum, Dad, this is Tim Hanson – he's in my form.'
'Hello, Tim,' said Mrs Patel.
Mr Patel turned to his wife: 'Come on Zahida, Yasmin, we must go.'
'Don't be silly, dear,' said Mrs Patel. 'Here's some money, Yasmin. You and Tim can go and buy four samosas for us all – and something to drink. We're all thirsty.'
'Tim won't like samosas,' said Mr Patel.
'But I love Indian food, Mr Patel,' said Tim. Mrs Patel smiled. 'Yasmin, dear, we'll meet you over there in twenty minutes.'
'Thanks, Mum,' said Yasmin.

→ P 12

▶ 10

'Your mum seems really nice!' said Tim. 'But my dad is so strict – and so rude! I'm sorry, Tim.' Yasmin was quite upset.
'Don't worry, Yasmin. Dads often think their daughters aren't able to look after themselves.
Look at my family,' Tim went on. 'I'm only 14 and I can stay out till 9 o'clock. But when my *sister* was 14, *she* wasn't allowed to stay out after 7 o'clock. So she phoned her friends. My parents were really angry when they saw the phone bill!'
Tim and Yasmin laughed.
'Anyway, you're right about my mum,' said Yasmin. 'She's the greatest! She often helps me when there's a problem with Dad.'
Tim pointed at a BBC poster: 'A real hero!'

→ S 5: 3 (p. 129)
→ P 9, 10 (D 3 ◆, p. 119)

FOCUS ON WORDS

Collect words that describe people and make networks.
What people can look like: tall, short, fat, thin, blond, dark, ...
What people can be: kind, friendly, rude, strict, intelligent, silly, nervous, shy, ...

▶▶▶ NOW YOU

In not more than five sentences, describe a person to your partner.
My person isn't tall. She's very beautiful. She isn't shy. She sings and dances.
- *Is she a famous pop star? – Yes, she is.*
- *Is it Madonna? – No, it isn't. She's is black.*
- *Is it Janet Jackson? – Yes, it is.*

LISTENING

Look at the pictures and listen to the song 'Ebony and Ivory' on the cassette/CD. What do the singers say about ebony and ivory? How should we live together?

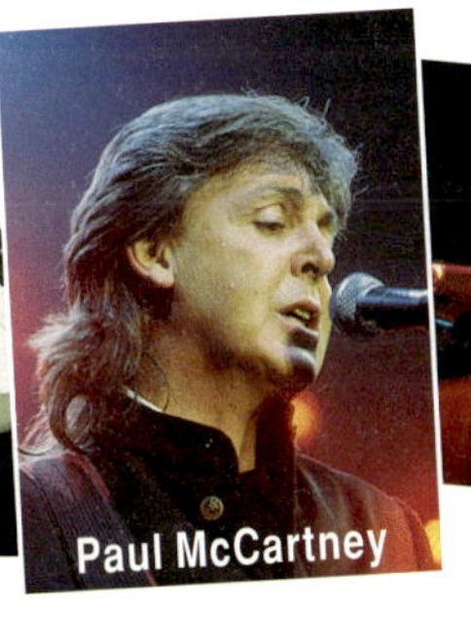

→ UK Mag, pp. 104–105

1 **REVISION** What in the world is …? – A quiz

Do you know who or what these are?
Find the answers, then write sentences with relative clauses like this:

1 *Jackie Chan is a film star who/that makes Kung Fu films in Hong Kong.*
2 *A döner is a kind of hamburger (that) you can get at a Turkish fast food place.*

1 Jackie Chan	a part of China	Indian women often wear it.
2 A 'döner'	a dress	It was part of India until 1947.
3 A sari	a kind of hamburger	It was British until 1997.
4 Hong Kong	a country	He makes Kung Fu films in Hong Kong.
5 Reggae	a film star	You can get it at a Turkish fast food place.
6 'Mela'	an Indian word	People first played it in the Caribbean.
7 Bangladesh	a kind of music	It means 'bazaar'.

◇ 2 ▶ **Selima's trip to Bradford** → D 1 ◆ (p. 119)

Last weekend Yasmin's cousin Selima came to Bradford.
Complete the sentences with the words in the box.

myself • yourself • himself
herself • ourselves • themselves

1 'I can look after *myself*, Dad,' Selima said as the train left Birmingham station.
2 'Well, enjoy … and phone us when you arrive,' called Selima's mum.
3 Mr Patel said to …, 'Selima is so tall – she looks like a young lady.'
4 'Don't worry,' said Mrs Patel. 'The girls can look after … .'
5 'I've taught … a song on the guitar,' said Selima at dinner.
6 'Great,' Yasmin said. 'I'll sing and we can record … .'
7 But when Yasmin heard … on cassette she said, 'Yuck, that can't be me!'

3 ▶ **Look after yourselves!**

Mrs Patel stayed with her sister in Birmingham for a few days and wrote a card home.
Complete the card. But be careful: you need these reflexive pronouns with three of the verbs in brackets.

myself
yourself • yourselves

Dear Yasmin,

First the bad news. I fell down some steps yesterday and (hurt)! I still can't (move) very well, but don't (worry). I (feel) much better now.
How's your father? And how are you? Try to (enjoy)!
Why don't you (meet) those two nice girls from your form after school? You could (watch) one of our new videos and (eat) something.
Be good and (look after), both of you!

Lots of love from Mum

4 ▶ **The Patels at home**

Read about the Patel family. Complete the sentences with each other *or* themselves.

1 Yasmin speaks English to her mum, and her mum speaks English to Yasmin. They speak English to *each other*.
2 Mr and Mrs Patel still like Urdu. At home they always talk in Urdu to … .
3 Mr Patel often thinks of his mother in Pakistan. They sometimes phone … .
4 The women in Mrs Patel's class have to learn a lot from their books at home. They have to teach … .
5 Mr and Mrs Patel are going to buy … a new car.
6 The Patels have still got a lot of friends in Pakistan. They write letters to … .

→ D 2 ■ (p. 119)

◆◆ 5 ▶ **Each other or themselves?**

Partner B: look at page 113. Partner A: look at the pictures on this page. You and your partner have the same pictures, but in a different order. Tell your partner about your pictures.

1

take photos

2
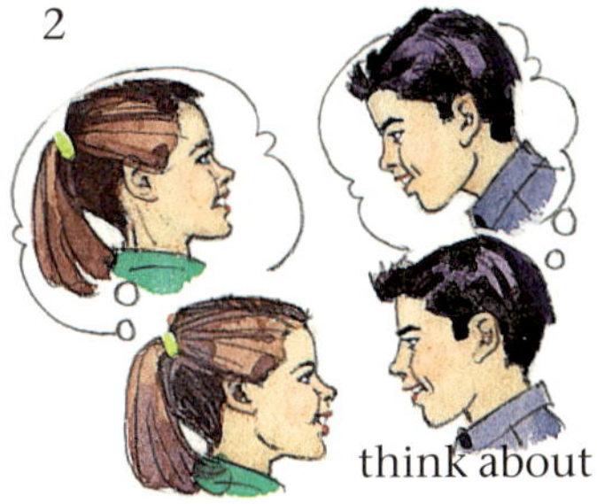
think about

3

laugh at

4

think about

5

laugh at

6

take photos

A In my picture 1 two kids are taking photos of each other.
B Oh, two kids are taking photos of each other in my picture 6.
A In my picture 2 a girl and a boy are ...

6 ▶ **The first and the last**

Match the two sentence halves.

1 Steffi Graf was the first German woman	to be secretary general of the UN.
2 A captain is always the last	to leave the classroom after a lesson.
3 Kofi Annan was the first black African	to hear about their children's problems.
4 A teacher should always be the last	to leave a ship when it sinks.
5 The first	to win at Wimbledon.
6 Parents are sometimes the last people	to arrive is often the last to leave.

7 ▶ **What can I do?**

Yasmin and Tim are both worrying about the Mela on Saturday.
Read what they are thinking and report:

What can I wear to the Mela?
How can I explain about Tim to Dad?
When can I get away from the family?
What can I say to Tim?
Who can I talk to about my feelings?

What should I wear?
Who can I ask about Yasmin?
Where can I go with Yasmin?
How much money should I take?
What can I tell my friends about Yasmin?

Yasmin is thinking about what to wear to the Mela.
She isn't sure / doesn't know ... .

Tim is thinking about what to wear ...

8 ▶ Write a poem

Read the poem.

GOOD
It's good to read
your letters.
It's even better to hear
your voice.
But it's best to be with you.

a *Write a poem like 'GOOD'. You can put it in your English album.*
Use one of the following beginnings:

NICE	BAD	BORING
It's nice to …	It's bad to …	It's boring to …
It's even nicer to …	It's even worse to …	It's even more boring to …
But it's nicest to …	But it's worst to …	But it's most boring to …

b *Now write your own poem. Choose an adjective for the title.*
Read out your poems. Then collect them and make a poster for the classroom wall.

9 ▶ You're allowed to, but I'm not

a *What are/aren't you allowed to do? Make two lists with five things each.*
I'm allowed to read in bed. … | *I'm not allowed to come home after eight in the evening. …*

b *Make a window like this:*

	My partner is allowed to	*My partner isn't allowed to*
I'm allowed to		
I'm not allowed to		

◆◆ **c** *Now talk to your partner and fill in the window:*

A I'm allowed to read in bed. What about you?
B I'm allowed to read in bed, too. / No, I'm not allowed to … .
A I'm not allowed to … . What about you?
B I'm allowed to … . / I'm not allowed to … either.

◆ 10 ▶ A problem letter → D 3 ◆ (p. 119)

a *Read this letter to TOPS magazine. Choose the right form of* be able to *or* be allowed to.

Dear Claire,
I've got a problem with my parents.
I' … to go out on school days. Last week I … see my boyfriend – but I … get out of the house and we … meet. My parents were really angry! Now they've said I … go to a party next week. But they … stop me!
Diane, 16

won't be able to
were able to
was able to

won't be allowed to
wasn't allowed to
'm not allowed to

b *Write a letter to TOPS magazine about a problem. (It needn't be true!)*

WORD WATCH

11 ▶ One school – many nationalities!

a *The pupils at Erich-Kästner-Schule in Bünde come from many different nations. Look at the alphabetical list on the right and read the text.*

country	number
Albania	3
Austria	1
Bosnia	4
Britain	3
Croatia	11
France	1
Germany	1297
Greece	~~1~~
Italy	15
Portugal	1
Poland	1
Spain	3
Turkey	103
Vietnam	2

Report on different nationalitites at my school

The German group is the biggest. The second biggest group is the Turkish group – with more than a hundred pupils.
The other groups are much smaller. We've got fifteen Italian pupils. Fifteen pupils are Bosnian or Croatian. There are three Spanish, three British, and three Albanian pupils. Two pupils are Vietnamese. One is French and one is Portuguese. We've got one Austrian and one Polish pupil, too. We had one Greek boy, but his family has just left Germany. We were all sad when Dimitrios had to go.

b *Copy this table and complete it with the names of countries from the list and with the adjectives from the report.*

country	adjectives (-ish)	(-n/-an)	(others)
Albania	–	Albanian	–

c *Now find out about the nationalities at your school. First make a list and then write a report.*

12 WORD LINK One verb, two different prepositions

Complete the sentences with the correct preposition from the box.

about • at • for • from
of • on • to

1 I talked … Tony yesterday. We talked … Sue's fantastic party last week.
2 I thought … the problem a lot. Then I suddenly thought … a great idea!
3 Tim is working upstairs … his computer. He's working … his school project.
4 Please phone soon. I want to hear … you. I want to hear … the family and the trip.
5 I asked my teacher … my homework. I also asked … some help.

13 LISTENING Oil drums and carnivals

a *Read the text and then listen to the cassette/CD. The underlined words are different there.*

1 What the Mela is for the Asians in <u>England</u>, the carnival is for us Afro-Caribbeans.
2 Your carnival in Germany is in <u>winter</u>, but ours is in <u>the summer</u>.
3 The best carnival is in London, in a part of <u>the city</u> called Notting Hill.
4 Steel drums. They're instruments with a <u>big story</u>.
5 Back home in Trinidad one of the biggest industries is oil. People put the oil into big drums for the <u>journey</u>. One day, I suppose someone hit an empty drum with a stick. It made a good, strong sound.
6 Perhaps that <u>someone</u> hit the drum on the other side, and there was a different sound.
7 So I suppose he or she started to think: 'There's music in this <u>old</u> drum.'

b *Listen again. Write the different words that you hear in your exercise book.*

5 T

'I Felt like a Monster'

Here are 4 Indian names:

Bhaji on the Beach • Punjabi
Delhi • Meera Syal

Which one is a person's name, the name of a film, a city, a language? Read the text and find out.

Actress and writer, Meera Syal, was born in a village near the town of Wolverhampton in the English Midlands. She lived in a little house with her parents and went to the village school, where her mum was a teacher.

In fact Meera had an ordinary English childhood. There was only one thing that was special about the Syal family: they were the only Asian family in the village. Their faces were the only faces that weren't white.

Barbara Derkow Disselbeck interviewed Meera Syal for English G 2000.

BARBARA *When did your parents come to England, Meera?*

MEERA They came in 1960, from Delhi, the capital of India.

BARBARA *Did they speak English when they arrived?*

MEERA Oh, yes. They spoke English well. My first language was English. I had to learn Punjabi when I was a bit older.

BARBARA *Punjabi?*

MEERA Yes. *Their* first language was Punjabi. All my family in India speak Punjabi.

BARBARA *You were born in England, but you still have family in India. Have you ever been to India?*

MEERA Yes, lots of times.

BARBARA *When was your first visit?*

MEERA When I was four years old.

BARBARA *Can you remember that first trip?*

MEERA Oh, yes! I remember the heat and the noise. And I remember that we spent most of the time outside. It was so exciting – cold, grey England and then that!

BARBARA *And the language?*

MEERA Punjabi! I couldn't speak a word at that time, but it was fine. My cousins spoke Punjabi, I spoke English and ... well, we understood each other – kids always do!

BARBARA *Back in England, you started school. Did you like it?*

MEERA I loved it.

BARBARA *Lots of kids hate school! Why did you love it?*

MEERA Well, firstly my mum was a teacher. She really made it fun to learn. And secondly my parents, like all Asian parents, always said to me: 'Meera, education is a gift. Don't throw it away!' So when I was young I thought of school as a kind of present!

BARBARA *Were there any problems?*

MEERA Yes, sometimes, of course. I remember I cut myself on a bottle and the whole form came and looked: they couldn't believe my blood was red, just like their blood! I felt like a monster.

BARBARA *Now you're a famous actress and writer. How did that happen?*

MEERA I did English and Drama at university. In my last year I did a one-woman show. Someone saw it and said, 'You're good: come and be an actress.' I was lucky.

BARBARA *And soon you were acting in London's West End theatres.*

MEERA Yes.

BARBARA *And then you started to write.*

MEERA Yes. I wanted to write a film script about Asian women in this country.

BARBARA *'Bhaji on the Beach'.*

MEERA Yes.

BARBARA *It was a wonderful film and it got lots of international prizes. And now you've written your first book.*

MEERA It's about Meena Kumar, an Indian girl who grows up in a village near Wolverhampton.

BARBARA *Is there a bit of Meera Syal in Meena Kumar?*

MEERA Oh, a lot!

BARBARA *Well, Meena wants to be famous one day and Meera is famous now! Thank you for the interview, Meera.*

WORKING WITH THE TEXT

1 ▶ About Meera Syal

Read the interview with Meera Syal again. Look at the following table and fill in the missing information. Write notes only.

Name: *Meera Syal*	Education:
Place of birth:	Languages:
Information about parents:	Work:

2 ▶ 'Anita and Me'

In this extract from Meera Syal's book, Meena's white friend Anita comes to dinner for the first time:

'What's that?' Anita asked, as if there was a sheep's head on her plate.
'Oh that's mattar-paneer,' mama said proudly. 'A sort of Indian cheese, and those are peas ...'
'Cheese and peas?' said Anita. 'Together?'
'Well,' mama went on quickly. 'This is chicken curry. You have had chicken before, haven't you?'
'What's that stuff round it?'
'Um, just gravy, you know, tomatoes, onions, garlic ...'
'Chicken with tomatoes? What's garlic?'
'Don't you worry!' papa said quickly. 'We've also got fish fingers and chips. Is tomato ketchup too dangerous for you?'

- *Why does Anita ask questions about the food Meena's mother has cooked?*
- *Do you think Meena's father is angry, or is he trying to be funny when he offers Anita fish fingers and chips?*

▶▶▶ NOW YOU

Collect names/examples of food we can buy from other countries. What's your favourite food that is not from Germany?

3 ▶ What's different? What's the same?

Do you know kids whose families come from other countries? Were you born in another country? Compare their/your situation with Meera's. What's different/the same?

HOW TO ... persuade people

1 LISTENING 'You must go to ...'

a *Listen to the cassette/CD. What are the people talking about?*

The first speaker is talking about ...

b *Listen again. Which event sounds most exciting? Say why you think it sounds good.*

You can use these expressions

I think the film/ ... sounds best/most exciting.
I'd like to go to the ... because the girl/the advertisement/ ... says ... .
I like the way the ... speaks.

◆◆ **c** *Do you remember these words and phrases from the cassette/CD?*

Waterlow Park • most exciting • the best
really cool • enjoy • at 11 • you'll love it
this Saturday • don't forget • too hot to miss
from next Friday • music for teenagers
go and see • Second Hand Outfit Show
15 lovely models • why spend pounds?

Some of the phrases give you information, and some try to persuade you. Work with a partner and put the phrases in the right group.

gives information	tries to persuade
Waterlow Park	most exciting
...	...

2 READING That sounds great

A Bradford school wants to tell people about their charity bazaar.

Find words and phrases you can put in the text to persuade people to come.

3 WRITING AND SPEAKING Don't miss our form project!

a *Imagine it's your project week and you want to persuade people to come to your event.*

THE ENGLISH TEA-ROOM ✶ THE SCOTLAND EXHIBITION ✶ THE AMERICAN PLAY ✶ ...

- *Collect ideas: What is the event? – Where? – When? ...*
- *Collect words and phrases to persuade people. Use your lists from* **1**. *Write a text for the radio.*
- *Check your text carefully. Is the English correct? Is there enough information? Does it sound good?*

b *Experiment with different ways of reading your text before you record it on cassette.*

REMEMBER

- What do you want to tell people: What, when, where is your event?
- What is great about your event? Why mustn't people miss it? Find phrases that will persuade them.
- Does your text sound good? Try to read it in different ways.

6 UNIT 6 Free Time

Free time activities

You can also
go skiing
go sailing
listen to music
play the cello
play chess ...

FOCUS ON WORDS

Think of all the free time activities you know. Make a list.

LISTENING

Listen to the cassette/CD. List the free time activities that Lisa, Ryan and Mike each do. Choose from these verbs:

go • learn • listen to
meet • play • take

What are they all interested in?

▶▶▶ NOW YOU and your class

a *Write down three of your free time activities. Then find pupils who do the same things. Find two pupils for each activity. Example:*
Do you play chess? – Yes, I do. / No, I don't.

b *Report to your class. Example:*
I play chess. Nils and Nora play chess, too.

▶ 1

MIKE Come on, come on! Yes!
COMPUTER *(bleeps)* Your score is 9,993.
MRS BECK Mike! The phone! It's Lisa.
MIKE Not now, Mum. I'm busy!
MRS BECK Mike! Do you want to go out with Lisa and Ryan? Lisa is asking.
MIKE I don't know. I can't think ...
MRS BECK They're going to come round.
MIKE Oh, no, not now!

→ P 1

▶ 2

'Mike is so unfriendly, isn't he?' Lisa said to Ryan.
'Yes,' said Ryan, 'Mike, you just like your computer, don't you? Come on, Lisa, he doesn't want to go out with us.'
Mike said, 'But you just hang out around town. You don't *do* anything, do you?'
'We do!' said Lisa. 'We see friends, we talk ... But you're always here all alone, aren't you?'
'That's not true,' Mike said. 'I talk to people all over the world.'
The others looked at Mike. 'But they aren't real conversations, are they?' Lisa said.
'Yes, they are. I talk on the Internet.'
'Huh! You can't show us, can you?' said Ryan.
'Yes, I can. Ask a question.'
'OK,' said Ryan. 'Ask all those computer nerds about their plans for tomorrow.' Mike's fingers moved quickly around the keyboard.

FOCUS ON GRAMMAR

Find sentences like these in A2.
Mike is so unfriendly, isn't he?
You don't do anything, do you?
Write them in your exercise book. Underline the verbs and the phrases at the end of the sentences.

→ S 6: 1 (pp. 130–131)
→ P 2, (D ◆ 1, p. 120)
→ P 3, D 2 ■ (p. 120)
→ P 11

▶ 3

LISA Mickey isn't your name!
MIKE It's my nickname on the Net. We've all got one. Jo-Jo is Joe. And Bibi is Barbie Brandt from Berlin.
RYAN What are all those letters?
MIKE They're short forms. RL means 'real life'. HTH means 'hope this helps'. L8R means 'later'.
LISA Skiing? But it's summer! That can't be right!
MIKE Sorry, Lisa. You're wrong.

?
– *Why is Lisa wrong?*
– *Do you know what* :-) *and* :-(*mean? Clue: turn your book clockwise.*

→ S 6: 2 (p. 131)
→ P 4

PROJECT (PART 1)

a *What do you and your friends do in your free time? Do a project and find out. First make a questionnaire and collect information. You can start like this:*

You can use:
- yes/no *questions*
- *questions with* how much, how many, how often, how long
- *questions with* when, where, what, why, who
- *'fill-in' statements*

Free time activities questionnaire

We want to find out what all of us do in our free time. Please help us and fill in this questionnaire.

Section 1: TV

1. Do you watch TV every / almost every day?
Yes ☐ *No* ☐
2. How much TV do you usually watch every day?
0–1 hour ☐ *1–2 hours* ☐ *2–3 hours* ☐ *more* ☐
3. When do you usually watch TV? In the *morning* ☐ *afternoon* ☐ *evening* ☐
4. Where do you usually watch TV? In *the living-room* ☐ *your bedroom* ☐ *Other* ☐
5. Your three favourite programmes are:
*a)*________ *b)*________ *c)*________

b *Work in a group of four and discuss questions for* **sections 2** *and* **3**. *Write questions together. Put the best ones in the best order and write the sections. You can use these ideas:*

Section 2: Music
- What sorts of music do people like? Pop? Rap? Rock? Folk? Jazz? Classical? Other?
- Where / When / How often ... listen?
- How much money ... spend on music?
- ... play an instrument?

Section 3: Outdoor activities
Use your list from p. 71.

c *Copy your questionnaire. All the members of your group have to fill it in first. Then each of you talks to two more people from your group and writes down their answers.*

d *Work with your group again. Count all the answers and write down the results. Put them in a chart like the one on the right.*

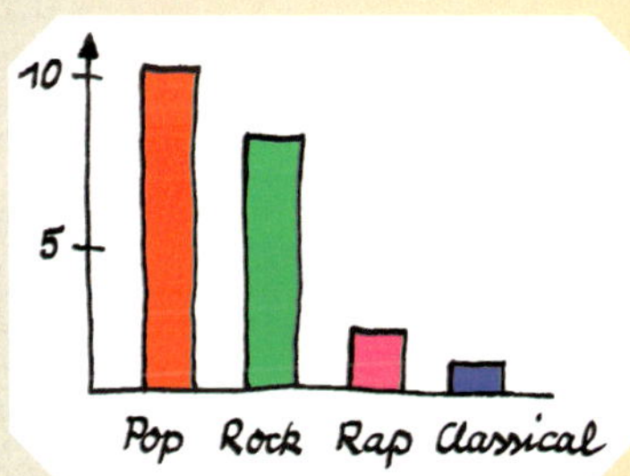

▶ 4

Lisa and Ryan were suddenly very interested in the Internet. They even joined the school computer club. Then, one evening ...

MRS BECK Plymouth 712356. Hello?
LISA Oh, hello, Mrs Beck. This is Lisa. Could I speak to Mike, please?
MRS BECK I'm sorry, Lisa. He's out at the moment.
LISA Oh, well, could you give him a message, please? Could he call me back after 6.00? It's about an Internet project.
MRS BECK Let me make a note ... Fine.
LISA Thank you, Mrs Beck.
MRS BECK You're welcome, Lisa.

→ P 5, 6

▶ 5

Mike called back and Lisa explained.

LISA We want to start a new page for the school's website about free time.
MIKE Nice. How do you want to do it?
LISA Well, first we want people to write lots of articles.
MIKE Would you like me to write something?
LISA No. We'd like you to set up our page.
MIKE Why me?
LISA Because you're the best!

FOCUS ON GRAMMAR

Compare these forms in A5:

We want to start ...	*First we want people to write ...*
verb + infinitive	verb + object + infinitive

Who is going to start? Who is going to write?

Find more examples of the two forms.
Write them in two lists in your exercise book.
Underline the objects in the second list.

→ S 6: 3 (p. 132)
→ P 7, 8

▶ 6

Two weeks later Lisa, Ryan and Mike had a name for the new page on their website and a lot of articles. Too many! So they had to choose just the best.

? *Look at the website directory below. Where would you click to find their new page?*

Netscape -
File Edit View Go Bookmarks Options Directory Window Help
Back Forward Home Reload Images Open Print Find Stop
Location: http://www.crownhill.edu.uk

Crownhill High School Computer Club

Welcome to the CCC directory

- Who's who at the CCC
- Crownhill High Magazine
- School dates for your diary
- Free time with Crownhill kids
- Crownhill High home page

Document: Done

Netscape -
File Edit View Go Bookmarks Options Directory Window Help
Back Forward Home Reload Images Open Print
Location: http://www.crownhill.edu.uk

FUN WITH ORIENTEERING
by Lisa Hall

I went orienteering last weekend – for the first time.
It was on Dartmoor, north of Plymouth.
I got there at 9.00, and they gave me a map and a compass. They said, 'You have to run to all these different places on the map.

Location: http://www.crownhill.edu.uk

Location: http://www.crownhill.edu.uk

MUSIC CORNER by Rod Stone and Sue West

In a new survey of young people in Plymouth, we asked about music and learned a lot:

- Almost 95 per cent like one or more sorts of music. Pop music is the most popular (87%). Not many people like jazz (13%) or classical music (4%).
- Some people (15%) spend over half their pocket money on music and music videos.
- Over 30% play an instrument. Number 1 and number 2 are the guitar and the piano. We think the most interesting instrument is the sitar: Rajiv Lal (Year 9) plays this with his father.

The first one back here wins.' I looked at the first place on the map: it was across a river and up a big hill! 'What am I doing here?' I thought. 'I should be at home – in bed!'
Well, I have to tell you I was wrong. I fell in that river three times, but I had a lot of fun – and I'm going to do it all again next weekend!
A great day, and very cheap! Try it!
Call Robin Tremaine on
01752 256361.

Plymouth Dome
by Ryan Price

This is where you should go if you want to find out more about Plymouth. You'll find it up on Plymouth Hoe above the sea. You can see and hear – and smell!!! – the town as it was 400 years ago. You can find out about the people and the ships that have sailed from Plymouth all over the world. (People like Sir Francis Drake, Captain Cook and Scott of the Antarctic.) You can try life on the big ships that carried people to America before everyone started to go by plane. You can use the radar equipment and 'watch' ships out at sea. It's fun and not too expensive.

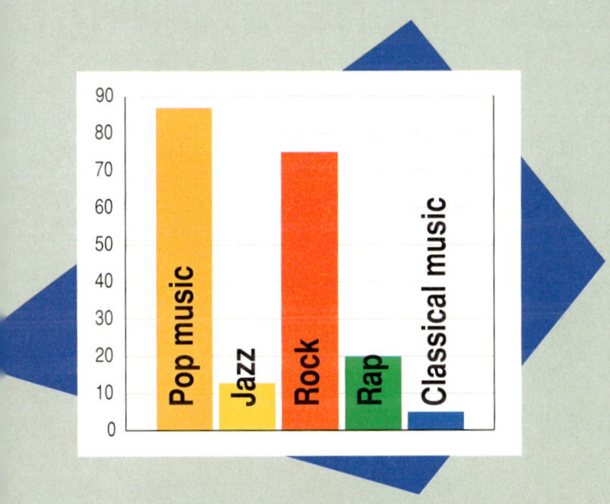

→ P 11, 12

7

After they had chosen their favourite articles, Mike collected all the pieces of paper together. He had already thought about the next step, and he explained to Lisa and Ryan, 'Now we have to scan everything into the computer.'
When they had done that, Mike started to work on-screen. The others watched and gave him ideas …
'Mike, move that picture up a bit.'
'And make the bar chart a bit bigger.'
'Can you change that colour? I hate brown!'
A lot later, when Mike had finished, he felt pleased with himself. 'Not bad, eh?' he said.
'Mm, but it really needs music,' Lisa said.
'Yes, and video, and … and … links to other websites,' Ryan added.
Mike turned slowly, made a face and said, 'Well, just listen to the biggest nerd of all!'

→ P 13

FOCUS ON GRAMMAR

Look at this sentence:
After they had chosen …, Mike collected …
What happened first? (past perfect)
What happened second? (simple past)

Look at A7. Find more sentences with the past perfect. Write them in your exercise book. Underline them as in the example above.

Now fill in the right verb forms in this sentence:
When he (finish), he (turn off) the screen.

→ S 6: 4 (pp. 132–133)
→ P 9, (D 3 ◆, p. 120)
→ P 10, D 4 ■ (p. 120)

PROJECT (PART 2)

You can now present information from your own survey. (Look at Rod Stone and Sue West's presentation.)
- *Divide your group in two. Decide which pair describes which section(s) of your survey.*
- *Discuss your ideas with your partner and write a text.*
- *Put all the texts from your group together. You can do this as a poster. You can add pictures or charts.*
- *If your school has a website, you can choose the best poster and start a new page like Mike and the others.*

→ UK Mag, pp. 106–109

◆◆ 1 **REVISION** Questions, questions, questions!

a *Partner B: look at page 113.*
Partner A: ask your partner about last Saturday. Make your questions from the following:

- (you be) out last Saturday?
- (you have) a nice time?
- What's it like? (be) there lots of things you can do?
- (you have got) a photo of the place?
- (it be) open next weekend?
- (you want to go) there again – with me?

Example:
A Were you out last Saturday?
B Yes, I was. I was at ...

b *Now your partner is asking you about last Saturday. Imagine you were at Woodlands Country Park. Study the advertisement on the right and answer your partner's questions. Say as much as you can about Woodlands Country Park.*

◇ 2 ▶ **The Internet is great, ...** → D1 ◆ (p. 120)
Find the correct question tag.

isn't	he? she? it?
aren't	you? we? they?

1 The Internet is great, ... it?
2 Mike is only interested in computers, ...
3 Lisa and Ryan are Mike's friends, ...
4 Lisa is angry with Mike, ...
5 We're going now, ...
6 You're always in front of your computer, ...

3 ▶ **You like computers, ...**
Choose the correct question tag.

doesn't he? • doesn't she?
don't they? • don't you?

1 Ryan: You like computers, ...
2 Lisa wants to learn about the Internet, ...
3 Ryan goes to town every Saturday, ...
4 Lisa and Ryan meet friends in town, ...
5 Mike: You just hang around, ...
6 Lisa thinks Mike is unfriendly, ...
7 Ryan: Your friends talk to you with their computers, ...

→ D 2 ■ (p. 120)

◆◆ 4 ▶ **What are you doing next week?**
Partner B: look at page 114.
Partner A: look at your plan for the week. You want to go swimming with your partner. But when? Find a time when both of you can go. Ask and answer questions like this:

A What are you doing on Monday afternoon?
B I'm ... . What about ... evening?
A That's no good. I'm ... . What about ...?
A/B I'm free then, too. Great!

Day	Afternoon	Evening
Mon	–	play basketball
Tue	help mum at home	–
Wed	play tennis with Alex	–
Thur	–	do tennis training
Fri	have a music lesson	–
Sat	–	go and watch Arsenal with dad

5 ▶ It's for you!

a *Ryan wants to talk to Lisa, but her mum has answered the phone. Put their conversation in the right order. (The phone conversation in A4 may help you.)*

- Bye.
- Fine. I've got that.
- Plymouth 714239. Hello?
- Hello, Ryan. Yes, of course. Lisa! It's for you! … Lisa? … I'm sorry, Ryan, she isn't here. Can I take a message?

- Thanks, Mrs Hall. Goodbye.
- Yes, please, it's this: everyone is meeting at the park at 4.00.
- Oh, hello, Mrs Hall. This is Ryan. Could I speak to Lisa, please?

◆◆ **b** *Now practise the conversation with a partner.*

6 LISTENING Phone messages

a *Copy the following twice. Then listen to the conversations and complete the messages.*

Message for: From:

Message:

◆◆ **b** *Make up more conversations with a partner.*
- *First write down a message. Example:* We're meeting at the pizza place at 5.00.
- *When you call, ask for someone. He/She is out. Then give your message.*
- *When you answer, take the message.*

A 756345. Hello?
B Oh, hello, (Niels). This is (Miriam). Could I speak to (Stefan), please?
A I'm sorry, (Miriam). He isn't here. He has gone to the shops / … .
B Well, could you give him …

7 ▶ The 'I want you to …' game

One person is 'it'. He/She has to do what other people say – very fast. If he/she finishes before the next instruction, the person who is 'it' changes. Example:

TEACHER Daniela, you're 'it'. Christian, give the first instruction.
CHRISTIAN I want you to open the door.
DANIELA *(starts to run to the door)*
TEACHER Nadine, you're next.
NADINE I want you to write your name on the board.
DANIELA *(starts to run to the board)*
TEACHER Julia, you're next.
JULIA Er … I want you to … er …
DANIELA *(finishes her name on the board)*
TEACHER All right. Julia, you're 'it' now!

Some ideas
say your name, address and phone number
put these books on that desk
take this book to (Stefan)
write your name on the board
clean the board
climb up on your chair and climb down again
open / close the window
open / close the door

8 ▶ What do/don't they want Lucy and Tony to do?

1 THEIR TEACHER Lucy and Tony, you must work harder. You mustn't be so lazy.
2 TONY'S FRIEND Please don't sing again, Tony!
3 THEIR MOTHER Tony and Lucy, go and tidy up your bedrooms.
4 LUCY'S SISTER Lucy, don't take my jeans again!
5 TONY'S FATHER Tony, you shouldn't listen to CDs when you're doing your homework.
6 THEIR MOTHER Now, you two, don't come home later than 8.00.
7 LUCY'S FRIENDS Why don't you go into town with us on Saturday?

Now say what they want / don't want Lucy and Tony to do – like this:

1 Their teacher wants them to work harder. He doesn't want them to be … .
2 Tony's friend doesn't … .

9 ▶ Lisa's bad day › D 3 ◆ (p. 120)

Write about Lisa. Use the simple past and the past perfect.

1 When Lisa (wake up), everyone else (already/get up).
2 When she (go) to the bathroom her brother (get) there first.
3 When she (get) downstairs for breakfast, her brother (eat) the last egg.
4 When she (reach) the bus stop, the bus (already/go).
5 When she (arrive) at school, the lessons (already/start).
6 When she (go) to the library at lunch-time, someone (take) the book that she wanted.
7 When she (get) to the school canteen, the others (have) the nicest things.

1 When Lisa *woke up*, everyone else *had already got up*.
2 *When she ...*

10 ▶ A visit to Plymouth

Finish Stefan's story of his visit to Plymouth. Put the verbs in the right forms – past perfect or simple past.

We (reach) Plymouth two hours late because our plane from Frankfurt (leave) late. We (find) the hotel easily because mum (phone) from Germany and the hotel people (send) us a map. After I (unpack) my things, I (decide) to go out and walk up onto the Hoe. The sea (be) beautiful that evening, and there (be) hundreds of boats on the water: I (never see) so many boats before I (come) here! Mum and dad (come) a few minutes later. The people at the hotel (tell) them about the old harbour, so next we (walk) down there together. We (have) dinner there because we (not eat) at the hotel. I (choose) fish and chips because I (never have) any really English food before. It (be) OK.

WORD WATCH

11 WORD BUILDING

a *You already know words like* unfriendly *and* unhealthy. *They come from the adjectives* friendly *and* healthy. *How does* un- *change the meaning of these adjectives? Say what the adjectives in the box mean (in English or in German).*

unhappy • unimportant
unkind • unpopular
unsafe • untidy

b *Complete these sentences with adjectives from* **a**.

1 You shouldn't eat so much chocolate: it's *unhealthy*.
2 The people who live opposite us are very … . They never talk to us.
3 Terry! Don't be so …! Give your brother some crisps.
4 You don't need to know that. It's … .
5 Ian is very … . He leaves things all over the house!
6 Mr Jones is the most … teacher at Mike's school. He always gives too much homework.
7 Tina was very … at her old school. She likes her new school much better.
8 The chair is … – one leg is broken.

12 WORD LINK

a *Match words from the boxes. How many combinations can you find?*

basketball • CD
chess • computer • newspaper
pop • radar • rock • school
sports • table

camp • centre • club
equipment • game • magazine
music • orchestra • player • room
shop • team • tennis

basketball camp, basketball centre, basketball …

❖ **b** *Make two teams. Your teacher will say a word from the top box. The teams must find as many combinations as they can. You can use words from the boxes and other words, too.*

TEACHER Computer.
TEAM A Computer game.
TEAM B Computer club.
TEAM A Computer magazine.
TEAM B We can't think of another one.
TEACHER What about you, Team A?
TEAM A Computer nerd.
TEACHER Very good! OK, that's one point for Team A. … And now, the next word is …

13 ▶ All about computers

a *Look at pages 72–75 again and make a network with words about computers.*

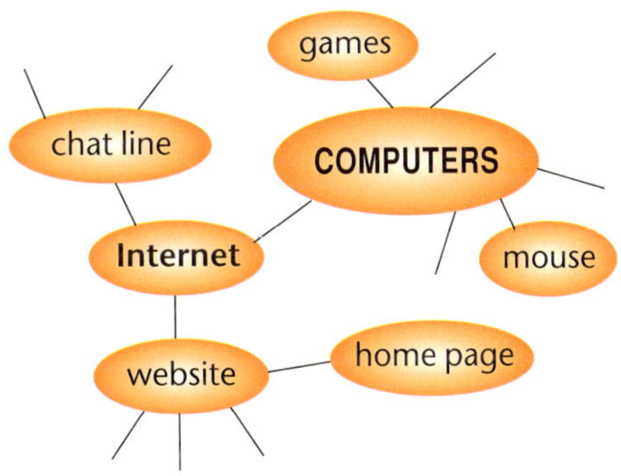

b *Now complete these sentences. Your network will help you.*

1 Mike's only interested in computers and nothing else. He's a real computer … .
2 If you want to get to talk to people on the Internet, you can join a … line.
3 Some people use computers to get information, others play computer … .
4 To do things on a computer you can use the mouse or the … .
5 You … on symbols with the mouse.
6 You look at things on the … .
7 A … is the first page of a website.
8 When you make a website, you type in texts and … in photos.

Dangerous Dartmoor

Look at the photo of Dartmoor. What might be dangerous there?

Julie Ruddock got on her pony Fred and said to her dad: 'Fred and I are going to go riding – up by Great Mis Tor.' She pointed up the valley, north to the big hill. Her dad turned from his work and smiled. 'Go carefully.' 'Of course,' she said. And she was careful. Very. Dartmoor was wild and could be dangerous, and a farm girl like Julie knew that. The sun was shining now, but that could change in just a few minutes. Julie checked her small rucksack: she had some chocolate, a map and a warm anorak.

An hour later, she was north of Great Mis Tor. She could see the small town of Princetown and the big, grey prison there. The sky was grey now, too, and Julie was cold. She took out her anorak and put it on. Then to the west she saw mist. 'It's coming fast,' she thought. 'I must get back quickly.' But the mist was quicker. Minutes later it reached her. She could see almost nothing.

*

Back at the farm, Julie's parents looked out of the dining-room window. The mist was coming down the valley. Her mum said, 'Bill, I think we should go and look for her.' Just then, the music on Radio Plymouth stopped, and the Ruddocks heard: 'Early this morning, a prisoner escaped from Dartmoor Prison at Princetown. The police have started a big search and have closed all roads from Dartmoor. The man, Ronald Black, is dangerous and people should not go near him.'
'You're right, Sally, we must go. Now!'

*

Julie did not know where she was any more. She could not see the path, and the ground was suddenly wet and muddy. 'We must be near Fox Mire!' Julie thought. The deep, black mud of Fox Mire was very dangerous, so she decided to go on foot. She climbed down from Fred and walked in front of him. She carefully touched the ground with each foot before she moved slowly forward. Three times she turned back and tried to find another way. She was frightened and very cold now. Night was coming.

*

The man was big and heavy, tired and very hungry. He came to a gate and stopped. Through the mist he could see a light.

'A house! Maybe I can get something to eat.' He opened the gate slowly and moved quietly towards the light.

*

Julie's parents were at the door. 'Wait,' said Mrs Ruddock suddenly. 'I know what Julie will do. She'll go to Liz Mitchell's cottage.'

'You might be right. Let's call Liz.'

Mrs Ruddock found the number and called. 'Liz? ... Listen, have you seen Julie? She was riding up near you before the mist.'

'No, my dear. But I can go out and look for her.'

'Thanks, Liz, but it's all right. Bill and I are going to do that. But she may come to you. If she does, can you call us on our mobile?'

'Yes, of course. ... But wait, I can hear someone outside now. It must be Julie.'

'Oh, that's wonderful, Liz!'

'I'm going to look.' The little old woman put the phone down and went to the door.

Mrs Ruddock turned to her husband. 'Someone has just arrived. It'll be Julie. I know it will.'

*

Mrs Mitchell opened the front door. 'Julie?' There was no answer. She went out. 'Julie, dear?'

Suddenly, she felt two big hands around her neck. 'Sorry, but it's not Julie,' a man said quietly into her ear. Mrs Mitchell tried to shout, but she couldn't.

'Let's go in, eh? Quietly.' The man pushed Mrs Mitchell inside and looked around. He saw one plate – Mrs Mitchell's dinner – on the table. 'Alone here, eh? Good.' Then he saw the phone off the hook. He pulled it from the wall. 'Now we can have a nice, quiet time together. Just you and me.' He threw Mrs Mitchell into a chair.

*

The ground was not so muddy now. 'Great!' Julie thought. Then through the mist she saw something tall and dark. It was not moving. Was it a man? She was frightened. 'Hello?' she said. No answer. She and Fred went nearer – slowly. Then she knew. 'It's the old Monk Stone! Now we know where we are, Fred!' She felt fantastic. 'Let's give ourselves a present.' She took out her chocolate and broke it into two pieces. They stood by the stone and enjoyed their chocolate. 'Good, now if we go right here,' she thought happily, 'we'll come to Mrs Mitchell's cottage, and I can phone home from there.' She got onto Fred, and turned his head to the right.

? *What do you think happened next?*

'Liz? ... Liz! Are you all right?' Mrs Ruddock shouted into the phone. Suddenly the phone was dead. Just then they heard the radio again. '... Do not go near Black. This man is dangerous.'
Mr and Mrs Ruddock looked at each other. They were thinking the same thing. 'The police,' she said. 'We must call the police!'

*

Julie reached the gate and saw the light. She and Fred went up the stone path. Inside Black heard Fred. 'A horse! I want it!' He said to Mrs Mitchell, 'Quiet! Or you'll be sorry!' Julie knocked. 'Hello? Mrs Mitchell?'
Mrs Mitchell jumped up and shouted as loudly as she could. 'Julie! Don't come in! Get back on Fred and go! Go, Julie! Go! ... Aagh!'
Black hit her hard and she fell back. Then he ran to the door and threw it open. Julie was turning away, but Black quickly caught her arm. 'Well, young Julie, not so fast!'
'Who ... who are you?' Her face was white.
'Don't worry about that.' He pushed her inside, to a chair next to Mrs Mitchell's.
'Mrs Mitchell! What's happening?'
'Sit quietly and we'll be all right.' Mrs Mitchell tried to smile because she did not want Julie to be frightened. But she was very scared, too!

First Black tied his prisoners to their chairs. Then he ate Mrs Mitchell's dinner. 'Very nice,' he said. 'And next I'm going to go riding!'
'You stupid man,' Mrs Mitchell shouted. 'You can't ride that little pony! You'll kill him!'
'We'll be fine, me and Fred.' And he left. Through the open door, Mrs Mitchell and Julie heard a car. Then another one. People were coming up the long path from the road. Black jumped onto Fred, and the poor pony almost fell. He hit Fred, shouted, and they disappeared down the path towards the Monk Stone – and towards Fox Mire.

The police pulled the ropes off. 'Thank God you're both all right!' Julie's mum said. 'But he has got Fred.' Julie was crying. 'Follow me,' Mrs Mitchell said. 'I know a short cut. And bring the ropes. We may need them.'

They heard Black before they reached the Mire. He was shouting for help. Fred was on dry ground, but the prisoner was deep in the mud. They threw the end of a rope to him and slowly pulled him out. He was black with mud. 'That animal!' he shouted. 'It threw me off.'
One police officer said, 'Well, after all this fun, prison life will be nice and quiet, won't it?'

WORKING WITH THE TEXT

1 ▶ Who thought it – and when?
Was it Julie, her mum or dad, Mrs Mitchell or Black?

1 'It's much colder now!'
2 'She's right. We must look for her.'
3 'No! I'm going the wrong way again!'
4 'Great! There's only this little old woman here.'
5 'What if Black is at Liz's cottage now?'
6 'People are coming! They'll help us!'
7 'Even prison is better than that mud!'

2 ▶ The police have got lots of questions
Write three police questions for one person in the story. Your partner reads the questions, says who the person is and answers them. For example:
What were you doing when Julie left the farm?
How did you hear about the prisoner?
Was it you who phoned Mrs Mitchell?

→ D 4 ■ (p. 120)

HOW TO ... nominate a hero

Here you can use what you've learned on the other *How to* pages in this book.

1 READING Letters about heroes

Do you remember the 'Our Heroes' poster on pages 6–7? People have written thousands of letters about their heroes to the BBC. They want to persuade the BBC to make a certain person one of the BBC's heroes of the year. How do they do it? Copy the table, then look at the letter excerpts and fill in the table.

beginning/end of letters	first sentences of letters	linking words	how you can persuade people	what people are like
Dear	I think your programme ..., ...	but, when, ...	(she) really did a great thing, ...	clever, ...

Dear Sir or Madam
I think your programme is a great idea. I would like to have my uncle, Sam Burnett, on the programme. He's a real hero.

Of course you'll have lots of heroes. But Mrs Jenkins really did a great thing. I'll never forget the time when

watched two men outside our house when we were on holiday. Lucy was really clever. She decided to phone the police. But before the police arrived, the men

I'm writing to you about my hero – Jenny Wells. So let me tell you what she did:

First she tried to pull him out of the car. Then she shouted as loudly as she could. Finally another car

is the kindest and bravest person in the world. Of course he was sad and lonely when his

I was quiet and frightened. But my little brother was very brave. Next he ran

That's why I think you should choose Sally Barker.
Yours faithfully
Doreen Shaw

2 WRITING Julie's hero

Mrs Mitchell is Julie's hero. Try and write a letter to the BBC for Julie. Read 'Dangerous Dartmoor', p. 82, lines 9–60, again for details and use your table from **1**.
Here's some more help.

... my hero: Mrs Mitchell / It all happened one day in ... when a prisoner escaped / didn't know where I was / she did some great things: ... .
So that's why ...

3 WRITING Your hero

Who would be your hero for the BBC Special? Nominate someone from the book or someone you know. Write a letter. You can put it in your English album.

7 UNIT 7 A Very Special TV Special

Look at the picture. The people on the stage are the BBC's everyday heroes and the people who nominated them. You know them all. Who do you think are the heroes? Who do you think are the people who nominated them? Make a list. Compare your list with your partner's. (You'll need your list again for page 89.)

A I think ... is one of the heroes.
B I agree. / No, I don't think he/she is one of the heroes. I think ...

LISTENING

a *Listen to the cassette/CD. You'll hear about different people and things. Look at the picture and try to find them.*

b *Now copy the two lists below into your exercise book. Listen again and match the names of the people to their jobs.*

Jack	carpenter
Maggie	electrician
Dave	presenter
Gerry	make-up person
Moira	floor manager
Eddie	director
Tina	assistant floor manager

▶▶▶ NOW YOU

Would you like to work in television? Why / Why not? Write a short text and read it to your class. These ideas may help you:

- TV is boring/fun/... .
- I'm good at ... at school.
- You can ... famous people.
- It's hard work / difficult / ... .
- I want to be famous / a star / ... .

You can start like this:
I would/wouldn't like to work in television because I think ...

10:30 'OK,' called Jack. 'Get ready for a rehearsal ...'
Megan was very nervous. Hannah was, too. She checked her hair in the mirror for the tenth time.
Suddenly Mrs Patel shouted, 'Careful, everybody! That step – it's going to break ... it's very dangerous.'
Jack looked at the steps up onto the stage. 'Tina, get the carpenter – quickly,' he shouted.
'Oh, no,' thought Tina as she left. 'I hope my last day isn't going to be too horrible!'
Jack spoke quietly into his walkie-talkie. 'Moira, sorry, we've got a problem ...'
'Young man,' called Mrs Patel. 'Excuse me, but I've seen two more dangerous things ...'

? *Can you find the other two dangerous things that Mrs Patel has seen? Look again at the picture on pages 84–85.* [→ S 7: 1 (p. 133)]

10:35 'Funny,' said Tina. 'I checked the steps at ten o'clock. They were OK then.'
'Well,' said Dave, 'Maybe somebody ...'

'I don't really care how it happened, Dave,' Jack said. 'Fix it!'
'OK, OK.' Quietly Dave said to himself: 'Do this, do that! I'm glad I'm leaving tomorrow!'

Meanwhile Tina was talking to the electrician. 'Just look at this cable, Eddie. It's so dangerous. How could this happen?'
'Don't ask me. I checked everything before my coffee break at 10.15. And don't ask me how my tool box got up there. I left it on the floor by camera 1 when I went to the coffee shop.'

'Jack.' It was Moira on Jack's walkie-talkie. 'The show starts at six and the lunch break is in two hours. We must start!' [→ S 7: 2 (p. 134)]

11:00 'Tina!' called Jack. 'I can't find my script. I had it when we stopped just after 10.30 ...'
'OK, I'll look for it,' said Tina.

Suddenly she saw something on top of a bin. It was Jack's script. She gave it to him and he opened it. 'Oh, no!' he whispered. 'Look at this.'

? *What do you think the letter tells you about the person who wrote it? What are his or her feelings?*

I think the person is ... because ... [→ S 7: 3 (p. 134)]

[ ] nicht in allen Bundesländern obligatorisch

11:21 Jack and Moira were sitting in the gallery. They looked at the anonymous letter.
'The step, the cable, the tool box, and now this ...,' Jack said. 'I think someone really is trying to sabotage the show.'
'But who could it be?' asked Moira.
'Maybe Tina? She was here very early this morning ... and this is her last day. She has got a new job at BBC Belfast.'
'I can't believe it's Tina. Eddie maybe? He's leaving for a six-week trip to Australia tomorrow.'
'Eddie? Never!' said Jack. 'I know Eddie well. Dave maybe? He's in a bad mood ... and he's leaving tomorrow.'
'Well, whoever it is, I'm worried. I'll call the police ...'
'... and I'll go back to the guests,' said Jack as he ran back down to the set.
'Tina,' he said, 'get ready for a rehearsal.'

? *How many suspects do you have? Write down their names.*

11:29 Up in the gallery Moira put the phone down. 'Ready, sound? – OK, then good luck, everybody. Five, four, three, ...!'

We don't need another ...

All the guests looked very surprised. Tina smiled. Moira shouted, 'Stop!'
'Sorry, Moira.' It was the sound engineer. 'Five minutes ago I had the right tape. Somebody has swapped it.'

LISTENING

Listen to the cassette/CD. Which song do you think the director wants? Why?
I think she wants the first/... song because it says / is about ...

? *There have been five incidents now. Find them. Do you know when they happened? Make notes.*

1 *step – between 10.00 and 10.30*
2 ...

11:35 'Take a break, everyone,' shouted Jack.
David and Aled came down from the stage.
'Hi,' said Aled to Hannah. 'I'm Aled and this is David.'
'And my name is Hannah.'
'Where are you from?' asked Aled.
'I'm from London ... oh, and this is Megan – she's from your part of the country.'
'Hello, Megan,' said David. 'So, you're Welsh?'

12:09 'Get ready, everyone,' shouted Jack.
'See you in the lunch break?' Aled whispered.
'OK,' said Hannah. 'Oh, Aled, who's the hero – you or David?'
'Guess!' said Aled.
'Quiet, *please*! Ten, nine, eight ...'

'... three, two, one ...'
'Good evening and welcome to the BBC's "Our Heroes Special". My name is Gerry Logan, and I'm very happy to be with ...'
Suddenly all the lights went out. There were screams. 'Help! Help!'
'Don't move till the lights are on again,' called Jack. 'I don't want any accidents: cables are lying all over the floor.'
When the lights went on, all the clocks still showed 12.10.

Just then the police arrived. 'Don't move. We're here to find the saboteur. We have to interview everyone. You're all witnesses – and suspects.'

◆◆ **ACTIVITY**

Now six things have happened in the studio. Who is trying to sabotage the show? The police soon have three suspects – Tina, Dave and Eddie. All of them are leaving tomorrow.

a *Copy this table into your exercise book or ask your teacher for a copy. Work with a partner. Read pages 86/87 again. Where do Tina, Dave and Eddie say they were at the times in the left column? Did anybody (a witness) see them? Where? Fill in all the information you can find so far. You'll get more information as you go on. Under the table write down all the other things that you find important.*

time	Tina	witness	Dave	witness	Eddie	witness
10.00–10.30 (*step, cable, tool box*)	*studio at 10.00* ...	*Jack, Mrs Patel* ...	?	?	?	?
10.30–11.00 (*letter*)	*studio at 10.35*	?	?	?	?	?
11.00–11.30 (*tape*)	?	?	?	?	?	?

Other clues: 1. Jack says that Dave is in a bad mood. 2. Jack knows that Tina ...

b *Partner B: look at page 114.*
Partner A: read the police interview with Tina. Add the new information to your table. Then tell your partner what you have found out. Your partner has the police interview with Dave. He/She will tell you what he/she has found out. Add this information, too.

POLICE When did you get here this morning, Miss McGough?

TINA Very early. I think I was the first person in the studio. I was busy with the guests till ten o'clock. I went to the coffee shop then. On my way I checked the steps onto the stage ...

POLICE And, were the steps OK?

TINA Yes, they were. Well, then I had my coffee. I saw Eddie in the coffee shop, too, but I was reading and I didn't want to talk. I was back in the studio at about 10.30. I don't know how that tool box got up onto the set wall – it's so heavy. I'm not strong enough to lift it.

POLICE When did you find the script with the letter in it?

TINA At eleven o'clock. It was on top of a bin, near the store room. After that I stayed in the studio and asked people questions. I wanted to know who was doing these terrible things.

POLICE Who did you talk to?

TINA Eddie, Da... no, Dave wasn't there.

POLICE And where were you at 11.30?

TINA I was here in the studio all the time. It was chaos! I'm glad I'm leaving tomorrow. Belfast can't be as bad as this!

c *Listen to the interview with Eddie on the cassette/CD together. Finish your tables. Who do you think is the saboteur? Why? Talk about your ideas with your partner.*

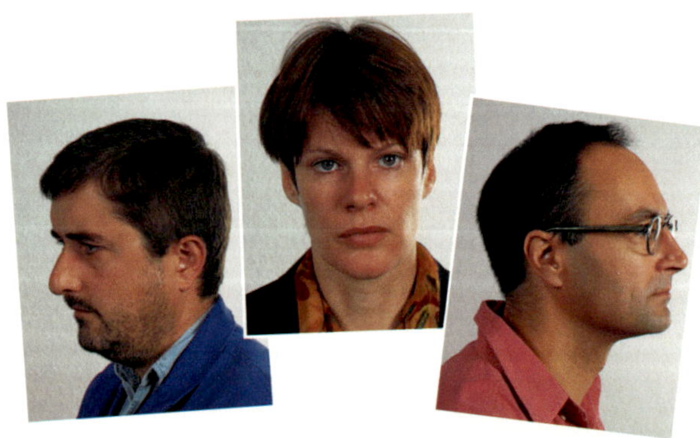

You can use these expressions
It may/might/must be ...
It can't be him/her because ...
He says he was ... but she says ...
What he/she says isn't true because ...

14:36 After lunch everyone felt better. Everything was ready for a rehearsal. Gerry Logan stood nervously and waited.
'... five ... four ... three ...'
'Good evening and welcome to the BBC's "Our Heroes Special". My name is Gerry Logan and I'm ...'
Suddenly there was a loud noise as one of the big lights broke loose. Tina shouted: 'Gerry – move!' He turned and took a step towards her just as the light crashed onto the floor only centimetres away from him. Tina looked up into the lights. 'It's Dave! I can see him! It's Dave!' She ran towards the metal stairs that led up to the lights. The policewoman got there first. 'This is a job for the police.' She ran up the stairs as the second police officer climbed up on the other side of the studio. They could see Dave now. He was trying to get back to the wall.
'I'm going to fall!' he screamed.
'You'll be all right. Just look at me ...'

The police got Dave down safely.
'They threw me out,' he told them. 'I hated the job, but it was a job. After tonight – no work and no money! I had nothing to lose.'
Five minutes later the police left – with Dave.

That evening millions of people sat down and watched the BBC Special. And not one of them knew that this was the end of a difficult day at the studio. They just heard: 'And now the BBC proudly presents – the OUR HEROES SPECIAL!'

LISTENING Our Heroes Special

At last the 'Our Heroes Special' is on television. Listen to it on the cassette/CD.
On page 85 you made a list of heroes and the people who nominated them. Look at that list while you are listening. Were you right?

▶▶▶ NOW YOU

Which of the heroes and people who nominated them is your hero? Why?
On page 1 of your English album is a hero. Have your ideas about heroes changed? Why/Why not? Your ideas from page 83 may help you.

○ REVISION Do-it-yourself exercises

You don't know all the words on these two pages. But you'll find them in the dictionary on pages 166–185.

◆◆ *Do you have problems with English? Here is some help for you and your partner. Try and make your own do-it-yourself exercises.*

Partner A: What problems do you have? Make a list and show it to your partner. Partner B: Help your partner with his/her problems. Choose an exercise from below. Read the instructions, make the exercise and give it to your partner.

How to spell words
Vocabulary
Prepositions (*at, behind*, etc.)
Verb forms (*heard, saw*, etc.)
Word order (*to the big city in July*, etc.)

1 ▶ What are the words? Spelling

Find words that belong together, for example, school words. *Write them down with the letters in the wrong order. Can your partner put the letters in the right order?*

arribly, enacten, chearet, stoihry → *library, canteen, ...*

2 ▶ Dictations Spelling

Read a text of 50–60 words to your partner. Your partner has to write down the text. You can give punctuation in English like this:

.	= full stop [ˌfʊl ˈstɒp]	‘	= Open quotation marks. [kwəʊˈteɪʃn mɑːks]
,	= comma [ˈkɒmə]	’	= Close quotation marks.
?	= question mark [ˈkwestʃn mɑːk]	:	= colon [ˈkəʊlən]
		;	= semicolon [ˌsemɪˈkəʊlən]
!	= exclamation mark [ˌekskləˈmeɪʃn mɑːk]	–	= dash [dæʃ]
		...	= three dots *or:* dot–dot–dot [dɒt]

Read with pauses (//) after groups of words – like this:

Breakfasts at the weekend were always special for Megan and her dad – no work, no school. → *Breakfasts at the weekend // were always special // for Megan and her dad (dash) // no work (comma) // no school (full stop)*

Your partner checks his/her work. Then you read the text again: he/she checks again.

3 ▶ Find the words Vocabulary/Spelling

Find words that belong together, for example, places in town. *Write them down as on the right. Can your partner find all the words?*

B	R	H	O	U	S	E	B	U	S	M	A	R	K	E	T
A	C	A	T	H	E	D	R	A	L	H	O	T	E	L	E
N	S	A	P	O	I	W	E	L	Y	T	O	K	H	I	P
K	D	O	G	S	M	U	S	E	U	M	V	P	E	Y	B
F	A	R	M	P	O	P	C	I	T	Y	W	A	L	L	S

4 ▶ Odd word out Vocabulary

Find words that belong together. Add one word that doesn't belong. Can your partner find the odd word out? Maybe he/she can say why the word doesn't belong.

department store, bank, supermarket, newspaper shop
↓
The odd word out is 'bank' because you can't buy things there.

5 ▶ **The fourth word** Vocabulary/Grammar

Find and arrange pairs of words as in the examples below. Leave one word out. Can your partner find it? You can ask for words or for grammatical forms.

fast	slow
good	?

man	men
mouse	?

→

fast	slow
good	*bad*

man	men
mouse	*mice*

6 ▶ **Fill in the right word** Prepositions/Vocabulary/Grammar

a *Copy a short text from this book, but leave out some of the words, for example,* prepositions. *You can write these words next to the text – but in the wrong order. Can your partner put them in the right places?*

in • for • to
to • with

I've been ... Wales. I was there ... a day last year when I stayed ... my cousins Nick and Debbie ... Chester. Have you ever been ... Chester?

→

I've been *to* Wales. I was there *for* a day last year when I stayed *with* my cousins Nick and Debbie *in* Chester. Have you ever been *to* Chester?

b *You can also take out every fifth word, for example. Can your partner fill in the missing words?*

I've been to Wales. ... was there for a ... last year when I ... with my cousins Nick ... Debbie in Chester.

→

I've been to Wales. *I* was there for a *day* last year when I *stayed* with my cousins Nick *and* Debbie in Chester.

7 ▶ **Fill in the right form of the verbs** Verb forms

Copy a short text from this book. For each verb, write the infinitive of that verb in brackets. Can your partner fill in the right verb forms? The list of irregular verbs on pages 191–192 will help you.

There (be) lots of kids and she (feel) very nervous. One girl (come) to talk to her.
'Hi!' she (say). '(Be) you new?'

↓

There *were* lots of kids and she *felt* very nervous. One girl *came* to talk to her.
'Hi!' she *said*. '*Are* you new?'

'Somewhere with no irregular verbs.'

8 ▶ **Put the words in the right order** Word order

Find sentences and write them with words and phrases in the wrong order. Can your partner write down the sentences correctly?

in a village / a town / Megan Owen / near Bangor / lived / in North Wales → *Megan Owen lived in a village near Bangor, a town in North Wales.*

and Megan / moved / Mr Owen / in July / to the big city → *In July Mr Owen and Megan moved to the big city. / Mr Owen and Megan moved to the big city in July.*

don't / I / anyone / know / at Tufnell Park → *I don't know anyone at Tufnell Park.*

◦ INTERPRETING[1]

AFTER UNIT 4

Situation 1

a *Look at the picture on the right:*

- What can you say about these people?
- Where are they?
- What's happening?

b *Now listen to the conversation on the cassette/CD. Then read it. Were you right about the situation?*

BOY Kann ich Ihnen helfen?
MAN Ich spreche leider kein Englisch. Es ist nett, dass du uns helfen möchtest.
BOY Can I help?
TOURIST Please! I'm trying to get to the market, but I can't find it.
BOY Die Dame sagt, sie sucht den Marktplatz. Ich bin nicht von hier. Wissen Sie, wo der ist?
MAN Ja, meint sie den neuen oder den alten Markt?
BOY He wants to know: Do you mean the old market or the new one?
TOURIST I think it's the old market I want.
BOY Sie sucht den alten.
MAN Das ist ja ganz einfach. Sag ihr, dass sie die Straße hier geradeaus gehen, dann rechts in die Hansastraße einbiegen soll. Der Markt ist dort.
BOY He says go along this street, then turn right into Hansastraße. The old market is there.
TOURIST Oh, thank you very much!

c *Now read the notes about interpreting.*

NOTES

Die kurze Szene hat dir sicherlich schon deutlich gemacht, worauf es beim Dolmetschen ankommt. Merke dir Folgendes:

1 **Ziel** ist es, den **Inhalt einer Aussage** weiterzugeben. Solange der Sinn der Aussage erhalten bleibt, kannst du unwichtige Wörter oder Sätze auslassen und den Satzbau verändern.

2 Im Deutschen wie im Englischen solltest du **Einleitungen** verwenden, z.B.:
Sie sagt/meint, dass ...
Er möchte wissen, ob Sie / wo Sie ...
She says/thinks ...
He wants to know: Are you ... / where do you ...

Situation 2

a *Try to explain the situation below.*

b *Listen to the cassette/CD and interpret like the boy in situation 1. Then practise the conversation with two partners.*

TOURIST Excuse me! I want to catch a bus to the castle. What time is the next one? Can anyone tell me?
YOU Die Dame sagt, ...
WOMAN Das ist kein Problem. Der nächste kommt gleich. Alle Busse, die hier abfahren, halten am Schloss.
YOU ...
TOURIST Oh, thanks very much.

[1] interpreting [ɪn'tɜːprɪtɪŋ] *Dolmetschen*

AFTER UNIT 5

a *Look at the picture and explain the situation.*

b *Listen to the conversation on the cassette/CD. Imagine you're Nina and interpret for Oma and Kate.*

OMA Sag Kate, dass ich mich freue, sie kennen zu lernen.
YOU …
KATE Nina has told me a lot about you, Mrs Berger. She always says that you tell great stories.
YOU …
OMA Danke, das ist ja nett von dir. … Wie gefällt es denn Kate hier in Düsseldorf?
YOU …
KATE It's great. But I'd like to speak German better. Now Nina has to interpret for me quite a lot.
YOU …
OMA Was habt ihr heute vor? Das Wetter ist so schön, ihr könntet doch eine Bootstour machen.
YOU …

c *Now practise the conversation with two partners.*

AFTER UNIT 6

a *Look at the picture and explain the situation.*

b *Listen to the conversation on the cassette/CD. Imagine you're Ute and interpret for Nils and Britta. Then practise the conversation with two partners.*

NILS Grüß dich, Britta! Tut mir Leid, aber mein Englisch ist schrecklich und ich kann kein Schwedisch. Sag mal, surfst du gern?
YOU …
BRITTA Well, my parents are trying to teach me, but I can't do it yet. I fall into the water all the time! Are you good at surfing?
YOU …
NILS Nein, aber ich wills lernen. Hör mal, ich hab eine Idee. Es gibt hier jeden Tag Surfkurse. Was hältst du davon?
YOU …
BRITTA Yes, that's a great idea! We can all go together.
YOU …

UK MAG

Welcome to the UK Mag(azine). Here you'll find articles, stories and photos that young people in Britain find in their magazines. You can read it on your own or with your form. Of course, as in any other English magazine, you won't know every word. But we think you'll understand most of it. If you need help, you'll find translations of the most important words on pages 164–165.
Have fun with the UK Mag!

The next day ...
Great, no school tomorrow! Let's go to the new CD shop, Kate.
I can't. I have to help mum to tidy up the house.
9
But then on Saturday ...
Look, there's Kate. Do you want to go and talk to her?
No, Mum, I don't!
10
That evening ...
11
Hi, Kate! Would you like to come over and watch *Baywatch*?
12
Sorry! I'm helping mum.
Later at Kate's house ...
I thought: maybe I can help, too?
Er, ... well, Diana is already ... er, helping me, er, us. Thanks.
13
14
I saw you with Diana this morning, too. I don't think you want to be my friend any more.
Well, Diana is more fun. But we can still meet sometimes, Mandy.
15
No, Kate. That's not what friends are about!
Next week at school ...
16
We've got another new pupil. This is Max.
Mmm, he looks nice!
After lessons ...
Of course you can, Max!
17
Hi, I'm Max. Are you Mandy? My sister knows you from dance class. ... Can I walk to the gym with you?

In and Out of School

Here in the UK kids have a long school day – from about 8.50 am to about 3.45 pm. After that they have school clubs and homework. Here's what one girl wrote. Next to her letter are some homework tips.

Debbie, 14, finds it a nightmare to study

'I've got a little sister and two little brothers so I can't do homework at home. I try to study in my bedroom but my sister, Angela, usually watches TV there or plays silly games with her friends. She says half of the room is hers, but I can't concentrate and we usually start arguing.'

FIND A SPACE

DO YOU HAVE A ROOM TOGETHER WITH A BROTHER OR SISTER? THEN TRY THIS: WHEN YOUR LITTLE SISTER IS WATCHING TV, DO SOMETHING ELSE. BUT SHE MUST AGREE TO LEAVE THE ROOM WHEN YOU WANT TO DO YOUR HOMEWORK. WITH A REGULAR 'HOMEWORK TIME' EVERY NIGHT YOU CAN CONCENTRATE MUCH BETTER, AND SHE AND YOU WILL GET WHAT YOU WANT.

Most kids in the UK have to wear school uniform. What are the advantages and disadvantages?

	School uniform	Your own clothes
What teachers say	'Put on your tie, please.'	'Does your mother really let you wear that?'
What pupils say	'I hate the uniform, terrible colour, silly tie.'	'Do you like my new clothes?'
What parents say	'You are growing fast, dear.'	'Can't you wear nice clothes to school?'
Advantages	Doesn't cost as much. You don't have to worry about what you're going to wear every morning.	Cost more, but you don't have to wear anything stupid.
Disadvantages	Everyone looks the same. It never fits.	You think more about clothes than school. You have nothing new you can wear outside school.

And the winner is: school uniform.

You look terrible, but all the others look terrible too, and you don't have to find a new outfit every day.

A VISIT TO WALES

MAE'R GYMRAEG YMA O HYD

When Gwenllian Ellis tells her great-grandson stories of the fairies in the valleys near their home in the North of Wales, she tells her stories in Welsh – of course.

But things weren't always like that. 'When I was a little girl in school, there was trouble if we spoke Welsh,' she remembers. '"Speak English," the teachers always told us. And we tried. But sometimes, when we were excited, we forgot. Just one word of Welsh – the language we spoke at home – and we had to wear the Welsh Not.

The teachers tied a piece of wood with the letters WN for "Welsh Not" round our necks, and we had to wear it all day. And everyone knew: that boy or girl spoke Welsh today. It was like something dirty. I only had to wear the Welsh Not once, but it was terrible.'

For a minute, Gwen didn't say anything. She looked out across the valley towards the sea. Slowly she started to smile. 'When I told my parents about the Not, they were angry. But they didn't go to the teachers and complain. We tried to speak English at home. Imagine, we stopped speaking our own language in our own home!

'Later I had children, too, and I never spoke Welsh to them. I remembered the Not, and I didn't want to see my children coming home with stories like mine.'

Today, of course, things are different. Gwen's great-grandson will speak Welsh and English at school. Some lessons will be in English, others in Welsh. He will listen not only to the best of English and American rock music, but also to Welsh pop and perhaps to traditional harp music, too.

'The Welsh language is very beautiful,' says Gwen. 'It's very good for poetry. The Welsh people have always been good at poetry and singing.'

Today people come from far away to Nant Gwrtheyrn (the National Welsh Language Centre), where they learn the language. Many of the people who are learning the old language are Welsh. They don't have to worry about the Welsh Not any more.

Mae'r Gymraeg yma o hyd – Welsh lives on.

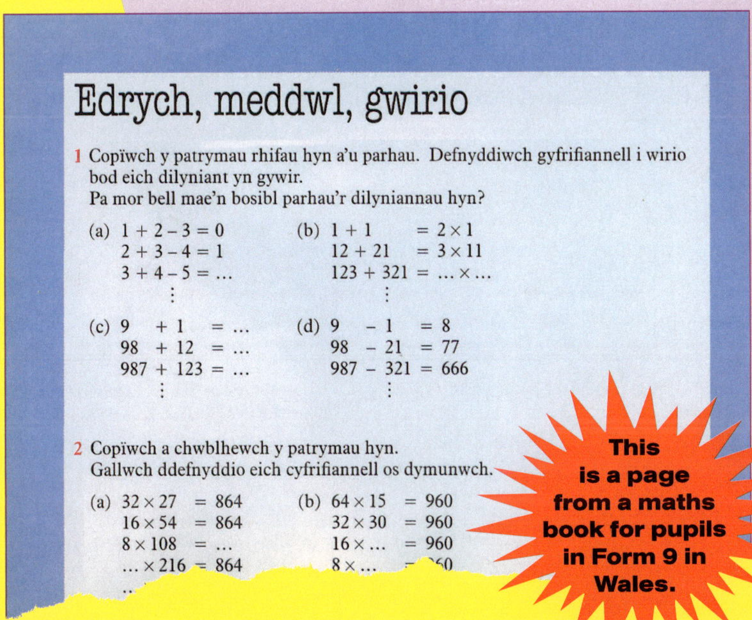

Edrych, meddwl, gwirio

1 Copïwch y patrymau rhifau hyn a'u parhau. Defnyddiwch gyfrifiannell i wirio bod eich dilyniant yn gywir.
Pa mor bell mae'n bosibl parhau'r dilyniannau hyn?

(a) $1 + 2 - 3 = 0$
$2 + 3 - 4 = 1$
$3 + 4 - 5 = \ldots$
⋮

(b) $1 + 1 = 2 \times 1$
$12 + 21 = 3 \times 11$
$123 + 321 = \ldots \times \ldots$
⋮

(c) $9 + 1 = \ldots$
$98 + 12 = \ldots$
$987 + 123 = \ldots$
⋮

(d) $9 - 1 = 8$
$98 - 21 = 77$
$987 - 321 = 666$
⋮

2 Copïwch a chwblhewch y patrymau hyn.
Gallwch ddefnyddio eich cyfrifiannell os dymunwch.

(a) $32 \times 27 = 864$
$16 \times 54 = 864$
$8 \times 108 = \ldots$
$\ldots \times 216 = 864$
..

(b) $64 \times 15 = 960$
$32 \times 30 = 960$
$16 \times \ldots = 960$
$8 \times \ldots =$ [illegible]60

This is a page from a maths book for pupils in Form 9 in Wales.

When people in other parts of Britain think of Wales, they think of music. If a Welsh school wants to have a special evening for parents and friends, it will usually be an evening of music. This is part of one school's programme.

YSGOL GYFUN EMLYN
yn cyflwyno / presents

OCEAN WORLD

1. Woodwind Ensemble	WATER MUSIC SUITE (Handel)
2. Choir	BEATLES MEDLEY
3. Recorder Group	SEA MEDLEY
4. Brass Quintet	ACAPULCO BAY
5. Ensemble	OCEAN WAVES
6. Cor Ysgol y Ddwylan ac Ysgol Penboyr	A FUOCH CHI 'RIOED YN MORIO
7. Sing along	I DO LIKE TO BE BESIDE THE SEASIDE
8. Stephen Jackson	FFLAT HUW PUW
9. Triawd 'Arbennig'	AR LAN Y MÔR

WHO WAS THE FIRST EUROPEAN IN AMERICA?

Story-telling has a long tradition in Wales. Sometimes you don't know if a story is true or not. Read this text about the first European in America. What do you think? Is it history or legend?

'Christopher Columbus, of course!' will be the answer from an American or English schoolchild. But if you ask a Welsh boy or girl, he or she may give you a different answer: Madog.

Who? Madog was a Welsh prince in the 12th century. When his father died, he and his brothers couldn't agree about what they should do with the king's money. Madog was angry, and he took his men and a ship and sailed west.

Over a year later, Madog came back to Wales and told people about a far-away land. A year after that, he took ten ships and sailed west again. No one ever saw Madog or the others after that. Columbus sailed to America 300 years later. As more and more people came from Europe to America, there were reports of 'white Indians' around Louisville, Kentucky. And some of the first Europeans in America said that they met Welsh-speaking 'Indians'!

A Taste of Scotland

This week *UK Mag* goes north for a taste of life in Scotland. Your guide is our star reporter – Fiona McPherson, from the West Highlands of Scotland. But first of all a word of warning for all visitors …

Hi! Well, the first thing is this: Scotland is *not* a part of England – it's different. And the people are, too. You can call us Scots and you can call us British. But English? – Never!

If you don't believe me, go to a big Scotland – England rugby match and see for yourself!

SCOTS HAMMER ENGLAND

Scotland was one big party last night after a great win against 'The Auld Enemy': 18–13 after 80 minutes of hard but brilliant play.

Of course, the Scots and the English are friends most of the time. Here's how the two countries put their flags together almost 300 years ago, back in 1707.

The English flag

+

The Scottish flag

=

The first British flag

Come with me to the Highlands where I grew up. It's a beautiful place, but you won't find many young people here because there aren't many jobs. People like me look for jobs elsewhere. But we all love to come home – for New Year and the summer festival for example.

New Year – 'Hogmanay' we call it – is big in Scotland. When midnight comes, everyone holds hands and sings *Auld Lang Syne* together. Most people don't really understand the old Scots words, but they sing it all over the world.

Should auld acquaintance be forgot,
And never brought to mind?
Should auld acquaintance be forgot,
For the sake of auld lang syne?
Chorus: For auld lang syne, my dear.
For auld lang syne,
We'll take a cup of kindness yet
For the sake of auld lang syne.

It means something like this: So we don't forget our old friends, let's drink together for the old times.

After *Auld Lang Syne* people go 'first-footing': they visit friends and neighbours with a piece of coal. That's for a warm and lucky home all year. And there's always something to eat – a piece of traditional Scottish shortbread, maybe. Here's my mum's old recipe. Why not try it?

Shortbread

1 Mix 150 g flour, 50 g sugar, 100 g butter and a little salt.
2 Make a ball.
3 Roll out the ball till it's about 1 cm thick.
4 Put it in the oven. Bake for 45 minutes at 150°C.
5 Take the shortbread out of the oven and cut it.

The summer festival is a great time, too. There's a regatta with all kinds of boats. And there's a ceilidh – a party with music and dancing – that goes on for three days!

And then at the end the piper plays from across the water and you look out to the mountains of the Isle of Skye. And you know you'll have to come back again next year!

Skye! And there's a story about Skye, too – the story of Bonnie Prince Charlie and Flora Macdonald. It happened after the Scottish fought their last battle against the English – the Battle of Culloden. Thousands of Highlanders died for their Prince that day in 1746.

After the battle Prince Charlie escaped. The English tried to find the Prince and kill him. But a brave Highland woman, Flora Macdonald, saved the Prince. She got him an Irish passport and some women's clothes. He then travelled with Flora (as her servant, Betty Burke) over the sea to Skye. The English looked everywhere for him. They offered £30,000 for information about him, too. But not one Highlander said a word. Later he escaped to France. He was never able to return to Scotland. Many Scots remember the story sadly because Culloden meant the end of the old Highland way of life.

Netscape - File Edit View Go Bookmarks Options Directory Window Help
Back Forward Home Reload Images Open Print Find Stop

Virtual London

You want to go to London, but you don't have the CASH?

You want to go to London NOW, but you have to be at school tomorrow morning?

You want to go to London, but your parents are AGAINST it?

NO MORE EXCUSES!

Through the magic of CYBERSPACE, you can visit Virtual London. Turn on your computer and warm up the modem for a WWW trip to the CAPITAL.

What's out there? – UK Mag shows you the BEST places in town.

Number 10 Downing Street
The home of the British Prime Minister!
http://www.number-10.gov.uk

The British Museum
One of the great museums of the world!
http://www.british-museum.ac.uk

The Natural History Museum
Find out about the awesome dinosaurs!
http://www.nhm.ac.uk

The British Monarchy Website
The Queen online!
http://www.royal.gov.uk

The Tower of London The virtual tour
http://www.toweroflondontour.com/kid

The London Aquarium
Meet the fish!
http://www.londonaquarium.co.uk

WHAT'S ON STAGE

UK Theatre Web What's on in the West End?
http://www.uktw.co.uk/index2.html

Document: Done

And what's behind the home pages?

Do the quiz on the kids' Tower of London Website!

Enjoy the underwater world at the London Aquarium!

The Reef & Living Corals

Be dazzled by the sheer brilliance and variety of exotic creatures such as sea-horses, clown fish, regal tang, dogface puffers, angel fish and invertebrates of the reef and tropical seas.

And the OTHERS?

You'll have to GO there yourself.

Enjoy your TRIP to Virtual London!

Coloured

What do kids think about colour? *UK Mag* tried to find out.

POETRY COMPETITION

Are you black, brown, white or yellow? Write a poem about how you see the world. Send it to us, here at *UK Mag*. We'll print the ten best poems – and the winners each get a *UK Mag* T-shirt. Maybe you can write a poem like this one? Milly Maceba, 13, from Birmingham sent it to us:

BLACK
is beautiful,
black is strong.
Sometimes black is lonely
but never white, always black.
Black and white together
can be beautiful,
and strong –
FRIENDS

OUT OF THE MOUTHS OF BABES?

'Come and meet my friend on
Sports Day, Mummy.'
Sports Day came.
'Where's your new friend, Paul?'
'He's sitting on the front
bench.'
There were ten on the front
bench.
'He's wearing red shorts.'
There were three boys with
red shorts.
'His hair's curly.'
'Oh, the black one,'
said Mummy.

Kathryn Clarke, 15 years

COLOURED

LaMont Humphrey, an American reggae singer from Frankfurt, has adapted a famous poem for his new single. Here are the words:

You got the nerve to call me coloured
And you got the nerve to call me coloured

When I'm born, I'm
When I grow up, I'm even more
When I'm in the sun, I'm still
When I'm cold, guess what – I'm
And when I die, I'm
too.
black

And you got the nerve to call me coloured
And you got the nerve to call me coloured

But you
When you are born, you are **pink**
When you grow up, you are **white**
When you are sick: man, look at yourself – you are **green**
When you go in the sun, you turn **red**
When you are cold, you turn **blue**
And when you die, you look **purple**

And you got the nerve to call me coloured
And *you* got the nerve to call me
coloured

So, who's coloured?

Meet the reggae band UB40 from Birmingham. The group takes its name from the number of a form you have to fill in if you are out of work in Britain. They have had lots of number one hits – … you can listen to *Guns in the Ghetto* on our special cassette/CD.

GUNS IN THE GHETTO

Daddy don't go out tonight
Just stay home till morning light
Me and momma don't feel right
Please hold us tight

Daddy why do you go to work
When you know just how much we
love you so
Please come back tomorrow

Chorus
They're giving out guns in the ghetto
They're saying they will set you free
One day I'll have children of my own
But I'm afraid they won't have me

UK Mag's own Laura Ann Silver went to the annual school drama festival and was delighted. Here is her favourite play, "Land ho!", by the drama group from Kingsway High School in Chester.

Land ho!

Scene 1 Plymouth

OLD MARY *(She is wearing a shawl and warming her hands by a fire, to one side of the action.)* I remember. It was a fine September day in 1620 when we left Plymouth, and I was just thirteen. Lots of kind people came to say goodbye. But the captain! He was shouting and shouting …

(Harbour wall. Captain Jones is hurrying people down the steps to the Mayflower.)

CAPT JONES Come on, you people, get on board! Quickly! Quickly – while the wind is right!

PEOPLE Good luck, friends! … Go safely!

MAN 1 Can anyone tell me – who are all those people in dark clothes?

MAN 2 Don't you know? They're the Pilgrims. They wear dark clothes because of their religion.

WOMAN 1 They're so brave, those people! They're going to sail to America and start a new life there.

MAN 1 But why? There's nothing there! Just wild animals and Indians!

WOMAN 2 Well, they want to be free and start their own church. And England doesn't let them do that.

MAN 1 But look at them all! There must be a hundred! And all the things they're carrying, too! They'll sink that little boat!

CAPT JONES Excuse me, but that is *not* a little *boat.* That is my very fine *ship,* the Mayflower!

MAN 1 Oh, all right. Sorry, then. Ship. *(Quietly, away from Jones)* But I still think it'll sink!

MR CARVER *(He is standing by the steps and talking to the people.)* Good people of Plymouth. I am speaking for all of us Pilgrims – when I say thank you.

MAN 1 Who's that then?

MAN 2 You don't know anything, do you? That's John Carver, their leader. Listen!

MR CARVER Others have been bad to us here in England, but you have been kind, and we will always remember you.

CAPT JONES Mr Carver! This is no time for fine words. We must go!

MR CARVER I'm sorry, Captain, but I've finished now. Goodbye, all of you. *(He goes.)*

CAPT JONES Now, is everyone on board? Good! Eh … What? Who's that girl? Come here!

OLD MARY *(She interrupts.)* It was me! That terrible old Captain Jones was shouting at me!

YOUNG MARY I … I'm s-s-sorry, Captain. I'm looking for my little white mouse. It has run away.

MAN 1 Clever mouse!

CAPT JONES Little white mouse! We don't have little white mice on *my* ship! We only have big, fat, brown rats! So forget the mouse, and get on board. *Now!!!*

YOUNG MARY Y-y-yes, sir … *(She runs to get on board.)*

PEOPLE Goodbye! … Good luck! … Go carefully!

MAN 1 And try not to sink! America is a long way to swim!

Scene 2 On the Mayflower

(Below decks on the Mayflower, now at sea for 22 days. The Pilgrims all move together from side to side as the ship rolls in the heavy waves.)

OLD MARY The weather was terrible, and it got worse and worse – week after week. Down below deck, life was very hard. I remember the day the ship almost sank …

GILES *(On the floor, on his knees)* I'm going to be sick!

YOUNG MARY Oh, no! Giles Hopkins! Don't do it here! This place is getting so smelly!

GILES I can't move, Mary. Be a good friend and give me the bucket, please! Quickly!

YOUNG MARY Yuck! Father, can't we go up and get some fresh air?

MR CHILTON The Captain says no. His men can't move around and work if we're up there.

MRS CHILTON When will we ever get to America, James? This wind and rain – and the waves! We go up and down and round and up and down again.

GILES Ugh … stop, Mrs Chilton! I'm going to be sick again!

MRS CHILTON It never stops, James! And everything is always wet and cold! And so dirty!

MR CHILTON I know, Susanna. It's very hard. But think. Soon we'll see the New World.

YOUNG MARY Oh, won't that be wonderful, Mother! And we'll be free. And then we'll …

MR CHILTON Sh, Daughter! Listen! *(He cups his hand to his ear.)* Did you hear that? I think something is breaking …

MRS CHILTON James! Do you mean this ship is going down?

Scene 3 Under the beam

(Below decks the captain and his men are looking up at a very large beam that goes across the middle of the ship. The beam is badly cracked and the men are worried.)

OLD MARY Well, we all thought that was the end – even terrible old Captain Jones …

CAPT JONES That beam is breaking. And when it does, the sea will smash this ship in minutes.

SAILOR 1 We'll have to go back.

SAILOR 2 But it's almost as far to England as it is to America now.

SAILOR 3 And if we go back, the Pilgrims won't pay us.

CAPT JONES Listen, and get this into your stupid heads! If we don't change this beam, we won't see England or America.

SAILOR 1 But we can't change the beam, can we? We haven't got another one.

OLD MARY *(She interrupts.)* But my father had a wonderful idea – an idea that saved the ship …

MR CARVER Excuse us, Captain. James Chilton and I heard the noise. We think we can help.

SAILOR 2 Rubbish! What do people like you Pilgrims know about ships?!

MR CARVER James, you can explain.

MR CHILTON We've got a printing press. We think it'll hold the beam up, and make it safe.

SAILOR 3 That's a crazy idea!

CAPT JONES Mm, maybe it isn't. Let's try it.

OLD MARY *(She interrupts.)* So we got the press, put it under the beam and turned the screw round and round …

PILGRIMS & SAILORS Push! … A bit more! … Not too much. … Yes! … That's it! … It has done the job! … The ship is safe!

Scene 4 Plymouth Rock

OLD MARY So we didn't sink after all, and we went on and on. Then on the 66th day …

LOOK-OUT *(With hand over eyes)* Land ho! Land ho! I can see America from up here!

OLD MARY *(She interrupts.)* Those were wonderful words. We were so happy, and we shouted and sang! But it still wasn't the end because there were no good harbours.

GILES We've been here for a month, and we still haven't found a harbour!

YOUNG MARY What are we going to do? It's so cold, now it's winter!

MR CHILTON We must go on. God will help us. You'll see.

OLD MARY *(She interrupts.)* Then, at last, we found the right place, with good land and clean water, too. And our leader, John Carver, had a wonderful idea …

MR CARVER Let's give this lovely place a lovely name. Plymouth! For our friends in England.

PILGRIMS Fantastic! … Great idea! … Wonderful!

OLD MARY *(She interrupts.)* And soon we left our smelly ship. I couldn't wait to be on dry land again! I was the first in the ship's little boat. And I couldn't sit quietly! …

MR CHILTON Child, don't jump around. You'll turn the boat over!

YOUNG MARY But I'm so excited, Father!

CAPT JONES Come on, men! Pull on those oars!

SAILORS *(They pull on their oars.)* Heave! … Heave! … Heave!

CAPT JONES We're almost there. That's it. Lift oars.

YOUNG MARY I'm going to jump onto that rock! Here I go!

MR CHILTON No, Mary! You'll fall into the water! *(Mary jumps.)* You stupid …

YOUNG MARY I'm all right, Father. Look. This is Plymouth and I'm on Plymouth Rock. *(She waves excitedly.)* Come on and jump like me.

MR CHILTON Well, let's follow my crazy daughter. *(He jumps and holds out a hand to his wife.)* Come on, Susanna, you're next.

MRS CHILTON Thank you, James. … Oh, but look at our daughter. She's running up the hill now. Something terrible will happen to her one day. The Indians will kill her!

YOUNG MARY *(She waves.)* Come up the hill, everyone. It's lovely up here. You can see for miles!

Scene 5 A new start

OLD MARY That winter was terrible! We were cold, hungry and ill. Half of us died – my poor, dear father and mother, too. … But spring came at last. The Indians came, too, and they were friendly. One of them, Squanto, spoke English, and he helped us.

(Three Pilgrims are talking as they dig and plant. Squanto, with a basket, is watching.)

PILGRIM 1 Just think, in a few months this place will be a sea of corn!

SQUANTO *(He laughs quietly.)* It won't if they go on like that. Well, … maybe I'll help them.

PILGRIM 2 Oh, my back is almost broken! I'm tired. I'm going to stop.

PILGRIM 3 If you don't work, you can forget our sea of corn!

PILGRIM 2 Don't talk to me like that. I've planted lots.

SQUANTO You've planted lots, but it won't grow. You're doing it all wrong.

PILGRIM 1 All wrong? What are you talking about, Squanto?

SQUANTO Listen. Corn needs food. Food makes corn grow.

PILGRIM 2 What food? What do you mean?

SQUANTO Fish. You use fish. Listen. Give me some corn. Now watch. *(He takes a small fish from his basket.)* Here's some baby corn. Here's a baby fish. *(He kneels to plant.)* Put them together in the ground. Now this corn will be happy. It'll grow well.

PILGRIMS 2/3 Fish?! … You're joking!

PILGRIM 1 I think we should do what Squanto says. He knows the land here, and we don't.

Scene 6 The first Thanksgiving

OLD MARY Squanto was right. The corn grew very well. Then it was autumn again. And we had a special dinner for ourselves and our new friends, the Indians. It was a 'thank you' to the Indians – and to God.

(Pilgrims and Indians are talking and laughing together at a long table.)

MRS WINSLOW Giles! Mary! Take these to the table. *(She gives them large bowls of food.)*

GILES It smells great! Your food is the best, Mrs Winslow. Can we have a bit?

MRS WINSLOW No, Giles, you cannot! You must wait until all of us eat!

YOUNG MARY Oh, but we're so hungry and we haven't eaten anything all day, Mrs Winslow!

MRS WINSLOW Well, here's a bit for now. (*She gives them a little.*) But don't let the others see!

GILES / MARY Thank you, Mrs Winslow! Mmm! ... Ooh, nice! We love you, Mrs Winslow!

MRS WINSLOW Now hurry and take the food to the table. *(Mary and Giles go to the table.)*

MR WINSLOW *(He bangs on the table.)* Friends, Brothers and Sisters, please listen for a minute. Let William Bradford, our new Governor, speak.

PILGRIMS Quiet! ... Sh! ... Listen! ... Let William speak.

MR BRADFORD Thank you, everyone. And thank you, Edward Winslow, our new Assistant Governor. Well, we arrived here a year ago – and what a year it has been! Many have died, including our dear friend and first leader, John Carver.

PILGRIMS Poor man. ... So many good people have gone.

MR BRADFORD But God has been kind to us, too. And we have our good friends – you, Squanto, and your people. You have helped us in many ways and we want to thank you.

PILGRIMS To Squanto! ... To our new friends!

MR WINSLOW Yes, William is right. Because of you, we have enough food for the next winter. You've been good friends to us. And we want to stay good friends with you.

MR BRADFORD So now, this autumn of 1621, we give thanks. We know now that we can live through the next winter – and years – in our new home in America.

PILGRIMS Hear, hear! ... Well said.

Scene 7 The next ship

OLD MARY I remember when my friend Giles and I were up on the hill a few days later. We were talking about that dinner, and we had a fantastic idea. *(Mary and Giles are walking and talking together.)*

YOUNG MARY That dinner was wonderful. All that good food.

GILES And it was so nice to laugh and talk and not work.

YOUNG MARY We should have one every year – a thank you for our new life here in America.

GILES Yes, and we should call it a thanksgiving. Wonderful! But ... *(He hesitates.)*

YOUNG MARY What is it, Giles?

GILES Do you really think we'll always stay here in America?

YOUNG MARY Yes, I'm sure. And there'll be more and more people like us. I know.

GILES How? How do you know that?

YOUNG MARY I'll tell you how. Look. See that bit of white? It's a sail. It's a ship!

GILES Wow! You're right! Another ship! Quick! Let's run and tell everyone! *(They wave and call and run.)*

OLD MARY And that was the end of the beginning. Now we knew for sure: our New World was real!

1 B

Unit 1

1 **REVISION** They moved, too

Not all the other kids in Megan's form are from London. Look at this information. Ask about Mark, Sandra and Thomas. Write down the missing information in your exercise book.

	Mark	Sandra	Thomas
Where ... did live before?	In Cardiff.	In Aberdeen.	?
When ... his/her family move?	?	Last summer.	?
Why ... move?	His mum got a new job.	?	His dad died.
... worry about the new school?	Yes, a lot.	?	?

A Where did Mark live before?

B In Cardiff. When did his family ...?

2 B

Unit 2

Are You a Sports Freak – or a Couch Potato?

Your score

1	A = 1	B = 3	C = 5
2	A = 0	B = 3	C = 5
3	A = 3	B = 5	C = 0
4	A = 3	B = 0	C = 2
5	A = 5	B = 3	C = 0
6a	A = 3	B = 0	C = 0

6b 1 point for each correct answer:
A = 4 B = 2 C = 6 D = 3 E = 1 F = 5

10 points or less
You're a couch potato. You spend too much time at home in front of the TV. Go out and do some sport. It's healthy, and you'll feel better, too.

11 to 25 points
You like sport. You know it's healthy and keeps you fit.

26 points or more
You're a real sports freak. Too much sport isn't good for you. You should relax sometimes, too – it's healthier!

2 **REVISION** Guess the Game
a Monopoly b Volleyball

Unit 2

6 ▶ A trip around 'Nameshire'

Here is a map for a trip around the county of Nameshire. Some of the information about activities in Nameshire is missing. Ask your partner.

A What can I do if I go to Peterpool?
B If you go to Peterpool, you can spend the night in a castle.
What can I do if …?

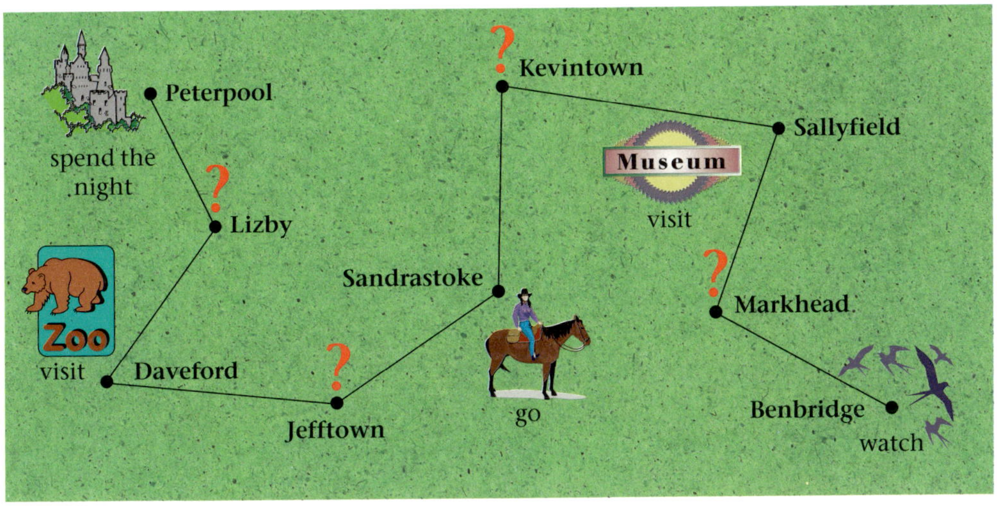

Unit 3

8 ▶ A person who … and a thing that …

Match the clues to the pictures.
Then talk about the pictures like this:

B It's a person who designs new gadgets.
A Is it a …? / It must be a … .
B That's right. / No, sorry. Try again.

person … designs new gadgets
person … goes to school
thing … keeps your food cold
thing … shows you the time
thing … carries people across water
person … plays CDs on the radio

7 ▶ At a party

Look at the picture with food and drinks at a party. Your partner has got a different picture.

Answer your partner's questions with a few / lots *or* a little / a lot. *Then ask about the things in the list below.*

B Have you got any sandwiches?
A Yes, I've got a few / lots.
No, I haven't got any.

B Have you got any chocolate?
A Yes, I've got a little / a lot.
No, I haven't got any.

9 ▶ How to explain words

a *Try to explain these words to your partner. Can he or she guess the words?*

doctor • ball • secretary

The following expressions will help you
It's someone / a person (who) …
It's an animal (that) …
It's something / a thing (that) …

B It's a person who sometimes works at a hospital. He or she helps people who are ill.
A Do you mean a …?
B Yes, that's right. / No, guess again.

b Relative clauses can be very useful when you want to explain a German word you don't know in English. A really clear explanation will help people to understand you better. Compare:

- A 'Taschenrechner' is something (that) you use for maths.
- A 'Taschenrechner' is a gadget (that) …
- A 'Taschenrechner' is a small gadget (that) …

Now try to explain these German words to your partner. Can he or she guess the words?

Museumsdirektorin • Schulzeugnis
Staubsauger • Torwart

Unit 5

5 ▶ Each other or themselves?

Look at the pictures on this page. You and your partner have the same pictures, but in a different order. Tell your partner about your pictures.

1
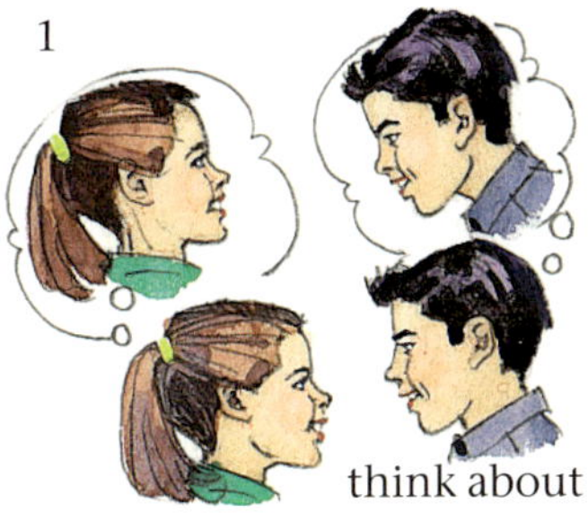
think about

2

think about

3

laugh at

4

take photos

5

laugh at

6

take photos

A In my picture 1 two kids are taking photos of each other.
B Oh, two kids are taking photos of each other in my picture 6.
A In my picture 2 a girl and a boy are …

Unit 6

1 REVISION Questions, questions, questions!

a *Your partner is asking you about last Saturday. Imagine you were at Dart Country Park. Study the advertisement on the right and answer your partner's questions. Say as much as you can about Dart Country Park.*

b *Now ask your partner about last Saturday. Make your questions from the following:*

- (you go) out last Saturday?
- (you enjoy) yourself?
- What's it like? (be) there much you can do there?
- (you have got) a picture of the place?
- (it be) open in the summer holidays?
- (you like to go) there again with me?

Example:
B Did you go out last Saturday?
A Yes, I did. I went to …

4 ▶ **What are you doing next week?**

You want to go swimming with your partner. But when? Find a time when both of you can go. Look at your plan for the week. Ask and answer questions like this:

A What are you doing on Monday afternoon?
B I'm seeing my grandma in hospital. What about Monday evening?
A That's no good. I'm … . What about …?
…
A/B I'm free then, too. Great!

Day	Afternoon	Evening
Mon	see grandma in hospital	–
Tue	–	work on a Science project
Wed	–	go to the chess club with Tina
Thur	help dad in the garden	–
Fri	–	go to Jim's party
Sat	–	go shopping with mum and dad

7 B

Unit 7

Read the police interview with Dave. Add the new information to your table. Your partner has the police interview with Tina. He/She will tell you what he/she has found out about Tina. Add this information, too. Then tell your partner what you have found out about Dave.

POLICE And when did you start work today, Mr Smith?
DAVE I'm not sure when I got in – about half past nine, I think – I don't wear a watch.
POLICE Did you meet anyone else when you arrived?
DAVE I didn't meet anybody, no. I saw Eddie – he was up in the lights. Oh, and I saw Tina. She was going to make-up with some guests.
POLICE What did you do then?
DAVE I went to the store room and read my newspaper. And at 10.30 Tina fetched me.
POLICE What did you do next, sir?
DAVE I fixed the step, of course – that floor manager always wants me to do things quickly. I'm not sorry that this is my last day – even if I haven't got another job yet.
POLICE Did you leave the studio at any time after that?
DAVE No … oh, maybe I went to the toilet …
POLICE When was that?
DAVE I can't remember. Well, you don't look at the clock every time you go to the toilet, do you?
POLICE No, sir, I don't – you're right!

1 REVISION A letter to an old friend

Write Megan's letter again. Put the verbs in brackets in the correct forms.

Dear Ruth,   London, 11th September

Thanks very much for your letter. It (come) on Monday morning. I (meet) the postman in our road and he (give) it to me. I (be) so excited!

You know Dad and I (move) to London only six weeks ago, but it feels like five months ago! Do you remember our goodbye party? I (be) so sad – I (not want) to leave you!

Last week we (go) shopping for things for our new flat. We (buy) a new sofa for the living-room and we (look) at a new cupboard for the kitchen. The sofa (be) expensive – but it looks great! Yesterday, Dad (open) a lot of our boxes from Wales. In one of the boxes I (find) a picture of you. I (be) so sad. I miss you. Please write soon.

Love,

Megan

2 REVISION Megan and her father have moved in

Look at the pictures and say what Megan and her father have done and haven't done. Use the verbs in the box. The list of irregular verbs on pp. 191–192 can help you.

buy • close • cook
hurt • open • put

1 *Megan's dad has ...*   2 *Megan hasn't ...*

3 ▶ A phone call to Wales

Megan is phoning her friend Ffion in Wales. Complete their dialogue with the right form of the verbs in the box – simple past or present perfect. (Look at the time words carefully!)

be (x 2) • come • come in
not get • go (x 2) • make

MEGAN Hi, Ffion – it's me, Megan.
FFION Hi Megan! How's the new school?
MEGAN Well, I already ... some new friends. So my first day today wasn't bad. But yesterday I ... really nervous.
FFION And how's London now?
MEGAN Well, you know I hated it when we ... . But I think it's OK now. Dad and I ... to the Tower of London last week. It was great! ... you ever there?
FFION Yes, I ... there last year, in June. Megan, I ... your letter yet.
MEGAN Oh, Dad just ... . Sorry, Ffion, I must go now. Bye.

1 REVISION Sport, sport, sport

Make a network with sport words.

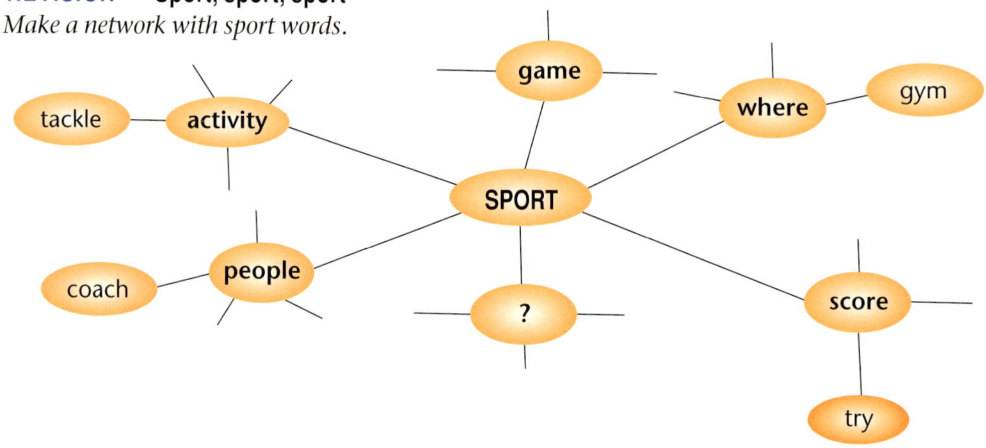

2 REVISION Julia's room

a *What do you think Julia usually does in her room? Think of five activities.*

Julia usually listens to CDs in her room.

...

b *And you? What did or didn't you do in your room yesterday? Think of five things.*

I read a book in my room yesterday.

...

◆◆ **c** *Ask a partner what he/she has done in his/her room this week.*

What have you ...?

3 ▶ David is thinking ...

Fill in the right forms of the verbs.

1 If we *don't play* (not play) well on Saturday, we (not be) in the championships.
2 If I (be) in bad form the coach (be) angry.
3 If I (be) hurt I (not go) to the match.
4 If we (not win), mum and dad (not be) sad.
5 If Emma (not want) to do a bike tour with me this summer, I (not go).
6 If we (not do) a bike tour, it (be) a boring holiday.
7 And if it (rain), I (not go) out much.

4 ▶ Bike Tour 11

David and Emma talked some more about Bike Tour 11 in the brochure. What did they say? Complete these sentences. Use if, will, won't *and* can. *Example:*

EMMA do tour 11 – stay in Cardiff for the weekend
If we do Tour 11, we can stay in Cardiff for the weekend.

EMMA don't go to Cardiff – save money.
DAVID see many interesting things – go to Cardiff
EMMA stay at the youth hostel – spend a few days in Cardiff
DAVID go to Cardiff – visit the science museum, Techniquest
EMMA you visit the science museum – I visit Cardiff Arms Park
DAVID go on this tour – also walk in Brecon Beacons National Park
EMMA maybe we – go to the Breacon Hill Music Festival – be there at the right time
DAVID it rains – not be a festival

1 ▶ What is it? Who is it?

Make sentences about the pictures. Use who *or* that.

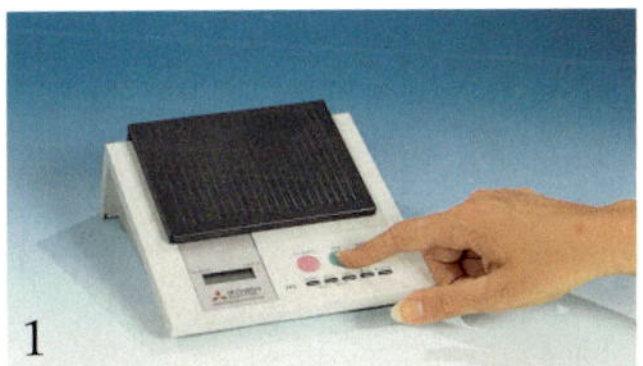

1 It's a …	never has time to talk.	4 He's …	everyone loves.
2 She's a …	opens tins.	5 They are …	loves to read.
3 It's a …	answers the phone.	6 It's a …	shout a lot.

2 ▶ Scottish people and places

Use a phrase from **a** *and a phrase from* **b** *and make sentences with* that *or* who *about the pictures.*

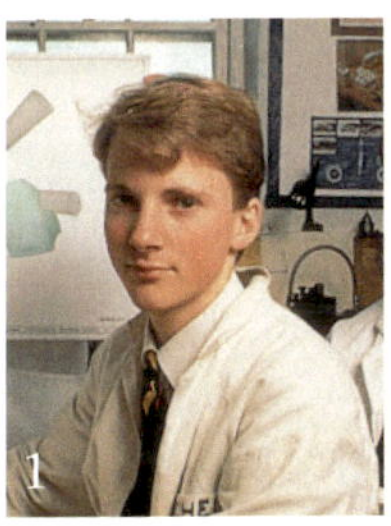
Andrew Mitchell

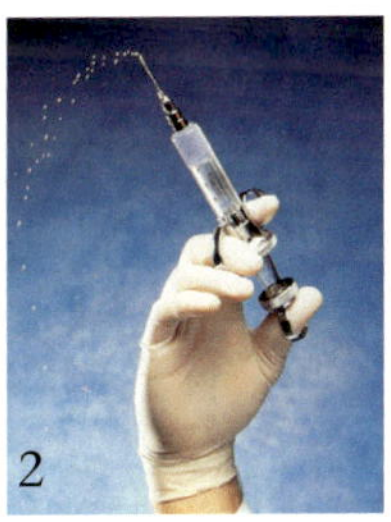
Penicillin

Lisa McKenna

Aviemore

James Thomson

a
1 the boy
2 the great discovery
3 the girl
4 a ski area
5 the Scottish inventor

b
1 he has only got one hand
2 Alexander Fleming made it
3 she designed an automatic cat feeder
4 it gave Sheena a great idea
5 he invented the fridge

Andrew Mitchell is the boy who has only got one hand.

3 ▶ That little cat again!

What were these people doing when the accident happened? Use the past progressive or the simple past.

BOY my dog (run) after a cat – I (stop) him
My dog was running after a cat when I stopped him.

GIRL I (ride) home – I (see) a cat in the road

WOMAN I (stand) at the bus-stop – a cat (go) across the road

CAR DRIVER I (drive) along the road – that stupid cat (run) in front of me

OTHER DRIVER I (go) along behind the other car – it suddenly (stop) and … CRASH!

Unit 4

1 ▶ What are they?

Use relative clauses and describe these people and things. Make a graffiti poster for the classroom.

A teacher is someone who …
Parents are people who …
A car is a thing that …
Computers are machines …
…

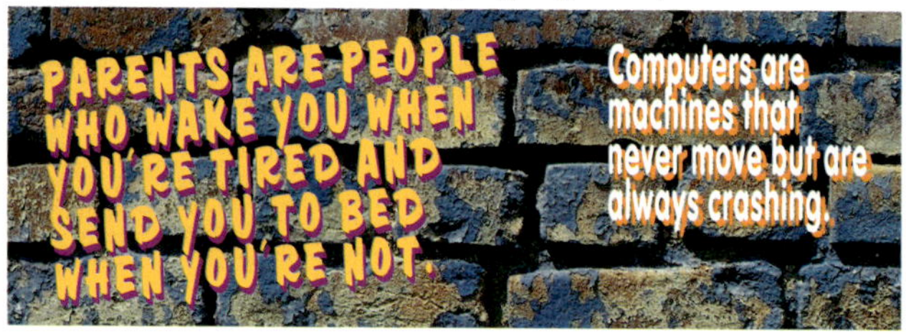

2 ▶ A trip to London

Join the sentences together. Use contact clauses.

1 London is a city. I have always wanted to visit it.
London is a city I have always wanted to visit.
2 Look! there is the cathedral. We are going to see it tomorrow.
3 St Paul's Cathedral is a beautiful building. Mr Martin really loves it.
4 Madame Tussaud's is a famous museum. You can visit it in London.
5 Ben has got a postcard of Trafalgar Square. He bought it in Chinatown.
6 Mr Martin didn't like the skiing machine. He saw it at the Trocadero.

3 ▶ In London

Make sentences with relative clauses. Where can you leave out who *or* that?

1 William Shakespeare …

2 St Paul's Cathedral …

3 The Queen …

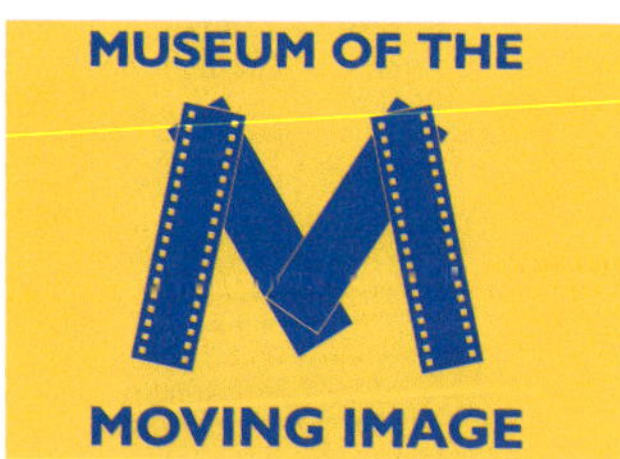

4 The Museum of the …

5 Hyde Park …

6 The London Dungeon …

a very big church • a museum
an attraction near London Bridge
a park • the man • the woman

(it) shows you some of London's violent history
(it) tells you about films and how they make them
Sir Christopher Wren built (it)
(he) wrote 'Romeo and Juliet'
you can see (her) on all British stamps and money
you can visit (it) in London

1 *William Shakespeare is the man who wrote 'Romeo and Juliet'.*

1 ▶ Selima's trip to Bradford

Last weekend Yasmin's cousin Selima came to Bradford. Complete the sentences.

1 'I can look after *myself*, Dad,' Selima said as the train left Birmingham station.
2 'Well, enjoy … and phone us when you arrive,' called Selima's mum.
3 Mr Patel said to …, 'Selima is so tall – she looks like a young lady.'
4 'Don't worry,' said Mrs Patel. 'The girls can look after … .'
5 'I've taught … a song on the guitar,' said Selima at dinner.
6 'Great,' Yasmin said. 'I'll sing and we can record … .
7 But when Yasmin heard … on cassette she said, 'Yuck, that can't be me!'

2 ▶ Yasmin and Sheila

Read the information about Yasmin and Sheila. Complete the sentences with each other, themselves *or* them.

1 Yasmin and Sheila are in the same class. They see … in school every day.
2 Sometimes they phone … in the evenings, too. They talk for hours!
3 Yasmin's parents speak Urdu, but Yasmin only speaks English with … .
4 Yasmin and Sheila always speak English to … .
5 Yasmin and Sheila are interested in Urdu, so they are teaching … the language in their free time.
6 Sometimes it's a bit difficult and Yasmin's mum has to help … .
7 They bought … a new CD-Rom in Urdu last weekend.

3 ▶ A problem letter

a *Read this letter to TOPS magazine. Put in the right form of* be able to *or* be allowed to.

b *Write a letter to TOPS magazine about a problem. (It needn't be true!)*

Dear Claire,
I've got a problem with my parents. I'm … to go out on school days. Last week I … see my boyfriend – but I … get out of the house and we … meet. My parents were really angry! Now they've said I … go to a party next week. But they … stop me!
Diane, 16

Unit 6

1 ▶ The Internet is great, ...

Complete with the correct question tag.

1 The Internet is great, … it?
2 Mike is only interested in computers, …
3 Lisa and Ryan are Mike's friends, …
4 Lisa is angry with Mike, …
5 We're going now, …
6 You're always in front of your computer, …

2 ▶ Your partner

Write five sentences with question tags and ask your partner. Example:

A You always watch MTV, don't you?
B Yes, that's right. / No, not really. I usually …
You don't ..., do you?
A No, I don't. / Oh yes, I do.

Some ideas

You always watch/listen to …
You came to school/go home by …
Your brother loves/doesn't like …

3 ▶ Lisa's bad day

Use the sentence parts and write about Lisa. Use the simple past and the past perfect.

1 Lisa – wake up / everyone else – already – get up
2 go – bathroom / brother – get – there first
3 get – downstairs for breakfast / brother – eat – last egg
4 reach – bus stop / bus – already – go
5 arrive – school / lessons – already – start
6 go – library – lunch-time / someone – take – book that she wanted
7 get – to – school canteen / the others – have – all – nicest things

1 *When Lisa woke up, everyone else had already got up.*
2 *When she ...*

◆◆ 4 ▶ A radio interview

a *A reporter from Radio Plymouth wants to interview Julie. Work with a partner. First write some questions for the interview.*

b *Then write Julie's answers to your questions. Work like this:*

REPORTER What's your pony's name?
JULIE Fred.
REPORTER Where did you go …?

c *Next, practise the interview with your partner. Then record it. Swap cassettes and listen to other interviews.*

LANGUAGE SUMMARY

Die folgenden **LANGUAGE SUMMARY**-Seiten fassen zusammen, was in den Units dieses Buches vermittelt wurde.

Links stehen die Regeln und Hinweise sowie Lerntipps und Merkkästen.
Rechts stehen Beispiele und Übersichten.
Warndreiecke (⚠) weisen auf Fehlerquellen und wichtige Regeln hin. Ein Hinweis wie → P 6, 7 (p. 16) bedeutet, dass zu diesem Abschnitt die Übungen 6 und 7 von Seite 16 gehören.

Die mit **REMEMBER** gekennzeichneten Stellen enthalten Stoff, den du bereits kennst und an den du dich jetzt erinnern solltest.

Am Ende einer jeden Unit zeigt eine kleine Übersicht, was du schon auf Englisch ausdrücken kannst („In dieser Unit hast du gelernt ...").

In so gekennzeichneten Abschnitten findest du Zusatzinformationen. Sie sollen dir helfen, englische Texte besser zu verstehen.

Alexander und Dilek lernen wieder mit – ihre Fragen und Hinweise nutzen vielleicht auch dir. Und natürlich findest du ab und zu einen kleinen Cartoon. Er kann dir helfen, dir etwas zu merken – und darüber lachen kannst du hoffentlich auch.
Also: Los gehts!

Unit 1

Das *present perfect* und das *simple past* im Vergleich – Wiederholung

Man verwendet das ***present perfect***, wenn man ausdrücken will, **dass** etwas geschehen ist. Man verwendet das ***simple past***, wenn man ausdrücken will, **wann** etwas geschehen ist.

In Sätzen mit dem ***present perfect*** wird nie ein **genauer** Zeitpunkt genannt. Es werden aber oft unbestimmte Zeitangaben wie *already, always, before, ever, just, never, often, yet* benutzt.
In ***simple past***-Sätzen wird oft ein Zeitpunkt oder ein bereits abgeschlossener Zeitraum genannt. Typische Zeitangaben sind *yesterday, last week, an hour ago, in 1998, when I was younger* sowie das Fragewort *when*.
Das *simple past* wird auch verwendet, wenn man eine Geschichte erzählt.

The present perfect and the simple past in contrast – Revision

(1) Why isn't Megan here? **Has** she **moved**?
(2) Yes, she **has**. She **moved** to London in the summer.

(1) Jemand fragt, **ob** Megan weggezogen ist – **nicht wann**. Also: ***present perfect***.
(2) Es wird bestätigt, **dass** sie weggezogen ist („Yes, she has.") – ***present perfect***. Und dann wird gesagt, **wann** das war („She moved to London in the summer.") – ***simple past***.

Present perfect		Simple past
Megan hasn't **always** lived in London.	–	**A few months ago** she was still in Wales.
Have you **ever** been to Wales?	–	No, but we went to Scotland **in July**.
I've **never** seen a film with Loriot.	–	I saw a film with Otto **when I was younger**.
Megan has **often** sung in front of other people.	–	She started with the choir **a long time ago**.
I have**n't** done a project at my new school **yet**.	–	We did lots of projects **at my old school** (last year).
Have you finished your homework **yet?**	–	**When** did you finish it?

→ P 6, 7 (p. 16) / D 3 (p. 115)

In dieser Unit hast du gelernt ...

- zu sagen, ob und wann jemand etwas getan hat.
- Personen zu beschreiben.
- zu sagen, wie sich jemand fühlt.

▶ I've been to Florida. We went there last summer.
▶ My sister has red hair and green eyes.
▶ On her first day Megan was nervous about her new school, but now she feels good about it.

Unit 2

1 Das Stützwort *one/ones*

Wenn man ein schon genanntes (zählbares) Nomen näher bestimmen, aber nicht wiederholen will, braucht man die „Stützwörter" *one* (Singular) bzw. *ones* (Plural).
Wir nennen *one/ones* „Stützwörter", weil – anders als im Deutschen – Adjektive und der bestimmte Artikel ohne diese „Stützen" nicht allein stehen können.

The prop-word *one/ones*

There are two good music shops in town – **the one** in Oring Road and **the one** in Elm Street. Es gibt zwei gute Musikläden …, **den** in der Oring Road und **den** in der Elm Street.

Can you give me a pen, please?
– Of course. **The blue one** or **the red one**?
… **Den blauen** oder **den roten**?

I like most of their songs, but not **the sad ones**.
…, aber nicht **die traurigen**.

→ P 1 (p. 26)

2 Bedingungssätze I

Ein Bedingungssatz besteht aus zwei Teilen: einem Nebensatz mit *if* und einem Hauptsatz. Ein Bedingungssatz drückt aus, was geschieht, wenn eine bestimmte Bedingung erfüllt wird.

Conditional sentences, type I

If we **do** this tour, we'**ll see** Snowdonia.
Wenn / Falls wir diese Tour machen, sehen wir Snowdonia. / werden wir Snowdonia sehen.

If it **rains**, we **won't see** the mountains.
Wenn / Falls es regnet, sehen wir die Berge nicht. / werden wir die Berge nicht sehen.

Nebensätze mit *if* und *when* stehen im *simple present* (nicht im *will-future*), obwohl sich die Sätze auf die Zukunft beziehen.
Im Hauptsatz steht meist das *will-future*; statt des *will-future* können im Hauptsatz auch stehen:
- ein Modalverb (z.B. *can, must, should*) + Infinitiv
- ein Imperativ.

If you **come** to my party, you**'ll meet** Sue and Pete.
Wenn (= Falls) du zu meiner Fete kommst, wirst du Sue und Pete treffen.

When you **arrive**, you**'ll hear** the music out on the street.
Wenn (= Sobald/Dann wenn) du ankommst, wirst du die Musik schon draußen auf der Straße hören.

If you **go** to Wales, you **must try** and see a rugby match.
Sarah is a vegetarian. **If** she **comes** for dinner, you **shouldn't have** meat.
If you **need** the police in Britain, **phone** 999.

→ P 4, 5, 6, 7, 8 (pp. 27/28) / D 3, 4 (p. 116)

In allgemein gültigen Aussagen steht auch im Hauptsatz das *simple present*.

If you **add** blue to yellow, you **get** green.

In dieser Unit hast du gelernt …

- über Spielregeln zu sprechen. ▶ Players must kick the ball over the goalposts.
- zu sagen, was unter bestimmten Bedingungen geschieht. ▶ If we win today, we'll go to the championships.
- zu sagen, was vielleicht passieren könnte. ▶ It may be nice in the morning, but it might rain later.
- Landschaften zu beschreiben. ▶ My part of Germany has lots of small lakes.

Unit 3

1 Bestimmende Relativsätze I

a Gebrauch

Manchmal ist es notwendig, ein Nomen genauer zu bestimmen, damit klar wird, von wem oder was wir reden. Dafür verwenden wir **bestimmende Relativsätze**. Bestimmende Relativsätze werden auch **notwendige Relativsätze** genannt, weil ohne sie unklar wäre, wer oder was genau gemeint ist (welcher Mann? welches Gerät?).

⚠ Relativsätze haben die übliche Wortstellung: **S – V – O**.

Defining relative clauses I
Use

The man **who invented radar** was from Scotland.
Der Mann, **der das Radar erfunden hat**, kam aus Schottland.

Is that the gadget **that feeds the cat automatically**?
Ist das das Gerät, **das die Katze automatisch füttert**?

	Subject	Verb	Object
	That girl	**helped**	me.
That's the girl	who	**helped**	me.

Das ist das Mädchen, das mir **geholfen hat**.

b Das Relativpronomen als Subjekt: *who, that*

Die Relativpronomen *who* und *that* werden unterschiedlich gebraucht:

– ***who*** nur für **Personen**

– ***that*** für **Sachen** (und Tiere)

whO für PersOnen
thAt für SAchen

The relative pronoun as subject: *who, that*

I know **the woman** who wrote this book.
Ich kenne **die Frau**, die dieses Buch geschrieben hat.
It's about **a machine** that makes breakfast.
Es handelt von **einer Maschine**, die Frühstück macht.

→ P 2, 3, 8 (p. 40, 42) / D 1, 2 (p. 117)

Übrigens: Für Sachen (und Tiere) wird statt *that* auch *which* verwendet. Und manchmal findest du auch *that* für Personen.

It's about **a machine** which makes breakfast.
I know **the woman** that wrote this book.

c Das Relativpronomen *whose*

Das Relativpronomen *whose* entspricht dem deutschen „dessen, deren". Es bezieht sich meist auf Personen, kann aber auch für Dinge und Tiere verwendet werden.

⚠ Verwechsle *whose* nicht mit der Kurzform *who's* (= *who is*).

The relative pronoun *whose*

Sam is **the boy** whose mother works for the BBC.
Sam ist **der Junge**, dessen Mutter bei der BBC arbeitet.
Bina is **the woman** whose parents are from India.
Bina ist **die Frau**, deren Eltern aus Indien kommen.
That's **the gadget** whose inventor died last week.
Das ist **das Gerät**, dessen Erfinderin letzte Woche gestorben ist.

The boy whose **picture** is in the magazine is my friend.
The boy who's **sitting** next to you is my friend, too.

→ P 4 (p. 41)

2 Die Verlaufsform der Vergangenheit

The past progressive

a Wie du weißt, benutzt man das ***present progressive***, wenn jemand **gerade etwas tut** oder wenn ein Vorgang **im Gange ist.**

REMEMBER

Sheena is **work**ing on a project for school now.
She isn't **watch**ing TV.
What sort of project is she **do**ing?

Das ***past progressive*** verwendest du, wenn jemand **zu einem bestimmten Zeitpunkt in der Vergangenheit dabei war, etwas zu tun**, oder wenn ein Vorgang **im Gange war**.
Bildung: *was/were* + *-ing*-Form

Grandad was **danc**ing at midnight.
Um Mitternacht tanzte Großvater (gerade).
He wasn't **play**ing games.
What was he **do**ing at 12.30?
Was he **sing**ing songs?

→ P 6 (p. 41)

b Das ***past progressive*** wird auch häufig benutzt, um zu sagen, was gerade vor sich ging (Handlung A), als etwas anderes passierte (Handlung B).

now

I was washing my hair when you **phoned**.
past progressive — simple past
(Handlung A, im Gange … — … als Handlung B einsetzte)

→ P 7 (p. 42) / D 3 (p. 117)

Du findest das *past progressive* oft auch in Berichten und Erzählungen: Es beschreibt die Situation oder „Szene", in der etwas geschah.

Birds were singing and dogs were playing in the park. People were walking along the river or sitting on benches and talking. Suddenly there **was** a loud noise and everything **changed**. …

In dieser Unit hast du gelernt …

- über die Funktionsweise von Geräten zu sprechen.
  ▶ When you open the box, the cassette starts. When you turn the power off, the motor stops.
- zusätzliche Informationen zu geben, die für das Verständnis notwendig sind.
  ▶ Andrew is the boy who wants to be an engineer. That's the gadget that feeds the cat. Jenny is the girl whose family is always busy.
- zu sagen, was vor sich ging, als etwas anderes geschah.
  ▶ I was writing a letter when the lights went out.

Unit 4

1 a Bestimmende Relativsätze II / Das Relativpronomen als Objekt

Defining relative clauses II / The relative pronoun as object

REMEMBER

	Subject	
That's **the boy**	who	was at the party yesterday.
	(He	was at the party yesterday.)

Die Relativpronomen *who* und *that* (bzw. *which*) können nicht nur Subjekt des Relativsatzes sein, sondern auch Objekt.

	Object	Subject	
That's **the boy**	who	I	saw at the party.
Das ist **der Junge,**	den	ich	auf der Fete gesehen habe.

(Vergleiche: I saw **him** at the party.
Ich habe **ihn** auf der Fete gesehen.)

→ P 1, 2 (p. 53) / D 1 (p. 118)

b Relativsätze ohne Relativpronomen

Contact clauses

Wenn *who* oder *that* (bzw. *which*) Objekt des Relativsatzes sind, werden sie meistens weggelassen. Relativsätze ohne Relativpronomen nennt man ***contact** clauses*, weil das näher zu bestimmende Nomen (im ersten Beispiel: *man*) und das Subjekt des Relativsatzes (im ersten Beispiel: *we*) **Kontakt** haben: Es steht kein Relativpronomen dazwischen.

	Object	Subject
Is that the man	who	**we** met last week?
…,	den	**wir** … getroffen haben?
Is that the man		**we** met last week?

who = Objekt: kann weggelassen werden

aber:

	Subject	
Was Wren the man	**who**	designed St. Paul's?
…,	**der**	St Paul's entworfen hat?

who = **Subjekt**: darf **nicht** weggelassen werden

	Object	Subject
The bike	that	**my mum** bought me is great.
The bike		**my mum** bought me is great.

that = Objekt: kann weggelassen werden

aber:

	Subject	
The bike	**that**	is so dirty is my brother's.

that = **Subjekt**: darf **nicht** weggelassen werden

→ P 3, 4, 9 (pp. 53, 55) / D 2, 3 (p. 118)

2 *a little / a few*

Wie du bereits gelernt hast, gibt es zählbare und nicht zählbare Nomen. *Much* („viel") steht vor nicht zählbaren Nomen, *many* („viele") vor dem Plural zählbarer Nomen.

a little / a few

REMEMBER
How **much money** have you got? – Not **much**.
Wie **viel Geld** hast du? – Nicht **viel**.
How **many T-shirts** did you buy? – Not **many**.
Wie **viele T-Shirts** hast du gekauft? – Nicht **viele**.

A little und *a few* werden ähnlich gebraucht wie *much* und *many*:

- *a little* („ein bisschen, (ein) wenig") wird nur mit nicht zählbaren Nomen verwendet.

Nicht zählbare Nomen:
I've got **a little money**.
I've got **a little time**.
I've got **a little homework**.

- *a few* („ein paar, einige") wird nur mit dem Plural zählbarer Nomen verwendet.

Plural von zählbaren Nomen:
I've got **a few pounds**.
I've got **a few minutes**.
I've got to do **a few exercises**.

Wie *much* und *many* können auch *a little* und *a few* allein, anstelle eines vorher genannten Nomens, stehen.

Could we have more **time** for the test, please?
– Yes, **a little**.

Could I have more **crisps**, please?
– OK, but just **a few**.

nicht zählbar		zählbar	
How much water?		**How many cakes?**	

a lot of **lots of**	**not much** **a little**	**a lot of** **lots of**	**not many** **a few**

→ P 6, 7 (p. 54)

In dieser Unit hast du gelernt ...

- über öffentliche Verkehrsmittel und Verkehrsverbindungen zu sprechen.
  ▶ What's the best route to Eaton Square?
  – Take the number 4 bus to Oak Street, then get off and change to the number 19.
- jemandem den Weg zu beschreiben.
  ▶ Can you tell me the way to the post office, please?
  – Go past the bank and turn right. Then cross the next street. The post office is on your left.
- zusätzliche Informationen zu geben, die für das Verständnis notwendig sind.
  ▶ Who was the man you met in the museum? I mean the museum we visited yesterday morning.
- über kleine Mengen zu reden.
  ▶ I've just got a little money – a few pence.

Unit 5

1 Das Reflexivpronomen / The reflexive pronoun

a Formen und Gebrauch / Forms and use

Das Reflexivpronomen (*myself, herself, themselves* usw.) bezeichnet dieselbe Person oder Sache wie das Subjekt (*I, she, they* usw.).

I taught myself French. Ich habe **mir** Französisch beigebracht.
Be careful or **you**'ll **hurt yourself**. du verletzt **dich**
He can **look after himself**. auf **sich (selbst)** aufpassen
She often **talks to herself**. mit **sich selbst**
The cat is clean. **It washes itself** all day. putzt **sich**
We can **teach ourselves** a new game. **uns** beibringen
You can **listen to yourselves** on cassette. **euch** anhören
They can **look after themselves**. auf **sich (selbst)** aufpassen

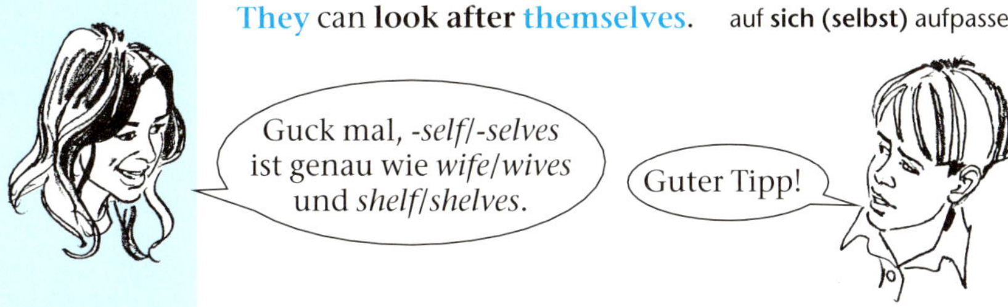

⚠ Beachte den Unterschied zwischen Reflexivpronomen und Personalpronomen.

He hurt **himself**.
(John hurt John.)
Er (John) hat **sich (selbst)** verletzt.

He hurt **him**.
(John hurt Tim.)
Er (John) hat **ihn** (Tim) verletzt.

Merke dir die Wendungen:

Enjoy yourself. *Viel Spaß! (Amüsier dich gut!)*
Help yourself. *Greif zu! (Bediene dich!)*

Did **you enjoy yourselves** at the party?

The food is on the table – just **help yourself**.

⚠ Es gibt eine Reihe von Verben, die im Deutschen reflexiv sind, im Englischen jedoch nicht:

(to) change	*sich (ver)ändern; sich umziehen*
(to) decide	*sich entscheiden*
(to) feel	*sich fühlen*
(to) imagine sth.	*sich etwas vorstellen*
(to) listen to sth.	*sich etwas anhören*
(to) meet	*sich treffen*
(to) move	*sich bewegen*
(to) open	*sich öffnen*
(to) relax	*sich entspannen*
(to) remember	*sich erinnern*
(to) sit down	*sich (hin)setzen*
(to) turn	*sich umdrehen*
(to) watch sth.	*sich etwas ansehen*
(to) worry	*sich Sorgen machen*

Megan **felt** miserable after her mother died.
Megan **fühlte sich** elend … .
Jenny and I **met** at the station.
Jenny und ich **trafen uns** am Bahnhof.
I **remember** my last holiday.
Ich **erinnere mich an** meinen letzten Urlaub.

→ P 2, 3 (p. 64) / D 1 (p. 119)

b Reflexivpronomen oder *each other*?

Reflexivpronomen:
„sich" (= sich selbst)
each other:
„sich" (= sich gegenseitig, einander)

Statt *each other* wird auch *one another* verwendet:
They are looking at one another.

-self/-selves = sich selbst
each other = einander, sich gegenseitig

Reflexive pronoun or *each other*?

Ann and Dan are laughing at **themselves**.

Ann and Dan are laughing at **each other**.

→ P 4, 5 (pp. 64/65) / D 2 (p. 119)

2 Der Infinitiv mit *to*

The *to*-infinitive

a ... nach *the first* / *the last* / *the next* / *the only*

Der Infinitiv mit *to* wird nach *the first, the last, the next, the only* verwendet. Im Deutschen benutzt man dafür einen Relativsatz. Nach ***the first, the last*** und ***the next*** **kann** ein Nomen oder das Stützwort *one/ones* stehen.

Nach ***the only*** **muss** ein Nomen oder *one/ones* stehen.

... after *the first* / *the last* / *the next* / *the only*

Hillary was **the first (person) to climb** Mount Everest.
Hillary war **der Erste**, **der** den Mount Everest **bestieg**.
The captain is **the last (person/one) to leave** the ship.
Der Kapitän ist **der Letzte**, **der** das Schiff **verlässt**.
James will be **the next (person/one) to go**.
James wird **der Nächste** sein, **der geht**.

Sue was **the only person/one to say** what she thought.
Sue war **die Einzige**, **die gesagt hat**, was sie dachte.

→ P 6 (p. 65)

b ... nach Adjektiven, Verben und Nomen

Der Infinitiv mit *to* kann stehen
- nach Adjektiven und ihren gesteigerten Formen
- nach bestimmten Verben *(agree, forget, learn, remember, start, try, ...)*
- nach bestimmten Nomen *(decision, plan, time, ...)*.

... after adjectives, verbs and nouns

Nice to meet you!
Schön, Sie **kennen zu lernen**.
I like Scotland, but I think it's **nicer to go** to Wales.
..., aber ich finde es **schöner**, nach Wales **zu fahren**.
It's **best to visit** England in the summer.
Es ist **am besten**, England im Sommer **zu besuchen**.

Tim **forgot to do** his homework last night.
Tim **hat** gestern Abend **vergessen**, seine Hausaufgaben **zu machen**.

It's **time to go** home now.
Es ist **Zeit**, nach Hause **zu gehen**.

→ P 8 (p. 66)

c **... nach Fragewörtern**

Der Infinitiv mit *to* kann nach Fragewörtern verwendet werden.

Wie im Deutschen kannst du stattdessen auch einen vollständigen Nebensatz benutzen:
what to do ... → *what I should do ...*
how to get ... → *how I can get ...*

I don't know **what to do** / **what I should do** in my free time.
..., was ich in meiner Freizeit machen soll.

Can you tell me **how to get** / **how I can get** to the station?
..., wie ich zum Bahnhof komme?

Tom never knows **when to stop.** / **when he should stop.**
..., wann er aufhören soll.

→ P 7 (p. 65)

3 ***be able to, be allowed to***

Wie du weißt, heißt *can* sowohl „können" als auch „dürfen".

be able to, be allowed to

REMEMBER

I **can** run faster than the other girls in my form.
Ich **kann** schneller laufen ...
Jeff **can** go to the school disco, but he has to be home at 9.
Jeff **darf** zur Schuldisco gehen, ...

Wenn man deutlich machen will, ob man „können" oder „dürfen" meint, verwendet man „Ersatzverben":
be able to = „können"
be allowed to = „dürfen".

Jenny **isn't able to come** to the phone.
Jenny kann nicht ... (z.B. weil sie unter der Dusche ist).
I**'m not allowed to go** to school discos.
Ich darf nicht ... (Meine Eltern erlauben es mir nicht.)

Diese Ersatzverben werden auch verwendet, um „können" und „dürfen" in anderen Zeiten auszudrücken.

I was so busy, I **wasn't able to phone** you.
..., ich konnte dich nicht anrufen.
When I was five, I **wasn't allowed to play** in the street.
..., durfte ich nicht auf der Straße spielen.
We **won't be able to see** the film. There's no time.
Wir können den Film nicht sehen. / Wir werden ... nicht sehen können.
When you're older, you**'ll be allowed to ride** a moped.
..., darfst du ein Moped fahren. /
wirst du ein Moped fahren dürfen.

→ P 9, 10 (p. 66) / D 3 (p. 119)

Im *simple past* wird statt der Ersatzverben *be able to* und *be allowed to* auch ***could/couldn't (could not)*** verwendet.

I **could** swim when I was two. But I **couldn't** walk.
Ich konnte schwimmen, ... Aber ich konnte nicht laufen.
How long **could** you stay out when you were eight?
Wie lange durftest du draußen bleiben, ...?

In dieser Unit hast du gelernt ...

- zu sagen, dass man sich verletzt/sich selbst zugesehen/... hat.
  ▶ I've hurt myself with a knife.
  We watched ourselves on video.
- zu sagen, dass man sich gegenseitig hilft/sich etwas zeigt/... .
  ▶ The kids in my form all help each other.
  We showed each other pictures of our parents.
- zu sagen, was jemand tun (bzw. nicht tun) konnte, oder was jemand tun können wird.
  ▶ I was late, so I wasn't able to go shopping. But I'm sure I'll be able to do the shopping tomorrow.
- zu sagen, was jemand tun (bzw. nicht tun) durfte, oder was jemand tun dürfen wird.
  ▶ Tina wasn't allowed to go to my party, but she will be allowed to go to Jackie's party.

Unit 6

1 Frageanhängsel

a Gebrauch

Frageanhängsel *(aren't you? / is she? / don't they?)* werden häufig in der gesprochenen Sprache verwendet, wenn man vom Gesprächspartner/von der Gesprächspartnerin **Zustimmung** erwartet. Deutsche Frageanhängsel sind zum Beispiel *nicht wahr? / oder? / ne? / gell? / woll?*

Question tags

Use

You're German, **aren't you?**
Du bist Deutsche, nicht wahr?
Steve can't play the guitar, **can he?**
Steve kann nicht Gitarre spielen, oder?
Marie isn't waiting for me, **is she?**
You've got a cat, **haven't you?**
Your friends live in London, **don't they?**

Auf Aussagen mit Frageanhängseln kann man mit Zustimmung oder Widerspruch reagieren.

You go to Heinrich-Heine-Schule, **don't you?**
Du gehst zur Heinrich-Heine-Schule, oder?

Zustimmung („Ja."/„Stimmt.")
Yes, I do. / Yes, that's right.

Widerspruch („Nein.")
No, I don't. (I go to ...)

You aren't from Germany, **are you?**
Du kommst nicht aus Deutschland, oder?

Zustimmung („Nein."/„Stimmt.")
No, I'm not. / That's right.

Widerspruch („Doch!")
I am! / Oh yes I am!

b Form

Ist der Hauptsatz bejaht, so ist das Frageanhängsel verneint.
Ist der Hauptsatz verneint, so ist das Frageanhängsel bejaht.

Hauptsatz **+** → *Anhängsel* **–**
Hauptsatz **–** → *Anhängsel* **+**

Form

You**'re** 13, **aren't you?**
bejaht → verneint
Hannah **isn't** 14 yet, **is she?**
verneint → bejaht

Wird im Hauptsatz ein Hilfsverb verwendet, so benutzt man dasselbe Hilfsverb im Frageanhängsel.

We **must** be home by 10 o'clock, **mustn't we?**
Winston **isn't** enjoying himself, **is he?**
You **haven't** been on holiday, **have you?**
You**'ve** got a cat, **haven't you?**
She**'s** going to phone her parents, **isn't she?**
The party **will** finish by 10.30, **won't it?**
Your mum **doesn't** like loud music, **does she?**
That **didn't** hurt much, **did it?**

Wird im Hauptsatz **kein** Hilfsverb verwendet, so benutzt man im Frageanhängsel *don't / doesn't / didn't*.

That boy and girl look good together, **don't they?**
He spends a lot of time at her house, **doesn't he?**
They danced most of the evening, **didn't they?**

c Intonation

Frageanhängsel werden mit fallender Intonation (*falling intonation*) gesprochen. Das heißt, dass die Stimme am Ende des Satzes **nach unten** geht, wie bei einer Aussage.

Intonation

You can't see very well, **can you?**
You need help with your homework, **don't you?**
The weather has been very nice, **hasn't it?**

→ P 2, 3 (p. 76) / D 1, 2 (p. 120)

He spends a lot of time at his computer, doesn't he?

2 Das *present progressive* für Pläne und Verabredungen

Wie du weißt, benutzt man das *present progressive*, wenn jemand gerade etwas tut oder wenn etwas gerade stattfindet.

Du kannst das *present progressive* auch verwenden, wenn eine Handlung für die Zukunft fest geplant bzw. verabredet ist. Dabei muss klar sein, dass es sich um etwas Zukünftiges handelt.

The present progressive for plans and arrangements

REMEMBER

I'm busy. I**'m making** a poster for my Art class.
Please stop! You**'re hurting** me.
Tom can't come to the phone. He**'s washing** his hair.
The dogs **are playing** in the garden now.

Tracy **is having** a party **on Saturday**. **Are** you **going**?
– I can't. I**'m visiting** my grandma **this weekend**.
Tracy gibt Samstag eine Party. Gehst du hin? / Wirst du hingehen?
– Ich kann nicht. Ich besuche dieses Wochenende meine Oma.
I**'m watching** football on TV with some friends **later**.
– Oh really? Who**'s playing**?

→ P 4 (p. 76)

3 Verb + Objekt + *to*-Infinitiv

Nach manchen Verben kann ein Objekt + *to*-Infinitiv stehen.
Im Deutschen steht meist ein Infinitiv mit „zu".

Verb + object + *to*-infinitive

REMEMBER

I **helped** my dad to clean the kitchen.
Ich habe meinem Vater geholfen, die Küche sauber zu machen.
Who **taught** you to play the guitar?
Wer hat dir beigebracht, Gitarre zu spielen?

Auch nach *want* und *would like* kann ein Objekt + *to*-Infinitiv stehen. Im Deutschen steht ein Nebensatz mit „dass".

Do you **want** me to clean the board?
Möchten Sie, dass ich die Tafel wische? / Soll ich die Tafel wischen?
I **would like** my parents to buy me a new bike.
Ich möchte, dass meine Eltern mir ein neues Fahrrad kaufen.
I **wouldn't like** Sam to come to my party.
Ich möchte nicht, dass Sam zu meiner Fete kommt.

⚠ Beachte die unterschiedliche Bedeutung:

Susan **wants** to help him.	Susan will ihm helfen.
Susan **wants** me to help him.	Susan will, dass ich ihm helfe.

→ P 7, 8 (pp. 77/78)

*Nach 'want' / 'would like'
(und das ist wichtig)
steht niemals 'that' –
mach das bloß richtig!*

4 Das Plusquamperfekt
a Form und Gebrauch

Wie du weißt, drückt das *simple past* aus, dass Handlungen oder Ereignisse zu einem bestimmten Zeitpunkt in der Vergangenheit stattfanden.

The past perfect
Form and use

REMEMBER

I **arrived** at the party at 9 o'clock.
Mike **was** late for school yesterday.
We **had** some cake this afternoon.

Wenn du sagen willst, dass etwas bereits **vor** einem Zeitpunkt in der Vergangenheit stattgefunden hat, verwendest du das *past perfect* (Plusquamperfekt, **Vor**vergangenheit).

geschah in der Vergangenheit	geschah noch davor: *past perfect*
When I **arrived**,	Sue **had** already **gone** home.
Als ich ankam,	war Sue schon … gegangen.
Mike **was** late because	he'**d missed** his bus.
Mike kam zu spät, weil	er seinen Bus verpasst hatte.
Ann **wanted** some cake	after I'**d washed** the dishes.*
Ann wollte noch Kuchen,	nachdem ich abgewaschen hatte.

Das *past perfect* wird mit *had* (Kurzform: *'d*) + Partizip Perfekt gebildet.

Tom was happy. He **had won** the race.
We **hadn't finished** dinner when the phone rang.
By the end of the day, we'**d visited** six churches!
Had you ever **eaten** Turkish food before today's lunch?

* In Nebensätzen mit *after* (= „nachdem") steht oft *simple past* statt *past perfect*, weil eindeutig ist, in welcher Reihenfolge die Handlungen oder Ereignisse stattgefunden haben:
Ann wanted some cake after I washed the dishes.

b **_Past perfect – simple past_**

Wenn man über mehrere aufeinander folgende Handlungen in der Vergangenheit berichtet, verwendet man für alle Handlungen das *simple past*.

Past perfect – simple past

First we **bought** some T-shirts, then we **stopped** at a café. After that we **went** home.
We **watched** TV until 10, and then we **went** to bed.

Wie die Beispiele zeigen, ändert sich die Bedeutung, je nachdem ob man *past perfect* oder *simple past* verwendet.

The lesson **had started** when Mike got there.
Der Unterricht hatte begonnen, als Mike kam.
The lesson **started** when Mike got there.
Der Unterricht begann, als Mike kam.

→ P 9, 10 (p. 78) / D 3, 4 (p. 120)

In dieser Unit hast du gelernt ...

- zu sagen, dass du Zustimmung zu deiner Aussage erwartest.
  ▶ This is a great game, isn't it?
  You haven't got a dog, have you?
- Nachrichten am Telefon zu hinterlassen und entgegenzunehmen.
  ▶ Could you give her a message, please?
  – Yes, of course.
  Can I take a message?
  – Yes, please. Tell her that I phoned.
- über feste Verabredungen und Pläne für die Zukunft zu sprechen.
  ▶ What are you doing after school?
  – I'm meeting some friends.
- zu sagen, dass du möchtest, dass jemand anders etwas tut.
  ▶ I want my brother to tidy up the living-room.
- zu sagen, dass etwas vor etwas anderem passiert ist.
  ▶ I had heard the joke lots of times, but when I tried to tell it I couldn't remember it.

Unit 7

[1] **Vorhersagen und Vermutungen über die Zukunft**

Predictions and suppositions about the future

a **Das Futur mit _will_**

Wie du weißt, werden **allgemeine Vorhersagen** und **Vermutungen** über die Zukunft mit dem *will-future* ausgedrückt.

The _will_-future

REMEMBER

The weather **will be** fine tomorrow.
Das Wetter wird morgen gut sein.
I'm sure the rain **will stop** soon.
Ich bin sicher, dass der Regen bald aufhört / aufhören wird.

b **Das Futur mit _going to_**

Wenn man sagen will, dass etwas **mit großer Wahrscheinlichkeit** geschehen wird, weil es bereits **Anzeichen** dafür gibt (z.B. die Wolken im ersten Beispiel rechts), verwendet man das *going to-future*.

The _going to_-future

Look at those clouds. It's **going to rain**.
... Es wird (bald) regnen. *(Die Wolken sind schon zu sehen!)*
That step doesn't look safe. It's **going to break**.
... Sie wird durchbrechen. *(Man kann schon sehen, dass die Stufe nicht sicher ist!)*

[ ] nicht in allen Bundesländern obligatorisch

[2] Pläne

a Das Futur mit *going to*

Das *going to-future* wird verwendet, wenn man sagen will, was jemand **vorhat**.

Plans and timetables

The *going to*-future

REMEMBER

I'm **going to write** a letter to the BBC this afternoon.
Ich habe vor, heute Nachmittag einen Brief an die BBC zu schreiben.

b Die Verlaufsform der Gegenwart

Um auszudrücken, dass etwas für die Zukunft **fest geplant** oder **verabredet** ist, verwendet man das *present progressive.*

The present progressive

REMEMBER

We'**re driving** to Birmingham at the weekend.
– **Is** Hannah **going**, too?
Ich fahre nächstes Wochenende nach Birmingham. / Ich werde nächstes Wochenende nach Birmingham fahren.
– Fährt Hannah auch mit? / Wird Hannah auch mitfahren?

c Die einfache Form der Gegenwart

Wenn ein zukünftiges Geschehen durch einen **Fahrplan**, ein **Programm**, einen **Kalender** oder Ähnliches festgelegt ist, verwendet man das *simple present.*

The simple present

You mustn't be so slow! The rehearsal **starts** at 10.
... Die Probe fängt um 10 an.
When **does** the next train to Birmingham **leave**?
Wann fährt der nächste Zug nach Birmingham?

[3] Angebote, Versprechen und spontane Entschlüsse

Wenn man **anbietet** oder **verspricht**, etwas zu tun, oder sich **spontan zu etwas entschließt**, verwendet man das *will-future.*

Offers, promises and spontaneous decisions

I'm really thirsty.
– I'**ll get** you something from the coffee shop.
Ich hole dir was aus der Kaffeestube.
What would you like to eat?
– Hmm, I'**ll have** some chips, please.
Ich nehme Pommes frites, bitte.

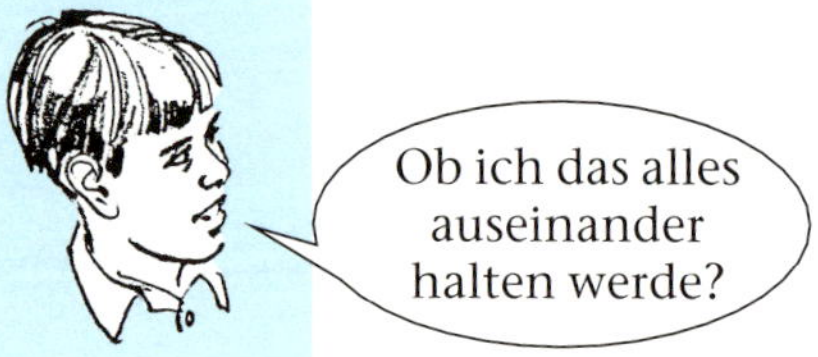

In dieser Unit hast du gelernt ...

- Vorhersagen aufgrund von äußeren Anzeichen zu machen. ▶ That step looks dangerous. It's going to break.
- über Absichten und Verabredungen zu sprechen. ▶ I'm leaving tomorrow. I've already packed. I'm having lunch with Sue in the canteen at 2 o'clock.
- über Fahrpläne, Programme u.Ä. zu sprechen. ▶ The next train to Birmingham leaves in half an hour. The show starts at six.
- plötzliche Entschlüsse auszudrücken und Angebote zu machen. ▶ I can't find the script. – I'll go and look for it.

VOCABULARY

Das *VOCABULARY* (Vokabelverzeichnis) enthält die neuen Wörter dieses Buches in der Reihenfolge, in der sie in den Units vorkommen.

- <u>Fett</u> gedruckte Wörter musst du verstehen und benutzen können.
  ➨ **brave** [breɪv] tapfer, mutig
- <u>Normal</u> gedruckte Wörter sollst du verstehen können, wenn du sie hörst oder liest.
  ➨ special ['speʃl] Sonderprogramm, -sendung
- Wörter aus Arbeitsanweisungen sind <u>*kursiv*</u> gedruckt. Du brauchst sie nur zu verstehen.
  ➨ *(to) explain* [ɪk'spleɪn] *erklären, erläutern*

Symbole

° Wörter und Ausdrücke mit einem **Kringel** sind nur in der Unit wichtig, in der sie vorkommen. *Beispiel:*
°busker ['bʌskə] Straßenmusikant/in

[ ] **Eckige Klammern** bedeuten, dass dieser Teil der Unit nicht Pflicht ist. Dein Lehrer / Deine Lehrerin wird dir sagen, ob du die Wörter lernen sollst.

~ Die **Tilde** in der dritten Spalte steht für das neue Wort. *Beispiel:*
hero – Batman and Superwoman are famous comic ~*es*. (= ... comic <u>hero</u>*es*.)

▸◂ Dies ist das „**Gegenteil**"-Zeichen.
Beispiel: (to) **sell** ▸◂ (to) **buy**
(to) buy („kaufen") ist das Gegenteil von *(to) sell („verkaufen")*.

⚠ Achtung, aufpassen – hier macht man leicht Fehler.

Betonung

['] und [ˌ] sind Betonungszeichen. Sie stehen <u>vor</u> der betonten Silbe.
['] zeigt die Hauptbetonung, [ˌ] die Nebenbetonung. *Beispiel:* **situation** [ˌsɪtʃu'eɪʃn]

Abkürzungen

P 3 = Practice 3 (Übung 3)
D 3 = Differentiation page, Practice 3 (Übung 3 auf den Differenzierungsseiten, S. 115–120)

p. = page pp. = pages
pl = *plural* *no pl* = *no plural*

adj = *adjective* *adv* = *adverb*
conj = *conjunction* *n* = *noun*
prep = *preposition* *v* = *verb*

sb. = somebody/someone
sth. = something
jd. = jemand
jm. = jemandem
jn. = jemanden

infml = *informal* (umgangssprachlich, informell)

Vor- und Nachnamen, Ortsnamen und Ländernamen findest du auf den Seiten 187–188.
Grammatische Fachbegriffe stehen gesammelt auf den Seiten 189–190.
Classroom phrases findest du auf der hinteren Umschlaginnenseite.

Englische Wörter wie *clown, gold, jazz, toast* oder *training*, die du ohne weiteres verstehst, werden nicht im *vocabulary* erklärt. Alle diese Wörter findest du aber mit Angabe ihrer Aussprache im *dictionary*.

▸▸▸ Our Heroes

pp.6/7	**hero** ['hɪərəʊ], *pl* **heroes** ['hɪərəʊz]	Held, Heldin; Idol	Batman and Superwoman are famous comic ~*es*. When I was a little boy, my grandpa was my ~.
	everyday *(adj)* ['evrideɪ]	Alltags-; alltäglich	Are you going to wear anything special tonight? – No, just my ~ clothes: jeans and a T-shirt.
	brave [breɪv]	tapfer, mutig (⚠ *nicht:* ~~brav~~)	She was very ~: she jumped into the river and saved the child's life.
	kind [kaɪnd]	freundlich, nett, gütig	It was ~ of you to help me yesterday.
	perhaps [pə'hæps, præps]	vielleicht	maybe
	special (on) ['speʃl]	Sonderprogramm, Sondersendung (über)	Watch tonight's TV ~ *on* German players in British football clubs!
	by 31st May	bis spätestens 31. Mai	We need your report ~ next Monday. (= not later than next Monday)
	office ['ɒfɪs]	Büro	
	album ['ælbəm]	Album	

TIPP **Das Wichtigste zuerst ...**

- **Nimm dir nicht zu viel vor** – 10 bis 15 neue Vokabeln auf einmal genügen! (Das ist wie beim Essen – wer zu viel auf einmal isst, kriegt Bauchschmerzen!)
- **Lerne nicht zu lange, aber regelmäßig!** Beim Vokabellernen sind 6 mal 10 Minuten mehr als eine Stunde!
- **Lerne nicht nur mündlich** – wenn du die Vokabeln aufschreibst, behältst du sie besser.
- **Wiederholung ist wichtig** – sieh dir deshalb regelmäßig auch die „alten" Wörter wieder an.

▶▶▶ Unit 1: New Places, New Faces

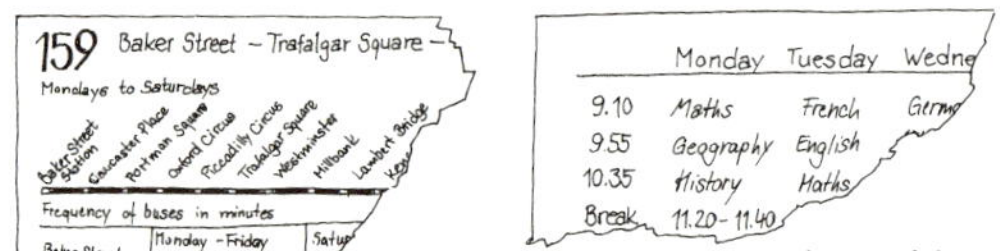

timetables

pp.8/9	**timetable** ['taɪmteɪbl]	Fahrplan	
	headteacher [ˌhed'tiːtʃə]	Schulleiter/in	
	(to) welcome ['welkəm]	willkommen heißen	When Liz and Pete arrived, Susan ~*d* them. ⚠ *(to) welcome* is a regular verb: *welcome – welcomed – welcomed*
	secretary ['sekrətri]	Sekretär, Sekretärin	
	(to) **include** [ɪn'kluːd]	(mit) einschließen, enthalten	*Does* the trip ~ a tour of London? The team ~*s* two women. (= Zum Team gehören zwei Frauen.)
	art [ɑːt]	Kunst	⚠ English *art* = „Kunst" • German „Art, Sorte" = *sort*
	athletics [æθ'letɪks]	Leichtathletik	I'm an ~ fan, I love sports like running and jumping.
	choir ['kwaɪə]	Chor	a group of singers choir Chor
	journey ['dʒɜːni]	Reise, Fahrt, Weg	Is it a long ~ from Chester to London?
p.10/A1	**until** [ən'tɪl]	bis	I'll have to work ~ 5 o'clock today. Can you wait for me ~ I come home?
	miserable ['mɪzrəbl]	unglücklich, elend; erbärmlich, armselig	I felt very sad when my father died. I was really ~. The weather was ~ – really cold and rainy.
	a year and a half	eineinhalb Jahre, anderthalb Jahre	*a year and a half* = one and a half year<u>s</u>
	(to) **sell** [sel], **sold, sold** [səʊld]	verkaufen	⧓ (to) buy
A2	(to) **move** [muːv]	(um)ziehen	After 18 months we ~*d* to London. We ~*d* to a small flat in Camden. – When *did* you ~ in? ⚠ *(to) move* = **1.** (sich) bewegen; **2.** (um)ziehen
	this way	so, auf diese Weise	Let's do it *this* ~: you draw the pictures and I'll write the texts. ⚠ It's better *this way*. = *So* ist es besser. Come on, *this way*. = Los, komm, *hier entlang*.
	(to) **miss** [mɪs]	vermissen; verpassen, verfehlen	It was great in London, but I ~*ed* my friends. She got up late today, so she ~*ed* the bus.

A3	(to) **be scared (about; of)** [skeəd]	Angst haben (wegen; vor)	My little brother *is* ~ *of* ghosts.
	nervous ['nɜːvəs]	nervös, aufgeregt	Are you scared before a test?– No, just a bit ~.
	Good luck. [lʌk]	Viel Glück.	
A4	°medical certificate [ˌmedɪkl sə'tɪfɪkət]	(ärztliches) Attest, Gesundheitszeugnis	
	(to) **fill** sth. **in** [ˌfɪl_'ɪn]	etwas ausfüllen	⚠ *(to) fill in* = **1.** einsetzen – *Fill in* the right verb. **2.** ausfüllen – *Fill in* the questionnaire.
	midday [ˌmɪd'deɪ]	Mittags-; Mittagszeit	We usually eat our ~ meal at 1 o'clock.

	form [fɔːm]	Formular, Vordruck	
	arrangement [əˈreɪndʒmənt]	Vereinbarung, Abmachung	What are your ~s for the weekend? Have you made any plans?
	(to) **return** [rɪˈtɜːn]	zurückkehren; zurücksenden, -bringen	I left London on 3rd May and ~*ed* on 14th May. Fill in the form and ~ it to the school secretary.
	(to) **tick** [tɪk]	mit einem Häkchen versehen, ankreuzen	There are three answers to each question – please ~ the right answer. ✓
p.11/A5	corridor [ˈkɒrɪdɔː]	Gang, Korridor	
	stairs *(pl)* [steəz]	Treppe; Treppenstufen	⚠ Geh *diese Treppe* hinauf. = Go up *these stairs*.
	floor [flɔː]	Stock(werk)	*first floor = erster Stock* / *ground floor = Erdgeschoss*  ⚠ *im* ersten Stock = *on* the first floor
	cloakroom [ˈkləʊkruːm]	Garderobe	
	staff room [ˈstɑːf ruːm]	Lehrerzimmer	
	assembly hall [əˈsembli hɔːl]	Aula	
	main [meɪn]	Haupt-	the ~ question = the most important question. There's always a lot of traffic on ~ roads.
	entrance [ˈentrəns]	Eingang	Let's meet at the main ~ to the disco.
	toilet [ˈtɔɪlət]	Toilette	
	focus on words / on grammar [ˈfəʊkəs]	*etwa:* Blickpunkt „Wörter"/„Grammatik"	
	(to) explain [ɪkˈspleɪn]	*erklären, erläutern*	
	another [əˈnʌðə]	*ein anderer/anderes, eine andere*	
A6	**friendly** [ˈfrendli]	freundlich, nett	Miss Hunt is a ~ teacher. She isn't often angry.
	to [tə, tu]	um zu	On Sundays we often stay at home ~ watch TV.
A7	**before** [bɪˈfɔː]	vorher schon mal	I've heard this song ~. Have you been here ~? – No, I haven't.

before

1. „vor": Wash your hands **before** dinner. *(prep)*
2. „bevor": Wash your hands **before** we eat. *(conj)*
3. „vorher schon mal": I've been here **before**. *(adv)* „vorher": You live in Cardiff now? Where did you live **before**? *(adv)*

p.12/A8	(to) **be good at** sth.	gut in etwas sein; etwas gut können	Megan likes Maths – and she*'s good* ~ it. ⧓ (to) be bad at sth.

Some more school subjects

Biology [baɪˈɒlədʒi]	Biologie	**History** [ˈhɪstri]	Geschichte
Chemistry [ˈkemɪstri]	Chemie	**Social Studies** [ˌsəʊʃl ˈstʌdiz]	Gesellschaftslehre
Physics *(no pl)* [ˈfɪzɪks]	Physik	**Spanish** [ˈspænɪʃ]	Spanisch
Design and Technology [dɪˈzaɪn], [tekˈnɒlədʒi]	Design und Technologie/Technik	**RE (Religious Education)** [ˌɑːr_ˈiː (rɪˌlɪdʒəs_edʒuˈkeɪʃn)]	Religion(sunterricht)

I'm **good/bad at** Maths.	Ich bin **gut/schlecht in** Mathematik.
My **favourite subject** is English.	Mein **Lieblingsfach** ist Englisch.
I **like** Biology **best**.	Ich **mag** Biologie **am liebsten**.
We **have** Mrs Neumann **for Spanish**.	Wir **haben Spanisch bei** Frau Neumann.
We **have two** History **lessons** every week.	Wir **haben zwei Stunden** Geschichte jede Woche.

p.13/A9	orchestra [ˈɔːkɪstrə]	Orchester	
	for the first time	zum ersten Mal	Today I'm going to play tennis *for the first* ~ in my life. (I've never played tennis before.)
A10	**fault** [fɔːlt]	Schuld; Fehler	You didn't wake me up this morning. It's your ~ that I'm late for school.
	(to) **play a trick on** sb. [trɪk]	jm. einen Streich spielen	
A11	(to) **smile (at** sb.**)** [smaɪl]	(jn. an)lächeln	The man ~*d at* his baby. 
	(to) **make** sb. **do** sth.	jn. dazu bringen, etwas zu tun; jn. zwingen etwas zu tun	Our teacher ~s us *speak* English in our lessons. I like comics. They ~ me *laugh* and they ~ me *feel good*.

	(to) **invite** [ɪn'vaɪt]	*(Gäste)* einladen	Who are you going to ~ to your birthday party? verb: *'(to) invite'* – noun: 'invitation'
	°lock [lɒk]	Schleuse	
	excited (about) [ɪk'saɪtɪd]	aufgeregt (wegen, über)	⚠ (to) be *excited* = *aufgeregt* sein an *exciting* trip = ein *aufregender* Ausflug
	on the top left	*links oben*	
	How do you know?	*Woher weißt du das?*	
	feeling ['fi:lɪŋ]	Gefühl	I feel funny. I've got a funny ~ in my head. verb: '(to) feel' – noun: *'feeling'*
	empty ['empti]	leer	an *empty* glass 
	snake [sneɪk]	Schlange	
P 1	*missing* ['mɪsɪŋ]	*fehlend*	
	before [bɪ'fɔ:]	vorher	You live in Chester now? Where did you live ~?
P 2	*phrases* ['freɪzɪz]	*Ausdrücke*	
[P 4]	*situation* [ˌsɪtʃu'eɪʃn]	*Situation*	
P 8	*(to) go with*	*passen zu, gehören zu*	
[D 1]	*postman* ['pəʊstmən]	*Briefträger, Postbote*	

The Boy with Green Hair

p.18	**stranger** ['streɪndʒə]	Unbekannte(r), Fremde(r)	No one in the village knew her. She was a ~.
	egg [eg]	Ei	What's this?  *Eggs on toast!*
	noisy ['nɔɪzi]	laut, lärmend	noun: 'noise' – adjective: *'noisy'*
	full (of) [fʊl]	voll (mit/von)	There's so much traffic, all the roads are ~ *of* cars. ⧓ empty  *full*  *empty*
	just then	genau in dem Moment; gerade dann	At three o'clock we wanted to go swimming in the lake, and *just* ~ it started to rain.
	stall [stɔ:l]	Stand	I bought this at the market yesterday – at that ~ with the cool T-shirts.
	canal [kə'næl]	Kanal	
	path [pɑ:θ]	Pfad, Weg	a *path* along a *canal* 
	°busker ['bʌskə]	Straßenmusikant/in	
p.19	(to) **look after** sb. [ˌlʊk_'ɑ:ftə]	sich um jn. kümmern, auf jn. aufpassen	Paul's sister is only three. He often ~*s after* her.
	worried (about) ['wʌrid]	beunruhigt (wegen), besorgt (wegen/um)	Sandra is ~ *about* her grandfather. He's very ill.
	the two of them	die beiden; alle beide	Hannah and Tony met at the stall, and then *the ~ of them* ran to the canal.
	half a mile [ˌhɑ:f_ə 'maɪl]	eine halbe Meile	⚠ Wortstellung: *half a* mile – eine halbe Meile *half an* hour – eine halbe Stunde

'half'

You need ***half* an apple** and ***half* a kilo** of grapes. ***Half* an hour** later we met at our favourite café.	… einen halben Apfel und ein halbes Kilo Trauben. Eine halbe Stunde später … .
After **a year and a *half*** he found a new job. (= After **one and a *half* years** …)	Nach eineinhalb Jahren … .
Look at **the first *half*** of page 9 again. Then match the **sentence *halves***.	… die erste Hälfte von Seite 9 … . … die Satzhälften …
At ***half*-time** all the players had some orange juice. Then **the second *half*** of the match began.	In der Halbzeit(pause) … . … die zweite Halbzeit …
It's ***half* past eight**, I have to go now.	Es ist halb neun, … .

	side [saɪd]	Seite	How can we get to the other ~ of the river? ⚠ Seite *(im Buch)* = page
	°aviary ['eɪviəri]	Vogelhaus	
	as [əz, *betont:* æz]	als, während	The bus made a lot of noise ~ it drove along the road.

panic ['pænɪk]	Panik	
(to) **be over** ['əʊvə]	vorbei sein, zu Ende sein	At 5.30 the match *was* ~. Everyone went home.

p.20 **How to ...**

how to do sth.	wie man etwas tun kann/soll	You can ask your teacher or your parents ~ *to do* your homework.
(to) sound [saʊnd]	*klingen, sich anhören*	
also ['ɔ:lsəʊ]	auch	Megan went to the canal, and Hannah went there, too. = Hannah ~ went there.
situation [ˌsɪtʃu'eɪʃn]	Situation	
(to) **describe** sth. **(to** sb.) [dɪ'skraɪb]	(jm.) etwas beschreiben	What does your room look like? Can you ~ it *to* me?
(to) **imagine** sth. [ɪ'mædʒɪn]	sich etwas vorstellen	I can't ~ why some people like punk music.

TIPP **Und jetzt ganz entspannt ...**

Am besten lernt man, wenn man ganz entspannt ist und den Kopf frei hat von anderen Dingen.

- Mach es dir gemütlich: Setz oder leg dich mit deinem Englischbuch ungestört hin.
- Wähle etwa 10 neue Vokabeln aus, die du lernen willst.
- Schau dir ein neues englisches Wort und dessen deutsche Entsprechung an. Dann schließ die Augen und stell dir bildhaft vor, was das Wort bezeichnet (es kann ein Einzelbild oder eine ganze Situation sein). Sag das englische Wort mehrmals laut, dann wird sich der Klang des Wortes fest mit deinem Bild verbinden und besser im Gedächtnis bleiben.

▶▶▶ Unit 2: Out and About

p.21

out and about	unterwegs, auf Achse	
°freak [fri:k]	Freak, Fanatiker/in	
°couch potato [ˌkaʊtʃ pə'teɪtəʊ] *(infml)*	„Dauerglotzer" (*wörtlich:* Sofakartoffel)	
score [skɔ:]	Spielstand, (Spiel-)Ergebnis, Punktestand	The English team lost the match. The ~ was Italy 3, England 1. / The ~ was 3–1 to Italy.
none [nʌn]	keine(r, s)	
winter ['wɪntə]	Winter	
spring [sprɪŋ]	Frühling	
autumn ['ɔ:təm]	Herbst	

spring *summer* *autumn* *winter*

Sports

aerobics [eə'rəʊbɪks]	Aerobic	**racing** ['reɪsɪŋ]	Rennsport
cricket ['krɪkɪt]	Kricket	**riding** ['raɪdɪŋ]	*(das)* Reiten, Reitsport
cycling ['saɪklɪŋ]	*(das)* Radfahren	**rugby** ['rʌgbi]	Rugby
golf [gɒlf]	Golf	**running** ['rʌnɪŋ]	*(das)* Laufen
ice-hockey ['aɪs hɒki]	Eishockey	**skiing** ['ski:ɪŋ]	*(das)* Skilaufen, Skisport
ice skating ['aɪs skeɪtɪŋ]	*(das)* Eislaufen	**table tennis** ['teɪbl tenɪs]	Tischtennis
jogging ['dʒɒgɪŋ]	*(das)* Joggen, Jogging	**windsurfing** ['wɪndsɜ:fɪŋ]	*(das)* Windsurfen

Remember: You **do** aerobics/judo/... . You **go** cycling/jogging/... . You **play** cricket/golf/... .

a **cup of** chocolate/tea [kʌp]	eine Tasse Schokolade/Tee	
(to) **cycle** ['saɪkl]	Rad fahren	(to) ride a bike
°Olympic Games [əˌlɪmpɪk 'geɪmz]	Olympische Spiele	
(to) **ride** (a horse) [raɪd], **rode** [rəʊd], **ridden** ['rɪdn]	(auf einem Pferd) reiten	

She*'s riding* a horse.

He*'s riding* a bike.

p.110 **Your score**

less [les]	weniger	▸◂ more
(to) **spend** time/money **(on)** [spend], **spent** [spent], **spent**	Zeit verbringen (mit) / Geld ausgeben (für)	I *spent* three hours at the chess club yesterday. My brother ~*s* a lot of money *on* clothes.

	healthy ['helθɪ]	gesund	It's very ~ to do sports. ▸◂ unhealthy
	(to) **relax** [rɪ'læks]	(sich) entspannen, sich ausruhen	
p.22/A1	**rubbish** ['rʌbɪʃ] *(infml)*	Quatsch, Blödsinn	⚠ *rubbish* = **1.** Abfall, Müll; **2.** Quatsch, Blödsinn
	(to) **throw** [θrəʊ], **threw** [θru:], **thrown** [θrəʊn]	werfen	*Don't* ~ things from the bridge. It's dangerous. throw werfen
	(to) **be interested (in)** ['ɪntrəstɪd]	interessiert sein (an), sich interessieren (für)	David is a sports freak. He *is* very *interested* ~ sports. ⚠ Betonung auf der ersten Silbe: *interested* ['ɪntrəstɪd] — interested in ⚠ (to) be *interested* (in) = *interessiert* (an) an *interesting* book = ein *interessantes* Buch
A2	county ['kaʊnti]	Grafschaft, Verwaltungsbezirk	

one/ ones

The boutique in Elm Street isn't as good as the **one** in our street.	… wie die in unserer Straße.
I've got three rabbits – a white **one** and two brown **ones**. The white **one** is called 'Henry'.	… – ein weißes und zwei braune. Das weiße heißt Henry.
I like all dogs, but I like little **ones** best.	…, aber mir gefallen kleine am besten.

⚠ *Nie:* three rabbits – ~~a white~~ and ~~two browns~~

Welsh [welʃ]	walisisch; Walisisch	Some people in Wales speak English and ~.
championship ['tʃæmpiənʃɪp]	Meisterschaft	
both [bəʊθ]	beide, beides	Let's listen to ~ *(the)* CDs. (= *beide* CDs) *B~ (of them)* are great. (= *Sie* sind *beide* …)

both

both + noun:	Let's listen to **both** CDs.	He lost **both** parents in 1984.
both the/my/these + noun:	Let's listen to **both the** CDs.	He lost **both his** parents in 1984.
	⚠ Word order: die *beiden* CDs / *both* the CDs	seine *beiden* Eltern / *both* his parents
both of us/you/them:	Tidy up your rooms now – **both of you!** Did you invite David or Colin? – **Both of them.**	
both:	David and Emma **both** want to go on a bike trip. Can we watch these two videos? They're **both** great!	

A3	**rule** [ru:l]	Regel, Vorschrift	I can't play chess, I don't know the ~s.
	oval ['əʊvl]	oval	
	round [raʊnd]	rund	
	(to) **kick** [kɪk]	treten	
	(to) **carry** ['kæri]	tragen; befördern	Sue is wearing her school uniform. She*'s ~ing* her school bag.  This bus can ~ 53 people.
	forward(s) ['fɔ:wəd(z)]	vorwärts, nach vorn	
	°(to) tackle ['tækl]	angreifen, fassen	
	(to) **give** sth. **up**	etwas aufgeben	I had to ~ *up* football. I don't have the time.
	°goal-line ['gəʊl laɪn]	Torlinie	
	°try [traɪ]	„Versuch" *(Rugby: ähnlich einem Tor beim Fußball)*	
	°goalpost ['gəʊlpəʊst]	Torpfosten	
	goal [gəʊl]	Tor *(im Sport)*	
p.23/A4	**popular (with)** ['pɒpjələ]	beliebt (bei)	Swimming is very ~ *with* girls in Wales.
	table ['teɪbl]	*Tabelle*	

A5	(to) **beat** [bi:t], **beat** [bi:t], **beaten** ['bi:tn]	besiegen; schlagen	I ~ my brother at tennis last Sunday.
	(to) **hope** [həʊp]	hoffen	I ~ you can come to my party. (= Ich hoffe, du kannst … . / Hoffentlich kannst du … .)
	He **may** be tired. [meɪ]	Vielleicht ist er müde. / Er könnte (vielleicht) müde sein.	**tired**
	tired ['taɪəd]	müde	
	athlete ['æθli:t]	(Leicht-)Athlet/in, Sportler/in	⚠ Betonung auf der ersten Silbe: *athlete* ['æθli:t]
	You **might** be right. [maɪt]	Du könntest Recht haben. / Vielleicht hast du Recht.	

Möglich / wahrscheinlich / sicherlich

My parents	**may**	be at home now.	Meine Eltern	sind jetzt **vielleicht** zu Hause.
	might			**könnten** jetzt **vielleicht** zu Hause sein.
	could			**könnten** jetzt zu Hause sein.
	should			**sollten/müssten eigentlich** jetzt zu Hause sein.
	must			**müssen** jetzt zu Hause sein.

	another [ə'nʌðə]	ein anderer/anderes, eine andere; noch ein/e	This pen doesn't write. Can I have ~ one, please? Would you like ~ cup of tea?
	beer [bɪə]	Bier	
	star [stɑ:]	Stern	
	(to) **wish** [wɪʃ]	wünschen	We ~ you a Happy Christmas! ⚠ Was *wünschst* du dir zum Geburtstag? = What *do* you *want* for your birthday?
	wish [wɪʃ]	Wunsch	verb: '(to) wish' – noun: *'wish'*
p.24/A6	coach [kəʊtʃ]	Trainer, Trainerin	⚠ *coach* = **1.** (Reise-)Bus; **2.** Trainer/in
	body ['bɒdi]	Körper	Arms, legs and hands are parts of the ~.
A7	**till** [tɪl]	bis	I'll have to work *till/until* 5 o'clock today. Can you wait for me *till/until* I come home?

until / till – by

until / till *(prep; conj)* = „bis"

(prep) I'll have to work **until/till** 5 o'clock today.
*Ich muss heute **bis** 5 Uhr arbeiten.*

(conj) Megan lived in Wales **until/till** she was 13.
*Megan lebte in Wales, **bis** sie 13 war.*

till is more informal than ***until***.

by *(prep)* = „bis spätestens", „nicht später als"

We needed your report **by** Friday midday **(= at or before 12 on Friday)**. Now it's too late.
*Wir brauchten Ihren Bericht **bis** Freitagmittag.*

All letters must be with us **by** 31st May.
*Alle Briefe müssen **bis** zum 31. Mai bei uns sein.*

	°league [li:g]	Liga	
	programme ['prəʊgræm]	*(Fernseh-)Sendung*	
	news *(no pl)* [nju:z]	Nachricht(en)	You won your match? Really? Well, that's good ~! It's nine o'clock. Here is the ~.

English singular – German plural

And what'<u>s</u> the good **news**?	Und was <u>ist</u> die gute **Nachricht**? *oder:* Und was <u>sind</u> die guten **Nachrichten**?
All this **information** <u>is</u> interesting.	All diese **Informationen** <u>sind</u> interessant.
That'<u>s</u> too much **homework**.	Das <u>sind</u> zu viele **Hausaufgaben**.
Your **hair** <u>is</u> too long.	Deine **Haare** <u>sind</u> zu lang.

p.25/A8	guidebook ['gaɪdbʊk]	Reiseführer	
	guide [gaɪd]	(Fremden-)Führer/in, Reiseleiter/in	

Numbers

11,400 = eleven thousand four hundred
⚠ 11.4 = eleven point four (*deutsch:* 11,4 – elf Komma vier)
1,100,000 = one million one hundred thousand
⚠ 1.1 million = one point one million (*deutsch:* 1,1 Millionen)

Im Englischen steht oft ein Komma in Zahlen, die größer als 1000 sind.

	sign [saɪn]	Schild; Zeichen	 a *sign*  a road *sign* (= Verkehrszeichen)

	hill [hɪl]	Hügel, Berg	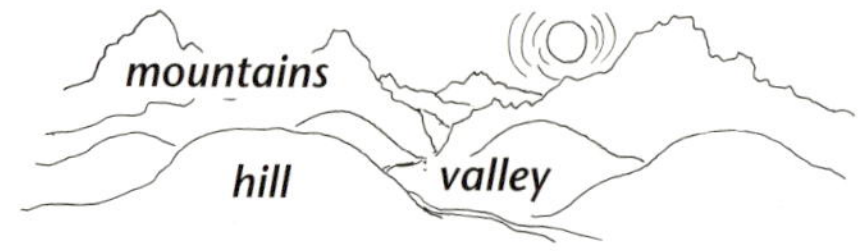
	°off-road [ˌɒf ˈrəʊd]	abseits der Straßen	
	valley [ˈvæli]	Tal	
	(to) **visit** [ˈvɪzɪt]	besuchen; besichtigen	My aunt lives in York. I'm going to ~ her on Friday.
	national [ˈnæʃnəl]	national, National-	▸◂ international
	railway [ˈreɪlweɪ]	Eisenbahn	
	capital [ˈkæpɪtl]	Hauptstadt	Berlin is the ~ of Germany.
	fact [fækt]	*Tatsache, Fakt*	
	(to) test [test]	*testen, prüfen*	
	if-clause [ˈɪf klɔːz]	Nebensatz mit „if", „if"-Satz	**sentence**: If we go south, we'll see lots of things. — ***if*-clause**: If we go south, — **main clause**: we'll see lots of things.
	clause [klɔːz]	(Teil-, Glied-)Satz	
P 1	*dialogue* [ˈdaɪəlɒg]	*Dialog*	
P 3	*with five things each*	*mit je fünf Dingen*	
	(to) **do the dishes**	das Geschirr abwaschen	(to) wash the dishes
P 6	*(to) be missing* [ˈmɪsɪŋ]	*fehlen*	
[P 9]	*radio commentaries* [ˈkɒməntriz]	*Radioreportagen*	
P 10	°word building	*etwa:* das „Bauen"/Bilden von Wörtern	
	(to) **build** [bɪld], **built** [bɪlt], **built**	bauen	It isn't easy to ~ a tree house. verb: *'(to) build'* – noun: 'building' (= Gebäude)
P 11	*(to) fit (-tt-)*[1] [fɪt]	*passen*	
P 12	trouble spot [ˈtrʌbl spɒt]	*hier etwa:* Falle	
	warm [wɔːm]	warm	
[D 3]	*youth hostel* [ˈjuːθ hɒstl]	*Jugendherberge*	
	festival [ˈfestɪvl]	*Festival, Festspiele*	

The Race

p.30	**article** [ˈɑːtɪkl]	(Zeitungs-)Artikel	
	(to) have sth. in common [ˈkɒmən]	etwas miteinander gemein haben	We're not interested in the same things – we *have* nothing *in* ~.
	win [wɪn]	Sieg	A football team gets three points for every ~.
	stadium [ˈsteɪdiəm]	Stadion	
	°(to) run/go for the try	*etwa:* versuchen Punkte zu erzielen	
	surprised (at) [səˈpraɪzd]	überrascht (über)	People say it usually rains in Scotland. So I was ~ *at* the weather there – it was great!
	local [ˈləʊkl]	örtlich, Lokal-; am/vom Ort	Find out what's happening in your town! Buy your ~ newspaper!
	(to) take third place	den dritten Platz belegen	
	junior [ˈdʒuːniə]	Junioren-, Jugend-	
	(to) come (in) third	als Dritter durchs Ziel kommen, einlaufen; Dritter werden	David *came (in) third* in the race, after Tom and Nathan. (= He took third place.) 
	favourite [ˈfeɪvrɪt]	Favorit, Favoritin	
	(to) be ahead (of sb.) [əˈhed]	führen, in Führung liegen (vor jm.); jm. voraus sein	Sometimes David *was ~ of* Aled, sometimes Aled *was ~ of* David.
	°checkpoint [ˈtʃekpɔɪnt]	Kontrollpunkt	
	°finish [ˈfɪnɪʃ]	Ziel; Finish	
	rival [ˈraɪvl]	Rivale, Rivalin; Konkurrent, Konkurrentin	David and Aled are *~s* – they both want to win the race.

p.31 **How to ...**

	detail [ˈdiːteɪl]	Detail, Einzelheit	

[1] Die Angabe „(-tt-)" zeigt, dass der Endkonsonant bei der Bildung von *-ing*-Form, *simple past*-Form und *past participle* verdoppelt wird: *fitting, fitted.*

(to) **make notes** [nəʊts]	sich Notizen machen	
programme ['prəʊgræm]	Programm, (Radio-, Fernseh-)Sendung	
(to) listen for sth.	auf etwas horchen, auf etwas achten	I'm going to work in the garden. Please ~ *for* the phone and fetch me if someone calls.
while [waɪl]	während	What's wrong with your leg? – I broke it ~ I was on holiday.

TIPP **Das Vokabelpuzzle**

- **Du brauchst:** einen Bogen weißen Karton (DIN A4 reicht für den Anfang), ein Lineal, eine Schere, Schreibzeug.
- Unterteile den Karton mit Lineal und Bleistift wie im Beispiel rechts in Drei- und Vierecke.
- Trage jetzt – wie im Beispiel rechts – die Vokabeln und ihre Übersetzung ein.
- Schneide nun die einzelnen Puzzleteile aus. Beim Puzzeln helfen dir die Form der Teile und deine Vokabelkenntnis.

Am besten, du arbeitest mit einem Partner/einer Partnerin, dann könnt ihr eure Puzzles tauschen.

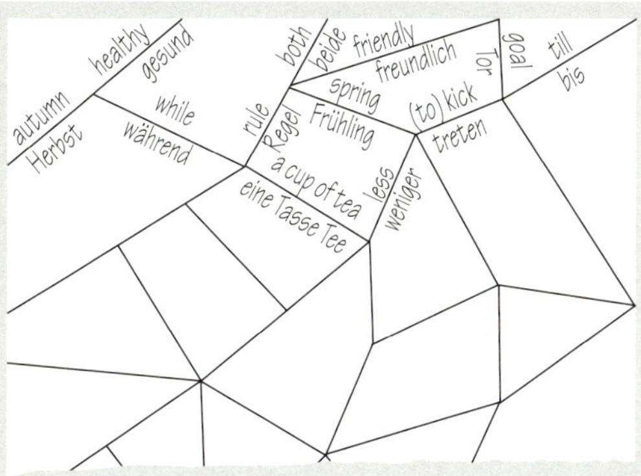

▶▶▶ Unit 3: Great Ideas

pp.34/35

invention [ɪn'venʃn]	Erfindung	
(to) invent [ɪn'vent]	erfinden	Alexander Graham Bell ~*ed* the telephone in 1876.
inventor [ɪn'ventə]	Erfinder, Erfinderin	⚠ *driv<u>er</u>, read<u>er</u>, winn<u>er</u>, …* – but: *invent<u>or</u>, sail<u>or</u>*
(to) **get ready** ['redi]	sich fertig machen, sich bereitmachen	It's half past eight. You must *get* ~ for school now.
ready ['redi]	bereit, fertig	Are you ~? Can we start? Paul! Linda! Dinner is ~.
fork [fɔːk]	Gabel	
spoon [spuːn]	Löffel	
gadget ['gædʒɪt]	Gerät, Apparat	

knife and fork

spoons

hat [hæt]	Hut	
coat [kəʊt]	Mantel	
umbrella [ʌm'brelə]	Regenschirm	

(to) **get dressed** [ˌget 'drest]	sich anziehen	(to) put on your clothes I got up, had a shower, *got* ~ and had breakfast.
as a present	*als Geschenk*	
(to) take the dog for a walk	*mit dem Hund rausgehen*	
discovery [dɪ'skʌvəri]	Entdeckung	The ~ of penicillin has saved many lives.
(to) **discover** [dɪ'skʌvə]	entdecken; herausfinden, feststellen	Alexander Fleming ~*ed* penicillin in 1928. Yesterday I ~*ed* that there's a new café in Elm Street.
fridge [frɪdʒ]	Kühlschrank	Food and drinks stay cold in a ~.
°penicillin [ˌpenɪ'sɪlɪn]	Penizillin	
Scotsman/Scotswoman ['skɒtsmən/-ˌwʊmən]	Schotte/Schottin	
television ['telɪvɪʒn]	Fernsehen; Fernsehgerät	
difficult ['dɪfɪkəlt]	schwierig, schwer	▸◂ easy
radar ['reɪdɑː]	Radar	
(to) **land** [lænd]	landen	
cooker ['kʊkə]	Herd	

a fridge

The plane *is landing.*

a cooker

	microwave ['maɪkrəweɪv]	Mikrowelle, Mikrowellengerät	 a *microwave*
	stereo ['steriəʊ]	Stereoanlage; Stereo	a *stereo* 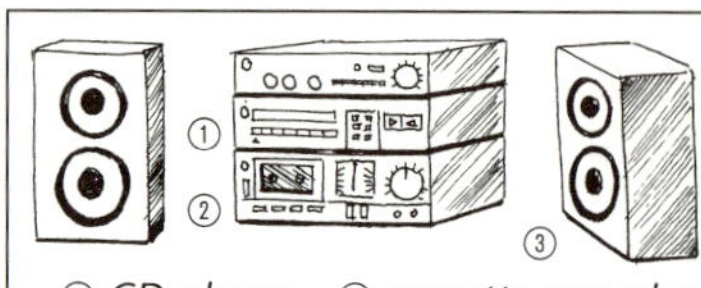 ① *CD player* ② *cassette recorder* ③ *speaker, loudspeaker*
	What things can you live without?	*Auf welche Dinge kannst du verzichten?*	
pp.36/37			
A1	instruction [ɪn'strʌkʃn]	Anweisung, Anleitung	Read the ~*s* carefully before you use the microwave.
A2	design [dɪ'zaɪn]	Entwurf; Design, Gestaltung, Konstruktion	The town planners looked at the ~*s* for the new shopping centre. This is our new school building. Do you like the ~?
	(to) design [dɪ'zaɪn]	entwerfen, konstruieren	Jill's parents ~*ed* and built their own house.
	(to) **explain** sth. **to** sb. [ɪk'spleɪn]	jm. etwas erklären, erläutern	I don't understand these instructions. Can you ~ them *to* me? ⚠ Never: *Can you ~~explain me~~ …?*

Verbs and their nouns

Beachte Schreibung und Aussprache! (Du kennst alle Verben und die meisten der Nomen.)

-ing			*-ion / -tion / -ation*		
(to) begin	**beginning**	Anfang, Beginn	(to) decide [dɪ'saɪd]	**decision** [dɪ'sɪʒn]	Entscheidung
(to) build	**building**	Gebäude	(to) describe [dɪ'skraɪb]	**description** [dɪ'skrɪpʃn]	Beschreibung
(to) feel	**feeling**	Gefühl	(to) explain [ɪk'spleɪn]	**explanation** [ˌeksplə'neɪʃn]	Erklärung
(to) meet	**meeting**	Treffen; Versammlung; Besprechung	(to) invent	**invention**	Erfindung
			(to) invite [ɪn'vaɪt]	**invitation** [ˌɪnvɪ'teɪʃn]	Einladung

	mark [mɑːk]	(Zeugnis-)Note, Zensur	Sue's French is very good. She has got very good ~*s* in French. ⚠ *mark* = Note, Zensur – *note* = Notiz
A3	the pupils **who** … / a person **who** …	die Schüler/innen, die … / eine Person, die …	The man/woman/child ~ wants to talk to you is waiting in my office. who für Personen
	something **that** … / a thing **that** …	etwas, was … / eine Sache, die …	A fridge is a sort of box ~ keeps food cold. that für Sachen
	skill [skɪl]	Fertigkeit, Fähigkeit	For this job you need language ~*s*. (= You have to be good at languages.)
	automatic [ˌɔːtə'mætɪk]	automatisch	This is an ~ door: it opens ~*ally*. adjective: *'automatic'* – adverb: *'automatically'*
	(to) **leave** [liːv], **left** [left], **left**	(zurück)lassen, hinterlassen	You can ~ your bag in the classroom. *Don't* ~ the door open, please. 
	board [bɔːd]	Brett	You need ~*s* to make a bookshelf.
	(to) **work** [wɜːk]	funktionieren	I can't phone my friends, our phone *isn't ~ing*.
	That feels great.	Das ist ein tolles Gefühl.	

Adverb oder Adjektiv nach bestimmten Verben

verb + adverb

Wie du weißt, werden nach Verben **Adverbien der Art und Weise** verwendet, um zu sagen, **wie jemand etwas tut**:

- All the kids are talking **excitedly**.
  Alle Kinder reden aufgeregt durcheinander.
  (Wie reden sie? – Aufgeregt.)

verb + adjective

Es gibt auch Verben, die nicht Tätigkeiten beschreiben, sondern **Zustände oder Eigenschaften (wie jemand oder etwas ist)**. Nach diesen Verben stehen **Adjektive**:

- All the kids felt **excited**.
  Alle Kinder waren aufgeregt.
  (Wie fühlten sie sich? Wie waren sie? – Aufgeregt.)
- It was dangerous, but she stayed **cool**.
  Es war gefährlich, aber sie blieb cool.

Vergleiche:

She looked **angrily** at Susan.
Sie sah Susan wütend an. (Tätigkeit)

She looked **angry**.
Sie sah wütend aus. (Zustand)

	engineer [ˌendʒɪˈnɪə]	Ingenieur/in, Techniker/in	My father is an ~. He designs cars.

Jobs ⚠ Im Englischen mit **unbestimmtem Artikel!**

My mum is **an** engineer / **a** teacher. — *… ist Ingenieurin … .*
My dad works as **a** shop assistant / **a** taxi driver. — *… als Verkäufer … .*
What do you want to **be** when you leave school? — *Was willst du **werden**, wenn du von der Schule abgehst?*

	(to) underline [ˌʌndəˈlaɪn]	*unterstreichen*	
	arrow [ˈærəʊ]	*Pfeil*	
	What words do the arrows point back to?	*Auf welche Wörter zeigen die Pfeile zurück?*	
A4	**whose** [huːz]	deren, dessen	Jane is the girl ~ mother is a bus driver. Can you give me the names of three countries ~ people speak English?
	oil rig [ˈɔɪl rɪg]	(Öl-)Bohrinsel	
p.38/A5	°Highland Games [ˌhaɪlənd ˈgeɪmz]	*Festival mit Musik und Sportwettkämpfen im schottischen Hochland*	
	quite [kwaɪt]	ziemlich, ganz	There were ~ a lot of people at the party. ⚠ *quite* [kwaɪt] = ziemlich, ganz – *quiet* [kwaɪət] = ruhig, leise, still
	midnight [ˈmɪdnaɪt]	Mitternacht	twelve o'clock at night **midnight** the **mid**dle of the **night**
	down south	unten im Süden	
	wonderful [ˈwʌndəfl]	wunderbar	very nice, great, fantastic
	industry [ˈɪndəstri]	Industrie	There's no ~ in our area, but there are a lot of farms. ⚠ Betonung auf der ersten Silbe: *industry* [ˈɪndəstri]
	across [əˈkrɒs]	(quer) über, durch; hinüber, herüber	Look at all those cars. We can't get ~ the street. Look at that stream. How can we get ~?
	land [lænd]	(Fest-)Land; Grund und Boden	We were happy to be on ~ again after a week at sea. ⚠ ein Land/Staat = *a country* auf dem Land = *in the country*

'of' in place phrases

the **city of** Aberdeen in Scotland — die Stadt Aberdeen in Schottland
the **town of** Doncaster — die Stadt Doncaster
the **Isle of** Skye on the coast of Scotland — die Insel Skye an der Küste Schottlands

	what else? [els]	*was sonst noch?*	
p.39/A6	**at first**	zuerst, anfangs, zu Anfang	I was very bad at English *at* ~, but I'm getting better. ⚠ *zuerst* (= als Erstes) = *first:* *First* turn left, then right. I'll come later. I have to finish my homework *first*.
	post [pəʊst]	Post(sendungen)	⚠ Kannst du bitte zur *Post* (= zum Postamt) gehen? = Can you go to the *post office*, please?
	useless [ˈjuːsləs]	nutzlos, zu nichts nütze	◄► useful
A7	**heavy** [ˈhevi]	schwer *(von Gewicht)*	Can you help me with this box? It's very ~. ⚠ *schwierig, schwer* = *difficult*
	(to) **notice** [ˈnəʊtɪs]	bemerken	Sue was at the party, too, but I *didn't* ~ her. ⚠ *(to) notice* = bemerken – *note* = Notiz
	(to) go on	*im Gange sein, vorgehen*	
	electric [ɪˈlektrɪk]	elektrisch	*Electric* cars are quiet and clean.
[P 1]	*(to) work* [wɜːk]	*funktionieren*	
P 2	**the only** boy/girl	der einzige Junge / das einzige Mädchen	The 'Pizza Palace' is *the* ~ restaurant in our street, but not *the* ~ one in our village.
P 4	Scottish-American [ˌskɒtɪʃ‿əˈmerɪkən]	Amerikaner/in schottischer Herkunft	
	modern [ˈmɒdn]	modern	⚠ Betonung auf der ersten Silbe: *modern* [ˈmɒdn]
P 5	*tick* [tɪk]	*Häkchen*	
	clear [klɪə]	klar, deutlich	Is the homework ~ to you now? Do you know what you have to do?
P 6	(to) run **after** sb.	hinter jm. herrennen	'Come back,' shouted the boy as he *ran* ~ his dog.

A Loch Ness Mystery

p.43	°loch [lɒx, lɒk]	See *(schottisch)*	
	mystery ['mɪstri]	Geheimnis, Rätsel	I don't know how I lost my book – it's a ~ to me.
	search (for) [sɜːtʃ]	Suche (nach), Durchsuchung	After a long ~ we found our tortoise. It was behind the cupboard.

Verbs and nouns with the same form

(to) **guide**	führen, lenken, leiten	(to) **return**	zurückkehren; zurücksenden
guide	(Fremden-)Führer/in	**return**	Rückkehr, Wiederkehr
(to) **hope**	hoffen	(to) **search** (for)	suchen (nach), durchsuchen
hope	Hoffnung	**search** (for)	Suche (nach), Durchsuchung
(to) **interview**	befragen, interviewen	(to) **smile**	lächeln
interview	Interview	**smile**	Lächeln
(to) **list**	auflisten, aufzählen	(to) **sound**	klingen, sich *(gut/...)* anhören
list	Liste	**sound**	Laut, Klang
(to) **report**	berichten, melden	(to) **visit**	besuchen; besichtigen
report	Bericht, Reportage	**visit**	Besuch

°mini-submarine ['mɪni ˌsʌbməˌriːn]	Mini-U-Boot	
line [laɪn]	Reihe; Linie	The footballers stood in a ~ in front of the goal. In Maths we had to draw a ~ between two points. ⚠ *line* = **1.** Zeile; **2.** Reihe; **3.** Linie
deep [diːp]	tief	How long and how ~ is your swimming-pool?
°sonar ['səʊnɑː]	Sonar	
equipment *(no pl)* [ɪ'kwɪpmənt]	Ausrüstung	⚠ *Without 'a/an':* I need new sports *equipment*. ... *eine* neue Sport*ausrüstung*.
kind (of) [kaɪnd]	Art, Sorte	What ~ *of* music do you like? – Pop music. ⚠ *Was für ein* Auto ...? = *What kind of* car ...?
(to) **sink** [sɪŋk], **sank** [sæŋk], **sunk** [sʌŋk]	sinken, untergehen; versenken	Small boats *sink* easily in storms. The storm *sank* the small boat.
outside lights/walls/toilet ['aʊtsaɪd]	Außenbeleuchtung/-wände/-toilette	
outside [ˌaʊt'saɪd]	draußen; nach draußen	I heard people ~. They were very loud, so I went ~ and asked them to be quiet.
inside [ˌɪn'saɪd]	drinnen; nach drinnen	⧓ outside
something **else** [els]	(noch) etwas anderes	I hate chess – let's play *something* ~, please.

... else

After the break we will do **something else**.	Nach der Pause machen wir **etwas anderes**.
I was busy, so **someone else** had to do the shopping.	..., also musste **jemand anders** einkaufen.
Do we need **anything else** from the supermarket?	Brauchen wir **sonst noch etwas** ...?
Did you see **anyone else** at the party?	Hast du **sonst noch jemand** ... gesehen?
(In a shop) Hey, you, can't you wait like **everyone else**?	..., kannst du nicht warten wie **alle anderen auch**?
What else do you know about Scotland?	**Was** weißt du **(sonst) noch** über Schottland?
Who else did you meet?	**Wen** hast du **(sonst) noch** getroffen?

(to) **push** [pʊʃ]	schieben, stoßen, drücken	
Hold on! [ˌhəʊld_'ɒn]	Festhalten! Halt dich fest!	
(to) **hold** [həʊld], **held** [held], **held**	(fest)halten	Can you ~ my bag for a moment? I'll be back in a minute.
(to) roll over [ˌrəʊl_'əʊvə]	sich (auf den Rücken) drehen, umkippen	There was a big wave, the boat *~ed over*, and we fell into the water.
(to) **go** black/hard/...	schwarz/hart/... werden	Something heavy fell on my head, and everything *went* black. The bread *has gone* hard – we can't have sandwiches.
(to) groan [grəʊn]	stöhnen, ächzen	
upside-down [ˌʌpsaɪd 'daʊn]	verkehrt herum, auf dem Kopf	This picture is ~-~. 

	°porthole ['pɔːthəʊl]	Seitenfenster, Bullauge	
	°controls *(pl)* [kən'trəʊlz]	Schalttafel, Steuerpult	
	(to) **rise** [raɪz], **rose** [rəʊz], **risen** ['rɪzn]	(an-, auf)steigen; aufgehen *(Sonne)*	Look at that river! It has rained so much that the water *has risen* almost a metre. The sun ~*s* in the east. 
p.44	°clunk [klʌŋk]	*dumpfes Geräusch*	
	(to) **pass** [pɑːs]	vergehen, vorüber-gehen *(Zeit)*	The lesson was so interesting that the time ~*ed* really quickly.
	(to) move **along** [ə'lɒŋ]	sich vorwärts bewegen, weitergehen	We *moved* ~ slowly with the other pupils until we reached the entrance.
	at last [ət 'lɑːst]	schließlich, endlich	We waited a long time, and *at* ~ the train arrived.
	(to) **be pleased (with)** [pliːzd]	zufrieden sein (mit), sich freuen (über)	Tom's work was very good. The teacher *was* very ~ *with* him.
	°dent [dent]	Delle, Beule	
	at the back (of)	hinten, am hinteren Ende (von)	Let's sit *at the* ~ *of* the bus today, not at the front. ⧓ at the front
	mark [mɑːk]	Abdruck, Spur	When the dog came in from the garden, it was very dirty. It left ~*s* all over the kitchen floor.
	beyond [bɪ'jɒnd]	über … hinaus, jenseits (von)	The road goes ~ the village and into the fields. You can't see it, but there's a lake ~ the wall.
	truth [truːθ]	Wahrheit	Where did you go last night? Tell me the ~.
p.45	**How to …**		
	(to) make sth. into sth.	*etwas zu etwas machen*	
	linking word ['lɪŋkɪŋ wɜːd]	Bindewort	'And', 'or', 'but', 'because' are ~ *words*, for example.
	spelling ['spelɪŋ]	(Recht-)Schreibung, Schreibweise	Your story is interesting, but your ~ is terrible.

TIPP

Zu zweit gehts besser …

Hier zwei Spielideen für das Lernen zu zweit oder in der Gruppe:

- Eine prima Sache für Freiarbeitsstunden ist das **Vokabel-Memory**. Ihr müsst dafür 10 bis 15 Kartenpaare anfertigen – es gehören immer zwei Karten zusammen. Als Paare könnt ihr wählen:
  - englisches Wort – deutsche Entsprechung ***(truth* – Wahrheit; *deep* – tief)** *oder*
  - Gegensätze ***(useful – useless; easy – difficult)*** *oder*
  - unregelmäßige Verben, Infinitiv und *simple past*-Form ***(go – went; say – said)*** *oder*
  - Teile von Wörtern ***(home + work → homework)***

  Die Karten liegen verdeckt auf dem Tisch. Abwechselnd darf jeder zwei Karten aufdecken – wer zusammengehörige Karten aufdeckt, darf sie behalten.

Arbeitet ihr mit einer **Vokabelkartei**? Dann probiert mal dieses Spiel:

- Nehmt 10 bis 15 Vokabelkarten und legt sie offen auf den Tisch. Partner **B** schließt die Augen, Partner **A** entfernt eine Karte und fragt:
  What have I changed?
  Partner **B** sagt, welche Karte fehlt; Beispiel:
  You've taken away 'excited'.
  Wenn die Antwort stimmt, kann **B** die Karte behalten.

  (In der Gruppe macht es noch mehr Spaß, weil es auf Schnelligkeit ankommt.)

▶▶▶ Unit 4: London

pp.46/47	**sights** *(pl)* [saɪts]	Sehenswürdigkeiten	Why do you want to go to London? – Because I want to see the ~.
	parliament ['pɑːləmənt]	Parlament	You can see the *Houses of Parliament* (= das Parlamentsgebäude in London) on page 46. ⚠ spelling: *parliament*
	bank [bæŋk]	(Fluss-)Ufer	

	complex ['kɒmpleks]	(Gebäude-)Komplex	There's a new stadium and sports ~ in our town.

	theatre ['θɪətə]	Theater	⚠ Betonung auf der ersten Silbe: *theatre* ['θɪətə]
	°Crown Jewels *(pl)* [ˌkraʊn 'dʒuːəlz]	Kronjuwelen	
	(to) learn about	etwas erfahren über/von, etwas herausfinden über	When *did* you ~ *about* their plans? Come to 'Water World' and ~ *about* dolphins and sea lions!
	violent ['vaɪələnt]	gewalttätig, gewaltsam	Some pupils often get ~ and hit other pupils.

Places and sights in London

Big Ben *die Glocke der Turmuhr des Parlamentsgebäudes (umgangssprachlich auch für Turm und Uhr des Parlamentsgebäudes gebraucht)*
Buckingham Palace [ˌbʌkɪŋəm 'pæləs] *Londoner Wohnsitz der Königin*
the **Houses of Parliament** *das Parlamentsgebäude*
the **London Aquarium** [ə'kweəriəm] *das Londoner Aquarienhaus (mit 30.000 Meerestieren u. -pflanzen)*
the **London Dungeon** ['dʌndʒən] *Museum nahe der London Bridge* (dungeon = *Kerker, Verlies)*
London Zoo *der Londoner Zoo (mit 12.000 Tieren)*
Madame Tussaud's [ˌmædəm tə'sɔːdz] *Madame Tussauds Wachsfigurenkabinett*
the **Museum of the Moving Image** ['ɪmɪdʒ] **(MOMI)** *Film- und Fernsehmuseum nahe der Waterloo Bridge*
Nelson's Column [ˌnelsnz 'kɒləm] *die Nelson-Säule (auf dem Trafalgar Square)*
Piccadilly Circus [ˌpɪkədɪli 'sɜːkəs] *Platz im West End mit Eros-Statue, Touristentreffpunkt*
St Paul's (Cathedral) [sənt 'pɔːlz] *die St. Pauls-Kathedrale (im Zentrum Londons)*
the **Statue of Eros** [ˌstætʃuː‿əv‿'ɪərɒs] *die Eros-Statue*
the **(River) Thames** [temz] *die Themse*
Tower Bridge *Klappbrücke beim Tower*
the **Tower (of London)** *mittelalterliche Festung, heute Aufbewahrungsort der Kronjuwelen*
Trafalgar Square [trəˌfælgə 'skweə] *Platz im West End mit Nelson-Säule*
the **Trocadero** [ˌtrɒkə'dɪərəʊ] *riesiges Vergnügungszentrum mit Computerspielen, Autoskootern u.Ä. nahe Piccadilly Circus*
the **West End** [ˌwest‿'end] *vornehmer Stadtteil im Zentrum mit zahlreichen Einkaufsstraßen, Hotels, Kinos, Diskotheken und Theatern*
Westminster Abbey [ˌwestmɪnstər‿'æbi] *die Westminster-Abtei (Krönungskirche der englischen Könige und Königinnen)*

avenue ['ævənjuː]	Allee, Boulevard
circus ['sɜːkəs]	(runder) Platz *(in einer Stadt)*
column ['kɒləm]	Säule
palace ['pæləs]	Palast, Schloss
square [skweə]	Platz *(in einer Stadt)*
statue ['stætʃuː]	Statue

p.48/A1	**the underground** *(no pl)* ['ʌndəgraʊnd] **the tube** *(no pl)* [tjuːb] *(infml)*	die U-Bahn die U-Bahn *(in London) (eigentlich:* Rohr, Röhre)	Take *the underground / the tube* to Oxford Street. There's an *underground* station / a *tube* station at Oxford Circus. ⚠ Wann fährt die nächste *U-Bahn* nach ...? = When's the next *(underground) train* to ...?
	over there [ˌəʊvə 'ðeə]	dort drüben, da drüben	

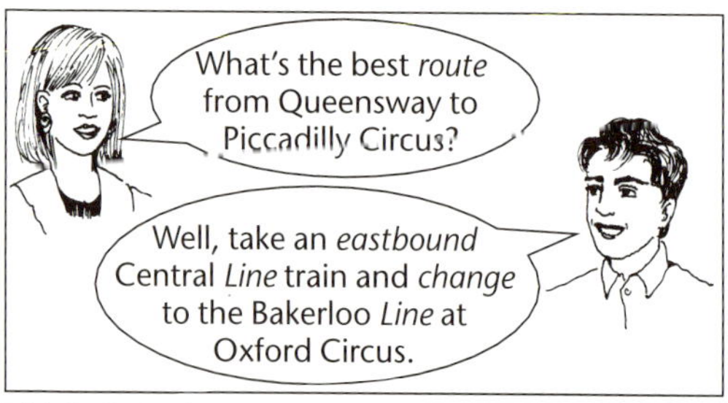

A2	**line** [laɪn]	(U-Bahn-)Linie	
	route [ruːt]	Route, Strecke	
	a southbound train ['saʊθbaʊnd]	ein Zug Richtung Süden	
	(to) **change** (trains)	umsteigen	
	(to) **get off** [ˌget‿'ɒf]	aussteigen	This is Oxford Circus. We have to *get* ~ here. ◂▸ (to) get in – There's the taxi. Let's *get in.*

German 'ein-/aussteigen'

(to) **get on** / (to) **get off** – **a bus**, **a train**, **a plane**, **a bike**

She *got on* the bus at 2.30.
He *got off* the train at Euston Station.
We *got in(to)* the car and drove away.
The driver helped me to *get out of* the taxi.

(to) **get in(to)** / (to) **get out of** – **a car**, **a taxi**

p.49/A3	wax [wæks]	Wachs	At Madame Tussaud's you can see ~ figures of a lot of famous people.

	°arcade [ɑːˈkeɪd]	Arkade, Passage *(mit Geschäften, Spielhallen usw.)*	
	pocket money [ˈpɒkɪt ˌmʌni]	Taschengeld	How much ~ *money* do you get from your parents?
	pocket [ˈpɒkɪt]	Tasche *(an einem Kleidungsstück)*	

A4	attraction [əˈtrækʃn]	Attraktion	Big Ben is one of the main tourist ~s in London.
	... the attractions **that** you must see	... die Attraktionen, die du sehen musst	

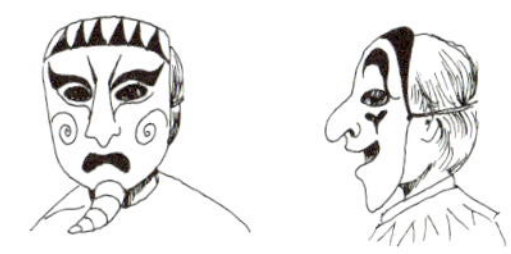

	mask [mɑːsk]	Maske	
	revolution [ˌrevəˈluːʃn]	Revolution	
	... the people **who** she modelled	... die Leute, die sie modellierte	
	(to) model (-ll-) [ˈmɒdl]	modellieren, nachbilden	verb: *'(to) model'* – noun: 'model'
	(to) **travel (-ll-)** [ˈtrævl]	reisen	I never go by plane. I always ~ by train.
	(to) translate [trænsˈleɪt]	*übersetzen*	
A5	**abroad** [əˈbrɔːd]	im/ins Ausland	Ron has left England. He's living ~ now. Where are you going on holiday? – We're going ~.
	virtual [ˈvɜːtʃuəl]	virtuell *(nicht echt, aber echt erscheinend)*	
	(to) **like** sth. **better/best**	etwas lieber/am liebsten mögen	I ~ milk *better* than lemonade, but I ~ cola *best*.
p.50/A6	**everywhere** [ˈevriweə]	überall, überallhin	I can't find my bag. I've looked ~.
	°Changing of the Guard [gɑːd]	Wachablösung *(vor dem Buckingham Palace)*	
	ceremony [ˈserəməni]	Zeremonie; Feier(lichkeit)	The Changing of the Guard is a famous ~ at Buckingham Palace. ⚠ Betonung auf der ersten Silbe: *ceremony* [ˈserəməni]
	°admiral [ˈædmərəl]	Admiral	
	°Lord [lɔːd]	Lord *(engl. Adelstitel)*	
A7	**as**	wie	There are too many cars in London, ~ in all big cities. London is the capital of England, ~ you all know.
	homeless [ˈhəʊmləs]	obdachlos	A person without a home is a ~ person.
	homelessness [ˈhəʊmləsnəs]	Obdachlosigkeit	adjective: 'homeless' – noun: *'homelessness'*
	issue [ˈɪʃuː]	(Streit-)Frage, Thema, Angelegenheit	Pollution is one of the big ~s of our time.
	off [ɒf]	von (... herunter/hinunter)	We must help homeless people to get ~ the streets. The child fell ~ the tree and broke his leg.
	(to) go a long way	viel erreichen, viel bewirken	£2 isn't much, but it can ~ *a long way* when you're hungry.
	(to) **mean** something **to** sb.	jm. etwas bedeuten	Her job ~s *a lot to* her. (= Her job is important to her.) The name ~s *nothing to* me. (= Der Name sagt mir nichts. / Ich kenne den Namen nicht.)
p.51/A8	**passenger** [ˈpæsɪndʒə]	Passagier/in, Fahrgast	All ~s for Euston Station should change trains here.
	conversation [ˌkɒnvəˈseɪʃn]	Gespräch, Unterhaltung	to have a ~ with someone = to talk to someone about something
	transport *(no pl)* [ˈtrænspɔːt]	Verkehrsmittel	Buses, trains and cars are all forms of ~.
	tram [træm]	Straßenbahn	a tram
	town hall [ˌtaʊn ˈhɔːl]	Rathaus	
	Continue to collect words. [kənˈtɪnjuː]	*Sammle weiter Wörter.*	
	rest [rest]	*Rest*	
A9	mime group [ˈmaɪm gruːp]	Pantomimengruppe	We listened to a jazz group and watched a ~ *group*.

	That's when we saw ...	In dem Moment sahen wir ...	I wanted to buy a ticket and looked in my pocket. *That's* ~ I noticed that my money wasn't there.
	°pickpocket ['pɪkpɒkɪt]	Taschendieb/in	
	(to) chase sb. (away) [tʃeɪs]	jn. (weg)jagen	The dog *is chasing* the cat. 
	(to) save the day	die Situation retten, der Retter sein *(in einer bestimmten Situation)*	We wanted to play tennis, but we had no ball. Then John arrived and had some tennis balls with him – he *~d the day* for us.
p.52/A10	**past** [pɑːst]	vorbei an, vorüber an	The bus didn't stop at the bus stop. It drove ~ it. ⚠ *an* der Haltestelle *vorbei* = *past* the bus stop
	Chinese *(adj; n)* [ˌtʃaɪ'niːz]	chinesisch; Chinesisch; Chinese/Chinesin	
	New Year [ˌnjuː 'jɪə]	Neujahr	
	parade [pə'reɪd]	Parade, Umzug	
	(to) ask sb. for directions [də'rekʃnz]	*jn. um eine Wegbeschreibung bitten; jn. nach dem Weg fragen*	
A11	(to) **be born** [bɔːn]	geboren sein/werden	When *were* you ~? – I *was* ~ on 15th March, 1987. ⚠ Wann *bist* du geboren? = When *were* you born? Never: I ~~am born~~ in 1987.
	exactly [ɪg'zæktli]	genau	adverb: *'exactly'* – Sue and John are ~ the same size.
	exact [ɪg'zækt]	genau	adjective: *'exact'* – What's the ~ size of Germany?
	wherever [weər'evə]	wohin (auch) immer; wo (auch) immer	I'll come with you, ~ you go. We'll find you, ~ you are.
P 9	**the following** expressions ['fɒləʊɪŋ]	die folgenden Ausdrücke	Look at *the* ~ words and tell me what they mean: 'underground', 'tube', 'tram', 'train'.
	(to) **mean** [miːn], **meant** [ment], **meant** [ment]	meinen (= sagen wollen)	He said Tuesday, but he *meant* Thursday. ⚠ ich meine (= ich denke, ich glaube) = I *think* ⚠ *(to) mean – meant – meant* = **1.** bedeuten; **2.** meinen ⚠ *meaning* = Bedeutung (nicht: ~~Meinung~~)
	(to) **compare** [kəm'peə]	vergleichen	Now ~ your answers with your partner's answers.
[D 1]	*graffiti (pl)* [grə'fiːti]	*Graffiti, Wandkritzeleien*	
	(to) crash [kræʃ]	*abstürzen (Computer)*	

Save the Crown Jewels

p.56	maze [meɪz]	Irrgarten, Labyrinth	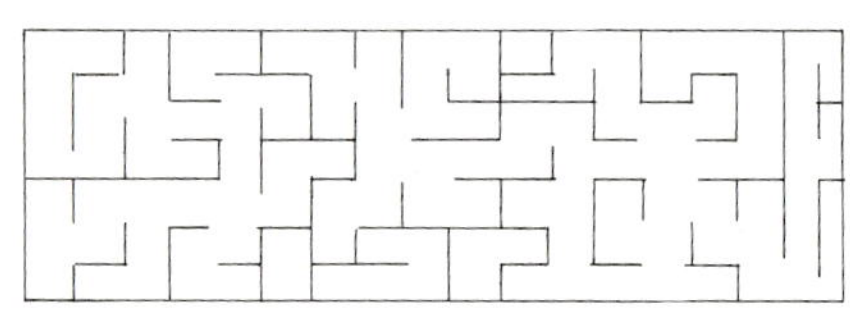 a *maze*
	agent ['eɪdʒənt]	Agent/in	
	step [step]	Schritt; Stufe	Try to do the exercise ~ by ~. (= Schritt für Schritt) 
	table ['teɪbl]	Tabelle	
	(to) **take**	dauern, *(Zeit)* brauchen	It *~s* about 20 minutes to do this exercise. How long *does* it ~ to get from Euston Station to Oxford Circus?
	enough [ɪ'nʌf]	genug	There aren't ~ chairs here for everyone.
	total ['təʊtl]	Summe, Gesamtbetrag	A ~ of 71 pupils are learning French at my school.
	°Secret Service [ˌsiːkrət 'sɜːvɪs]	Geheimdienst	
	(to) **ring** [rɪŋ], **rang** [ræŋ], **rung** [rʌŋ]	klingeln, läuten; anrufen	The phone *rang* while I was leaving the house. David *rang* while you were out. (= He phoned ...)
	bomb [bɒm]	Bombe	⚠ Stummes „b": *bomb* [bɒm]
	code [kəʊd]	(Geheim-)Kode	I can't read the letter, it's in ~.
	(to) **be alive** [ə'laɪv]	leben, am Leben sein	◂▸ (to) be dead ⚠ Aussprache: *alive* [ə'laɪv] – *(to) live* [lɪv]
	(to) **add** [æd]	addieren, hinzufügen, ergänzen	*Add* blue water to yellow water and you get green water.

alive
am Leben

TIPP **Reim dich, oder ich fress dich!**

Du kannst dir schwierige Wörter, z.B. unregelmäßige Verben, besser merken, wenn du sie in Reimform bringst und dann rhythmisch sprichst – du kannst dabei im Rhythmus klatschen, dann wird daraus so eine Art Rap.

ring - rang - rung sounds like *sing - sang - sung*
and *tell - told - told* sounds like *sell - sold - sold.*
sleep - slept - slept sounds like *keep - …*
and *drink - drank - drunk* sounds like …

Probiers mal mit diesen Verben: *blow, break, fly, wake.*

In der Liste der unregelmäßigen Verben (S. 191–192) findest du sicher noch weitere Paare.

	°Put that in your pipe and smoke it. *(infml)*	*etwa:* Lass dir das gesagt sein. / Schreib dir das hinter die Ohren.	
	pipe [paɪp]	(Tabaks-)Pfeife	
	(to) **smoke** [sməʊk]	rauchen	When you see this sign, you mustn't ~. 
	order ['ɔːdə]	Reihenfolge; (An-)Ordnung	Put the following words in the right ~: 'Can – help – you – me?'.
	directions *(pl)* [də'rekʃnz]	Anweisung(en)	
p.57	°hologram ['hɒləgræm]	Hologramm *(mithilfe eines Lasers erzeugtes dreidimensionales Bild)*	
	university [ˌjuːnɪ'vɜːsəti]	Universität, Hochschule	⚠ Betonung auf der dritten Silbe: *university* [ˌjuːnɪ'vɜːsəti]
	inside *(prep)* [ˌɪn'saɪd]	innerhalb, im Innern (von); in (… hinein)	It's raining. Let's wait ~ the boutique. ▸◂ outside
	mistake [mɪ'steɪk]	Fehler, Irrtum	Don't make too many ~*s* in the test.
	ticket ['tɪkɪt]	Fahrkarte, Fahrschein	
	platform ['plætfɔːm]	Bahnsteig, Gleis	The train to London leaves from ~ 3.
	(to) **catch a train/bus** [kætʃ], **caught** [kɔːt], **caught**	einen Zug/Bus nehmen, erreichen	We don't have to walk, we can ~ *a bus.* We had to run to ~ the bus. What are they doing?  *They're trying to catch a bus!*
	(to) **catch** [kætʃ], **caught** [kɔːt], **caught**	fangen; erwischen	You throw the ball, and I*'ll* ~ it. The assistant *caught* the thief and called the police.
	microchip ['maɪkrəʊtʃɪp]	Mikrochip	
	(to) **fit** (-tt-) [fɪt]	passen	That table is too big, it *won't* ~ into our kitchen. I tried on the jacket, but it *didn't* ~. It was too big.
p.58	**gun** [gʌn]	Schusswaffe	The policeman pulled out his ~ and shouted, 'Stop!'

How to …

(to) scan (-nn-) [skæn]	*(einen Text)* überfliegen *(um bestimmte Informationen zu finden)*	
technique [tek'niːk]	(Arbeits-)Verfahren, Technik, Methode	How do you learn new words? Do you have a special ~? ⚠ Betonung auf der zweiten Silbe: *technique* [tek'niːk]
(to) go with	*einhergehen mit, gehören zu*	
finger ['fɪŋgə]	*Finger*	
wavy lines [ˌweɪvi 'laɪnz]	*Wellenlinien, Schlangenlinien*	
edge [edʒ]	*Rand, Kante*	

TIPP

Werbung für Vokabeln!

Ist dir schon mal aufgefallen, dass du dir jede Menge neue Namen für Schokoriegel, Eissorten oder Waschmittel merkst, ohne dass du dich dafür anstrengen musst? Wie kommt das?

Ein Grund ist sicherlich, dass du diese Produktnamen ganz häufig zu sehen bekommst, auch wenn dir das gar nicht bewusst ist – denk nur mal an die Werbung in Sportstadien, die du ganz nebenbei wahrnimmst, während du ein Sportereignis verfolgst.

Diesen Effekt kannst du beim Vokabellernen ausnutzen:

- **Das Vokabel-Werbeplakat:** Gib den Popstars oder Fußballern auf deinen Postern Sprechblasen. Oder nimm ein A3-Blatt, Filzstifte und ein paar Fotos und gestalte dein eigenes Vokabelplakat.

- **Die Vokabel-Litfaßsäule:** Alles, was die Form einer Walze hat, eignet sich als Litfaßsäule. Mit Selbstklebeetiketten kannst du sie zum Werbeträger für Vokabeln machen.

Wenn du die Werbung gut platzierst, werden sich die Vokabeln ganz nebenbei einprägen – wie die Produktnamen. Also dann – Kreativität ist Trumpf!

►►► Unit 5: One Country, Many Cultures

p.59	**culture** ['kʌltʃə]	Kultur	
	festival ['festɪvl]	Festival, Festspiele	
	°bazaar [bə'zɑː]	Basar	
	Enjoy yourself … [ɪn'dʒɔɪ jə,self]	Amüsier dich … / Vergnüg dich …	I'm going to the theatre tonight. – Well, ~ *yourself*! (= Viel Spaß! / Amüsier dich gut!)
	(to) **enjoy** sth. [ɪn'dʒɔɪ]	etwas genießen, an etwas Spaß haben, etwas gern haben/tun	Do you play football? – No, but I ~ swimming. (Ich schwimme gern. / Schwimmen macht mir Spaß.) Did you like the film? – Yes, I really ~*ed* it.
	ethnic minorities [,eθnɪk maɪ'nɒrətiz]	*ethnische Minderheiten*	
	once [wʌns]	*einmal*	
	Pakistani [,pɑːkɪ'stɑːni]	Pakistani, Pakistaner/in	someone from Pakistan
	Bangladeshi [,bæŋglə'deʃi]	Bangale/Bangalin *(jd. aus Bangladesch)*	someone from Bangladesh
	Afro-Caribbean [,æfrəʊ kærə'biːən]	Afro-Karibe/-Karibin *(Schwarze/r karibischer Herkunft)*	a black person from the Caribbean (a group of small islands east of Central America, for example Jamaica, Trinidad and Tobago, Barbados)
p.60/A1	**Would** you …?	Würdest du …?	*Would* you help me, please? – Yes, of course.
A2	°Urdu ['ʊəduː]	Urdu *(in Pakistan und Indien gesprochene Sprache)*	
A3	She asked **herself** … [hə'self, *betont:* hɜː'self]	Sie fragte sich (selbst) …	

Reflexive pronouns (Reflexivpronomen)

I've hurt **myself**.	Ich habe **mir** wehgetan.	/ **mich** verletzt.	
You've hurt **yourself**.	Du … **dir** … .	/ **dich** … .	
He has hurt **himself**.	Er … **sich** … .	/ **sich** … .	
She has hurt **herself**.	Sie … **sich** … .	/ **sich** … .	
It has hurt **itself**.	Es … **sich** … .	/ **sich** … .	
We've hurt **ourselves**.	Wir … **uns** … .	/ **uns** … .	
You've hurt **yourselves**.	Ihr … **euch** … .	/ **euch** … .	
They've hurt **themselves**.	Sie … **sich** … .	/ **sich** … .	

⚠ Aussprache/Betonung:
-self [-'self]
-selves [-'selvz]

Reflexive in German – on-reflexive in English

Die folgenden Verben kennst du alle – aber sei vorsichtig:
Sie sind im Deutschen reflexiv, im Englischen jedoch nicht.

(to) **change**	sich (ver)ändern	The weather *is changing*.
(to) **decide**	sich entscheiden	Please *decide* quickly, we haven't got much time.
(to) **feel**	sich fühlen	Yesterday I didn't *feel* well.
(to) **imagine** sth.	sich etwas vorstellen	*Imagine* a trip into space.
(to) **listen to** sth.	sich etwas anhören	Now *listen to* the next song.
(to) **meet**	sich treffen	We're going to *meet* in front of the disco.
(to) **move**	sich bewegen	Help! I can't *move*.
(to) **relax**	sich entspannen/ausruhen	Good music helps me to *relax*.
(to) **remember**	sich erinnern	At ten or at eleven? – I can't *remember*.
(to) **sit down**	sich (hin)setzen	Why don't you *sit down*?
(to) **turn**	sich umdrehen	Susan *turned* and looked at me.
(to) **watch** sth.	sich etwas ansehen	Why don't we *watch* a video?

⚠ *(to)* ***buy*** kann mit Reflexivpronomen verwendet werden. Häufiger steht es jedoch ohne:
Ich habe mir einen neuen Computer gekauft. = I've bought (myself) a new computer.

	well *(adj)*	gesund	Yesterday I felt ill, but today I'm (feeling) ~ again. ⚠ *well* = **1.** *(adv)* gut *(Adverb zu 'good')* **2.** *(adj)* gesund
p.61/A4	builder ['bɪldə]	Bauarbeiter/in	someone who builds houses
A5	**minority** [maɪ'nɒrəti]	Minderheit	There are 16 girls and 11 boys in my form. The boys are in the ~. minority Minderheit
	population [ˌpɒpju'leɪʃn]	Bevölkerung, Einwohner(zahl)	the number of people who live in a country or city: Wales has got a ~ of about three million people.
	large [lɑːdʒ]	groß, umfangreich	◂▸ small

German 'groß'

large – big: *large* benutzt man hauptsächlich für Dinge, während *big* für Dinge und Personen verwendet wird.
▷ We've got a **big/large** house near Ashton. What's the **biggest/largest** ethnic group in Bradford? Lord Nelson was not a very **big** man.

tall: *tall (groß, hoch)* benutzt man für die Körpergröße von Menschen und die Höhe von (schmalen) Dingen.
▷ Is Janet **taller** than Karen? How **tall** is Nelson's Column?

great: *great* bedeutet
- *groß, beträchtlich* ▷ The children were in *great* danger. We're learning about the *Great* Fire of London in 1666.
- *großartig, toll* ▷ We had a *great* time at the festival. The music was *great*. *Great*! No homework today.
- *bedeutend, berühmt* ▷ Who do you think is the world's *greatest* pop singer? Do you know the CD '*Greatest* Rap Hits'?

	ethnic ['eθnɪk]	ethnisch, Volks-	There are people from lots of different ~ groups in our city: people from Turkey, Russia, Bosnia, … .
A6	**even** worse/better/taller ['iːvn]	(sogar) noch schlechter/besser/größer	I'm very tall, but my brother is ~ *taller*.
	even ['iːvn]	sogar, selbst	Our village is very beautiful, ~ in winter.
	each other [iːtʃ‿'ʌðə]	einander, sich (gegenseitig)	Paul likes Linda and Linda likes Paul. Linda and Paul like ~ *other*.
	celebration [ˌselɪ'breɪʃn]	(Gedenk-)Feier	My grandpa will be 90 next week and we're going to have a ~.
p.62/A7	°Lord Mayor [lɔːd 'meə]	*etwa:* Oberbürgermeister/in	
	mayor [meə]	Bürgermeister/in	
	He was **the first … to be …** .	Er war der erste …, der … war/wurde.	Who was *the first (person) to climb* Mount Everest? (= … the first person who climbed …?)
	racist *(adj; n)* ['reɪsɪst]	rassistisch; Rassist/in	He said, 'Blacks go home.' That's stupid and ~. People who say they don't like black people are ~*s*.

	racism ['reɪsɪzəm]	Rassismus	
A8	**perfect** ['pɜːfɪkt]	perfekt, einwandfrei, vollkommen; ideal	 Nobody is ~. This little park is the ~ place for a picnic. ⚠ Betonung auf der ersten Silbe: *perfect* ['pɜːfɪkt]
	I wanted to know **where to go and what to do**.	Ich wollte wissen, wohin ich gehen soll und was ich tun soll.	I don't know *what to do*. (= … what I should do.)
	(to) **become** [bɪ'kʌm], **became** [bɪ'keɪm], **become** [bɪ'kʌm]	werden	Kate Walker *became* a pop singer five years ago. She *became* famous after her second CD. ⚠ 'False friend': *(to) become* = werden • bekommen = *(to) get*

German 'werden'

(to) **become**
(to) **get**

Die wichtigsten Verben für das deutsche „werden" sind *(to)* ***get*** und *(to)* ***become***. In der Umgangssprache ist *(to)* ***get*** häufiger.

▷ (to) **become/get** | **angry, tired, nervous, old, …** | **cold, windy, dark, …** | **boring, funny, more interesting, …**

⚠ Mit Nomen nur *(to)* ***become***: She **became a doctor / a football fan / … .**
Aber: *Was willst du* ***werden****, wenn du von der Schule abgehst?*
What do you want to **be** when you leave school?

(to) **go**

(to) ***go*** wird oft mit Farbadjektiven verwendet. ▷ (to) **go red, brown, white, black, …**

(to) ***go*** wird auch benutzt, wenn etwas schlecht wird. ▷ (to) **go hard** *(bread)*, **bad** *(fish, eggs, cheese)*

	strict (with sb.**)** [strɪkt]	streng (mit/zu jm.)	Peter mustn't watch TV after 6 o'clock. His parents are very ~ *with* him. strict / streng
	(to) **let** sb. **do** sth. **(-tt-)**, **let, let** [let]	jm. erlauben, etwas zu tun; jn. etwas tun lassen	Peter's parents are so strict, they *don't* ~ him read in bed. That bag is so heavy. *Let* me carry it for you.

TIPP

So unregelmäßig sind die unregelmäßigen Verben gar nicht!

Wenn du dir die Liste der unregelmäßigen Verben (S. 191–192) einmal genauer ansiehst, wirst du feststellen, dass man Gruppen bilden kann, die sich viel leichter lernen lassen.

• Gruppe 1:

A	A	A
cost	*cost*	*cost*
let	*let*	*let*
…		

• Gruppe 2:

A	B	A
become	*became*	*become*
run	*ran*	*run*
…		

• Gruppe 3:

A	B	B
bring	*brought*	*brought*
feel	*felt*	*felt*
…		

• Gruppe 4:

A	B	C
begin	*began*	*begun*
blow	*blew*	*blown*
…		

Welche der unregelmäßigen Verben, die dir bekannt sind, passen in welche Gruppe?

p.63/A9	(to) blush [blʌʃ]	rot werden, erröten	I ~*ed* after I noticed my big mistake.
	°samosa [sə'məʊsə]	*dreieckige Teigtaschen mit würziger Gemüse- oder Fleischfüllung*	
	(to) be **thirsty** ['θɜːsti]	durstig sein, Durst haben	I'm not just hungry, I'm ~, too. Can I have a glass of milk, please?
A10	(to) **seem** (to be/do) [siːm]	(zu sein/tun) scheinen	Is there anything wrong? You ~ (to be) unhappy.
	rude [ruːd]	unhöflich, grob	She was ~ to me: she called me stupid and silly.

	upset [ˌʌpˈset]	aufgebracht, aufgeregt; betrübt	very nervous Jim was very ~ when he heard about your accident.
	(to) **be able to** do sth. [ˈeɪbl]	etwas tun können; fähig sein, etwas zu tun	Kevin won't *be ~ to* come to the party on Saturday because he's ill.
	(to) **go on** [ˌɡəʊ‿ˈɒn]	fortfahren, weiterreden	The speaker stopped and drank a glass of water. Then he *went ~*: 'And we should …'
	(to) **be allowed to** do sth. [əˈlaʊd]	etwas tun dürfen	*Are* you *~ to* watch TV after 8 o'clock? (= Do your parents let you watch TV after 8 o'clock?)
	bill [bɪl]	Rechnung	
	anyway [ˈeniweɪ]	jedenfalls, wie dem auch sei; außerdem, und überhaupt	I'm not sure when we'll arrive: 7.30 or 7.45. *Anyway*, we'll be there before 8 o'clock. No, you can't go out now. *Anyway*, didn't you want to wash the dishes?
	fat (-tt-) [fæt] **thin** (-nn-) [θɪn]	dick, fett dünn	a *fat* cat  a *thin* cat fat – fett thin – dünn
	intelligent [ɪnˈtelɪdʒənt]	klug, intelligent	▸◂ stupid
	shy [ʃaɪ]	scheu, zurückhaltend	I find it hard to meet new people because I'm so ~.
	°ebony [ˈebəni]	Ebenholz	
	°ivory [ˈaɪvəri]	Elfenbein	
P 1	°sari [ˈsɑːri]	Sari *(besonders von indischen Frauen getragenes Kleidungsstück)*	
P 2	**lady** [ˈleɪdi]	Dame	My grandma is a lovely old ~.
	guitar [ɡɪˈtɑː]	Gitarre	⚠ Sarah spielt *Gitarre.* = Sarah plays *the guitar.* 
P 6	°secretary general [ˌsekrətriː ˈdʒenrəl]	Generalsekretär/in	
	°UN (United Nations) [juː‿ˈen, juˌnaɪtɪd ˈneɪʃnz]	UN (Vereinte Nationen)	
P 11	**nationality** [ˌnæʃəˈnæləti]	Staatsangehörigkeit, Nationalität	My husband and I have different *nationalities*. He's French and I'm British.
	nation [ˈneɪʃn]	Nation, Volk	⚠ *nation (n)* [ˈneɪʃn] – *national (adj)* [ˈnæʃnəl]
[P 13]	*oil drum* [drʌm]	*Ölfass*	
	carnival [ˈkɑːnɪvl]	*Karneval, Volksfest*	
	called [kɔːld]	*mit Namen; genannt*	
	steel [stiːl]	*Stahl*	
	instrument [ˈɪnstrəmənt]	*Instrument*	
	stick [stɪk]	*Stock, Knüppel*	
	a strong sound [strɒŋ]	*ein kräftiger, voller Ton*	

'I Felt like a Monster'

p.68	**actress** [ˈæktrəs]	Schauspielerin	a woman who acts in a film or play
	actor [ˈæktə]	Schauspieler	a man who acts in a film or play
	°the Midlands [ˈmɪdləndz]	Mittelengland	
	in fact [ɪn ˈfækt]	eigentlich, genau gesagt; in Wirklichkeit	I think she's fifteen. Well, *in ~* I know she is. Ken says Sue lives in Chester, but *in ~* she lives in Bradford.
	ordinary [ˈɔːdnəri]	gewöhnlich, normal	You don't need any special clothes for the party – just wear your ~ clothes.
	childhood [ˈtʃaɪldhʊd]	Kindheit	your ~ = your years as a child
	That was special **about** the family.	Das war außergewöhnlich an der Familie.	The great thing ~ our teacher is that she is so funny.

°Punjabi [pʌn'dʒɑ:bi]	Pandschabi *(im Pandschab – einer Gegend in Nordpakistan und Nordindien – gesprochene Sprache)*	
heat [hi:t]	Hitze	It's so hot. I can't sleep *in this* ~. (= bei dieser Hitze.) adjective: 'hot' – noun: *'heat'*
firstly, …; **secondly**, …; **thirdly**, …	erstens …; zweitens …; drittens …	*Firstly,* we need something to eat. *Secondly,* we have to buy some lemonade. And *thirdly,* …
education [ˌedʒu'keɪʃn]	(Schul-, Aus-)Bildung; Erziehung	My school ~ started when I was 5 and finished when I was 16.
gift [gɪft]	Geschenk, Gabe	a kind of present ⚠ 'False friend': *gift* ≠ Gift
whole [həʊl]	ganze(r, s), gesamte(r, s)	I spent the ~ morning (= all morning) in bed today. ⚠ Stummes „w": *whole* [həʊl]
blood [blʌd]	Blut	Have you cut your hand? You've got ~ on it. 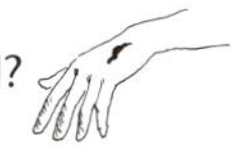
just like	genau wie	

just

I like all sorts of stories, not **just** cowboy stories.	…, nicht **nur** Cowboygeschichten.
(In a shop) I'm **just** looking.	Ich sehe mich **nur** mal um.
That's very good coffee – **just like** German coffee!	… – **genau wie** deutscher Kaffee.
I'm **just as** tired **as** you are.	Ich bin **genauso** müde **wie** du!
Just a moment!	Einen Moment **mal (eben)**!
They're **just** leaving. / They've **just** left.	Sie gehen **gerade**. / Sie sind **gerade** gegangen.
'Let's go', I said – **just then** the phone rang.	… – **genau in dem Moment** klingelte das Telefon.
I **just** can't understand why he's so silly.	Ich kann **einfach** nicht verstehen, warum … .

script [skrɪpt]	Drehbuch	
p.69 (to) **grow up** [ˌgrəʊ_'ʌp], **grew** [gru:], **grown** [grəʊn]	aufwachsen; erwachsen werden	When my grandparents *were ~ing up*, they had no television. Dave is 12. When he *~s up* he wants to be a doctor.
(to) **grow, grew, grown**	wachsen	Orange trees ~ only in hot countries. I*'ve ~n* a lot. I'm almost as tall as my father now.
birth [bɜ:θ]	Geburt	Please fill in your address, nationality, date of ~ (= Geburtsdatum) and place of ~ (= Geburtsort).
extract ['ekstrækt]	*Auszug*	
as if [əz_'ɪf]	als ob	The sky is very grey. It looks ~ *if* it'll rain soon.
proud (of sb./sth.) [praʊd]	stolz (auf jn./etwas)	Our daughter is the best pupil in her form. We're ~ *of* her.
pea [pi:]	Erbse	*peas* 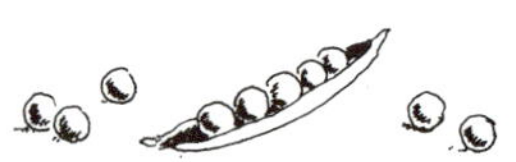
curry ['kʌri]	*scharfes, mit Curry gewürztes Gericht*	⚠ 'False friend': English *curry* = *ein Gericht*; German „Curry" = *ein Gewürz*
°…, haven't you?	oder? / nicht wahr?	
stuff [stʌf] *(infml)*	Zeug, Kram	What's that red ~ on your shirt? Ketchup?
round [raʊnd]	um … (herum)	*round* the car 
gravy ['greɪvi]	(Braten-)Soße	

	onion ['ʌnjən]	Zwiebel	⚠ Aussprache: *onion* ['ʌnjən] an *onion* 
	garlic ['gɑ:lɪk]	Knoblauch	 *garlic*
	fish finger [,fɪʃ 'fɪŋgə]	Fischstäbchen	*fish fingers* 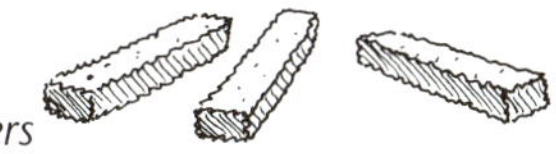
	finger ['fɪŋgə]	Finger	finger
	(to) offer ['ɒfə]	*anbieten*	

p.70	**How to ...**		
	(to) **persuade** sb. **(to do** sth.**)** [pə'sweɪd]	jn. überzeugen (etwas zu tun)	Sita didn't want to go at first, but then we were able to ~ her *to* come with us.
	event [ɪ'vent]	*Veranstaltung; Ereignis*	
	advertisement [əd'vɜ:tɪsmənt]	Anzeige, Inserat; Werbespot	If you want to sell your computer, you should put an ~ in the newspaper.
	outfit ['aʊtfɪt]	Kleider, Kleidung	I need a new ~ for our end-of-term party.
	charity bazaar ['tʃærəti]	*Wohltätigkeitsbasar*	
	exhibition [,eksɪ'bɪʃn]	Ausstellung	Have you seen the exciting new ~ at the museum?
	(to) experiment with [ɪk'sperɪmənt]	*experimentieren mit, ausprobieren*	
	different ways of reading your text	*verschiedene Arten, deinen Text zu lesen*	
	event [ɪ'vent]	Veranstaltung; Ereignis	Come to our school bazaar! The biggest ~ in town this month! The first day at school is a big ~ in a child's life.
	in different ways	auf verschiedene Weise(n)	Collect words for food and arrange them ~ *different ways.*

TIPP **Nun aber fix ...**

Folgende Wortschatzspiele könnt ihr in der Gruppe **nach Zeit** spielen:

- Eine/r von euch gibt einen **Oberbegriff** vor, die anderen müssen in der vorgegebenen Zeit – probiert es mal mit 2 oder 3 Minuten – so viele **Unterbegriffe** aufschreiben wie möglich.
  Beispiel:
  family*: mother, father, sister, uncle, ...*
- Eine/r von euch gibt einen **Anfangsbuchstaben** vor, die anderen müssen in der vorgegebenen Zeit so viele Wörter mit diesem Anfangsbuchstaben aufschreiben wie möglich.
  Beispiel:
  „c“*: clean, clothes, cold, colour, come, ...*
- Eine/r von euch gibt ein **langes Wort** vor, die anderen müssen in der vorgegebenen Zeit so viele Wörter aus den Buchstaben des vorgegebenen Wortes bilden wie möglich.
  Beispiel:
  breakfast*: a, as, are, eat, sea, tea, best, east, fast, rest, break, ...*

▶▶▶ Unit 6: Free Time

p.71	**free time** [,fri: 'taɪm]	Freizeit, freie Zeit	What do you do in your *free* ~?
	free [fri:]	frei; kostenlos	Animals don't like cages. They want to be ~. How much did the disco cost last night? – It was ~!
	free time activities [,fri:taɪm‿æk'tɪvəti:z]	Freizeitaktivitäten	
	cello ['tʃeləʊ]	Cello	
pp.72/73			
A1	°(to) bleep [bli:p]	piepen, piepsen	
	(to) **come round**	vorbeischauen, vorbeikommen	Why don't you *come* ~ for dinner tonight?

A2	**unfriendly** [ˌʌn'frendli]	unfreundlich	⧓ friendly — unfriendly / unfreundlich
	Mike is so unfriendly, **isn't he?**	Mike ist ganz schön unfreundlich, nicht? / gell?	
	(to) hang out [ˌhæŋ_'aʊt], hung [hʌŋ], hung *(infml)*	sich herumtreiben, rumhängen	After school we often *hang* ~ at the bus stop.
	(to) **hang** [hæŋ], **hung** [hʌŋ], **hung**	hängen, aufhängen	Sue came in and *hung* her coat over a chair. You could ~ the poster next to the bookshelf.

German 'Doch!'

You <u>don't</u> do anything, do you? – **We do!** We talk, … . *Ihr macht ja nichts, oder? – **Doch!** Wir reden, … .* Your conversations on the Internet <u>aren't</u> real, are they? – **Oh yes, they are!** *Deine Gespräche … sind nicht echt, oder? – **Oh doch!*** You <u>can't</u> show us, can you? – **Yes, I can.** *Du kannst es uns nicht zeigen, oder? – **Doch!*** You <u>haven't</u> got a computer, have you? – **I have!** *Du hast keinen Computer, nicht wahr? – **Doch!***	Im Deutschen widerspricht man einer verneinten Aussage meist mit „Doch!". Im Englischen benutzt man – wie bei den Kurzantworten – das Hilfsverb aus dem Aussagesatz, also: You don't … → (**Oh yes,**) We **do!** They aren't … → (**Oh yes,**) They **are!** You can't … → (**Oh yes,**) I **can!** You haven't … → (**Oh yes,**) I **have!**

	true [tru:]	wahr	adjective: *'true'* – noun: 'truth'
	°computer nerd [nɜ:d] *(infml)*	*etwa:* Computerfreak	
	keyboard ['ki:bɔ:d]	Tastatur	a *keyboard* 
A3	**camp** [kæmp]	(Trainings-, Zelt-)Lager	When I was 14 I was at summer ~ for three weeks.
	Lucky you!	Du Glückspilz!	My aunt has given me £1000. – *~ you!*
	nickname ['nɪkneɪm]	Spitzname	
	section ['sekʃn]	Abschnitt, Teil	I always read the sport ~ of the newspaper first.
	classical ['klæsɪkl]	klassisch	What do you like better – pop music or ~ music?
	instrument ['ɪnstrəmənt]	Instrument	⚠ Betonung auf der ersten Silbe: *instrument* ['ɪnstrəmənt]
	outdoor (activities) ['aʊtdɔ:]	(Aktivitäten) im Freien	Football is an ~ game. ⧓ indoor (activity) – Table tennis is an ~ game.
	member ['membə]	*Mitglied*	
	result [rɪ'zʌlt]	*Ergebnis*	
A4	(to) **join** [dʒɔɪn]	beitreten, eintreten in *(einen Verein usw.)*	I like football. – Then you should ~ the school football team.
	You're welcome.	Bitte sehr. / Nichts zu danken. / Gern geschehen.	Thank you for your help. – *You're ~.*

German 'bitte!'

• wenn man um etwas bittet: **please**	Could I have another cup of tea, **please**? Open the window, **please.**
• wenn man jemandem etwas gibt: **Here you are.** (Bitte sehr. / Hier bitte.)	Have you got a pencil for me? – Yes, **here you are.** Give me that ruler, please. – **Here you are.**
• nachdem sich jemand bedankt hat: **You're welcome.** (Bitte sehr. / Nichts zu danken. / Gern geschehen.)	Thank you very much, Mrs Beck. – **You're welcome.** Thanks for your help. – **You're welcome.**

pp.74/75

A5	website ['websaɪt]	*alle Seiten eines Anbieters im World Wide Web*	
	We **want people to write** lots of articles.	Wir möchten, dass die Leute viele Artikel schreiben.	⚠ The children *want to help their father.* (… wollen ihrem Vater helfen.) The children *want their father to help them.* (… wollen, dass ihr Vater ihnen hilft.) ⚠ *Nie:* They want/would like ~~that~~ …
	(to) set sth. up (-tt-) [ˌset_'ʌp], set, set	etwas aufbauen, einrichten	Can you help me to ~ *up* the video recorder and the TV?
A6	*(to) click* [klɪk]	*(an-, hin)klicken*	

	directory [də'rektəri]	Inhaltsverzeichnis *(Computer)*	
	home page ['həʊm ˌpeɪdʒ]	*erste Seite eines Angebots im World Wide Web*	
	°orienteering [ˌɔːriən'tɪərɪŋ]	Orientierungslauf, Orientierungsrennen	
	compass ['kʌmpəs]	Kompass	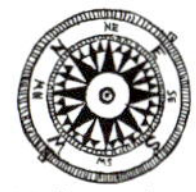 a *compass*
	°dome [dəʊm]	Kuppel, Gewölbe	
	up	oben	Where's my book? – It's ~ there, on the top shelf. ▸◂ down
	above *(prep; adv)* [ə'bʌv]	über, oberhalb (von); oben	The plane was flying ~ the clouds. The clouds ~ began to get darker.
	below *(prep; adv)* [bɪ'ləʊ]	unter, unterhalb (von); unten	Your eyes are above your nose, your mouth is ~ your nose. From the plane, we could see London ~. ▸◂ above
	(to) **smell** [smel]	riechen	I *~ed* the lovely cake that my mum was making. 'Mmmm, that *~s* good,' I said. 
	the Antarctic [æn'tɑːktɪk]	die Antarktis	
	survey (of) ['sɜːveɪ]	Umfrage, Untersuchung (über)	We did a ~ *of* people's favourite sports. Most of them like football best.
	per cent (%) [pə'sent]	Prozent	Two ~ ~ of two hundred is four.
	piano [pi'ænəʊ]	Klavier	⚠ Sarah spielt *Klavier.* = Sarah plays *the piano.*
	°sitar [sɪ'tɑː]	Sitar *(indisches Saiteninstrument)*	
A7	(to) scan (-nn-) [skæn]	(ein)scannen	*Have* you *~ned* the pictures into the computer yet?
	when	als, nachdem	**when** **wann?** **When** do you usually go shopping? **wenn** We'll be there **when** you come home. **als** Her mother died **when** she was eleven. **nachdem** They watched TV **when** they had eaten.
	on-screen [ˌɒn'skriːn]	am Bildschirm	
	bar chart ['bɑː tʃɑːt]	Balkendiagramm	a *bar chart* 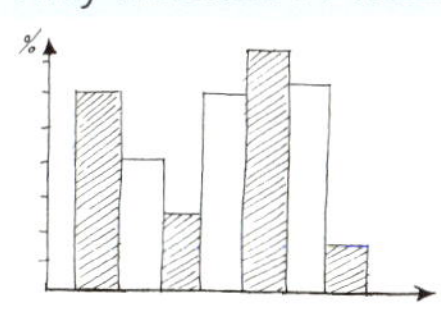
	Divide your group in two. [dɪ'vaɪd]	*Teilt eure Gruppe in zwei Hälften auf.*	
	pair [peə]	*Paar*	
P 1	*(to) study* ['stʌdi]	*studieren, sorgfältig durchlesen*	
	line [laɪn]	(Telefon-)Leitung	Helen, phone for you! Your mother is on the ~. 
P 4	**That's no good.**	Das geht nicht.	
P 5	**Can I take a message?**	Kann ich (ihr/ihm) etwas ausrichten?	
	(to) practise ['præktɪs]	*üben, trainieren*	
[P 6]	*twice* [twaɪs]	*zweimal*	
	(to) make sth. up	*sich etwas ausdenken, etwas erfinden*	
	(to) ask for sb.	*nach jm. fragen*	
P 8	**lazy** ['leɪzi]	faul, träge	My brother is very ~: he often doesn't do his homework, and he doesn't tidy up his room.
P 12	*combinations* [ˌkɒmbɪ'neɪʃnz]	*Kombinationen, Verbindungen*	

Dangerous Dartmoor

p.80	pony ['pəʊni]	Pony	⚠ two pon*ies* = zwei Pon*ys*
	(to) **shine** [ʃaɪn], **shone** [ʃɒn], **shone**	scheinen; leuchten	We had some rain this morning, but now the sun *is shining*. Sue's eyes *were shining* when she saw her presents.
	prison ['prɪzn]	Gefängnis	The police caught the thief, and he went to ~.
	prisoner ['prɪznə]	Gefangene(r)	someone who is in prison
	(to) **be/feel cold**	frieren	⚠ *Mir war kalt.* = *I was cold. / I felt cold.* *Mir war heiß.* = *I was hot. / I felt hot.*
	to the west/east/…	im Westen/Osten/…	Dartmoor is ~ *the north* of Plymouth.
	mist [mɪst]	Dunst, (feiner) Nebel	
	back at the farm	daheim auf der Farm	
	dining-room ['daɪnɪŋru:m]	Esszimmer	
	(to) **escape (from sb./sth.)** [ɪ'skeɪp]	fliehen (vor jm. / aus etwas); entkommen	Three men ~*d from* prison last night. The police don't know where they are. The police couldn't catch the thief – he ~*d* in a fast sports car.
	not … any more [ˌeni 'mɔ:]	nicht mehr; kein(e, n) … mehr	Joe does*n't* live here *any* ~. He has moved to Bristol. I do*n't* have a car *any* ~. I sold it last month.
	wet (-tt-) [wet]	feucht, nass	Why are your clothes all ~? – It's raining. ◂▸ dry
	muddy ['mʌdi]	schlammig, matschig	
	mud [mʌd]	Schlamm, Matsch	The football field is full of ~ after all this rain. noun: *'mud'* – adjective: *'muddy'*
	on foot	zu Fuß	to go *on* ~ = to walk
	(to) **turn back**	umkehren, kehrtmachen	There was an accident, so we couldn't go any farther. We had to *turn* ~.
p.81	**gate** [geɪt]	Tor, Pforte	Close the ~ so the dog can't get out of the garden.
	cottage ['kɒtɪdʒ]	(kleines) Landhaus, Häuschen	a small house in the country
	mobile (phone) ['məʊbaɪl]	Mobiltelefon, Handy	⚠ German: „Handy" = English: *mobile (phone)* (*nicht:* ~~*handy*~~)
	neck [nek]	Hals	
	off the hook [hʊk]	ausgehängt, nicht aufgelegt *(Telefon)*	Sorry you couldn't reach me. I had left the phone *off the* ~.
p.82	**horse** [hɔ:s]	Pferd	
	(to) **knock** [nɒk]	klopfen, anklopfen	Please ~ (on the door) before you go in. ⚠ Stummes „k": *k̲nock* [nɒk]
	(to) catch sb.'s arm	jn. am Arm packen, fassen	I wanted to leave but she *caught my* ~ with both hands.
	(to) **tie (to)** [taɪ]	binden, anbinden (an)	Sometimes we ~ our dog *to* a tree in the garden. ⚠ -ing form: *t*y̲*ing*
	Thank God! [gɒd]	Gott sei Dank!	The leg isn't broken – ~ *God*!
	short cut ['ʃɔ:t kʌt]	Abkürzung	a route that makes a journey shorter. We took a ~ *cut* across the field to get home earlier.

p.83 How to …

(to) nominate ['nɒmɪneɪt]	nominieren, vorschlagen	
a certain person ['sɜ:tn]	*eine bestimmte Person*	
excerpt ['eksɜ:pt]	*Auszug, Ausschnitt*	
Dear Sir or Madam [sɜ:, 'mædəm]	Sehr geehrte Damen und Herren	
finally ['faɪnəli]	schließlich, endlich	We waited a long time, and ~ (= at last) the train arrived.
That's why …	Darum/Deshalb …	Andrew is ill. *That's* ~ he can't come to your party.
Yours faithfully	Mit freundlichen Grüßen / Hochachtungsvoll	

Letters	Name des Empfängers / der Empfängerin bekannt	Dear **Mrs Barker,** … **Yours sincerely,** (Your name)	Name des Empfängers / der Empfängerin unbekannt	Dear **Sir or Madam,** … **Yours faithfully,** (Your name)

TIPP **Make your own WORD GAMES**

Selbst gestaltete Vokabelrätsel eignen sich prima zum Wiederholen von Vokabeln mit Partnern/Partnerinnen oder in der Gruppe – hier sind zwei Vorschläge:

- **VERSTECKTE WÖRTER:**
  1) Zeichne ein Rätselgitter mit 10 mal 10 Feldern.
  2) Wähle einen Oberbegriff, z.B. *clothes*, und suche 8 bis 10 Unterbegriffe dazu *(shirt, trousers, socks, …)*.
  3) Trage die Unterbegriffe in das Gitter ein – waagerecht, senkrecht oder diagonal, vorwärts oder rückwärts.
  4) Ergänze die noch leeren Felder mit beliebig gewählten Buchstaben. (Achtung, es dürfen keine neuen Wörter entstehen!)

  Nun tausche dein Rätsel mit einem Partner/einer Partnerin – wer findet am schnellsten die versteckten Wörter?
  (Im Beispiel rechts sind die Lösungen hervorgehoben.)

clothes

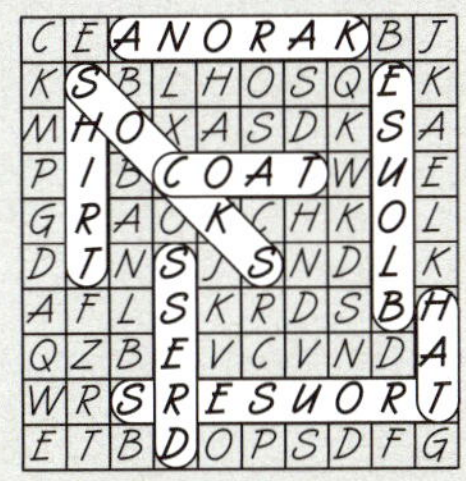

- **KAMMRÄTSEL:**
  1) Zeichne einen „Kamm" wie im Beispiel rechts und lege ein Lösungswort mit 8 bis 10 Buchstaben fest, z.B. *breakfast*.
  2) Suche Wörter, die mit dem 2., 4., 6. und 8. Buchstaben deines Lösungsworts beginnen. Diese Wörter sollten alle gleich viele Buchstaben haben, damit das Rätsel die Form eines Kamms bekommt, z.B. *road; aunt; fast; shop*.
  3) Gib deinem Partner/deiner Partnerin Hinweise, welche senkrechten Wörter gesucht sind, z.B. 2: *another word for 'street'* 4: *your mother's or your father's sister* 6: *not slow, but …* 8: *Here you can buy things.*
  4) Gib deinem Partner/deiner Partnerin einen Hinweis auf dein Lösungswort, z.B. _ _ _ _ _ _ _ _ _ *is the first meal of the day.*

  Kann dein Partner/deine Partnerin dein Lösungswort finden?

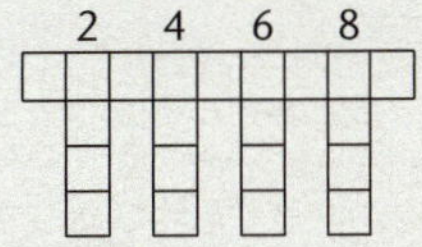

▶▶▶ Unit 7: A Very Special TV Special

pp.84/85	°set [set]	Bühnenbild, Kulisse	
	tool [tu:l]	Werkzeug	
	°gallery ['gæləri]	Regie(raum)	
	stage [steɪdʒ]	Bühne	At 9 o'clock the band came on ~ and started to play.
	cable ['keɪbl]	Kabel	
	carpenter ['kɑ:pəntə]	Zimmermann	
	electrician [ɪˌlek'trɪʃn]	Elektriker/in	There's a problem with the lights. We need an ~. 
	presenter [prɪ'zentə]	Moderator/in	Thomas Gottschalk is the ~ of 'Wetten, dass …'.
	make-up ['meɪkʌp]	Make-up	⚠ Betonung auf der ersten Silbe: *make-up* ['meɪkʌp]
	°floor manager ['flɔ: ˌmænɪdʒə]	Aufnahmeleiter/in	
	director [də'rektə]	Regisseur/in	
	(to) work **in** television	beim Fernsehen arbeiten	
p.86	rehearsal [rɪ'hɜ:sl]	Probe *(Theater, Film)*	
	mirror ['mɪrə]	Spiegel	Peter looked at himself in the ~. 

everyone/ everybody, ...

everyone/everybody ['evribɒdi]	jeder, alle		
someone/somebody ['sʌmbədi]	jemand	**anyone?/anybody?** ['enibɒdi]	(irgend)jemand?
no one/nobody ['nəʊbədi]	niemand	**not ... anyone/not ... anybody**	niemand

walkie-talkie [ˌwɔːki 'tɔːki]	Walkie-Talkie *(tragbares Funksprechgerät)*	
(to) **fix** [fɪks]	reparieren, in Ordnung bringen	The chair is broken. – Well, you're a carpenter, ~ it!
(to) **be glad** (-dd-) [glæd]	froh sein, sich freuen	(to) be happy, (to) be pleased
meanwhile ['miːnwaɪl]	inzwischen, währenddessen	I went to bed at 10 pm. *Meanwhile* in Japan, the sun was going up.
just after/before 10.30	kurz nach/vor 10.30	Do I have to go to bed now? It's only ~ *after* 9!
°(to) sabotage ['sæbətɑːʒ]	sabotieren	
p.87 anonymous [ə'nɒnɪməs]	anonym	Many old songs are ~: we don't know who wrote them. ⚠ Betonung auf der zweiten Silbe: *anonymous* [ə'nɒnɪməs]
(to) **be in a bad mood** [muːd]	schlechte Laune haben, in schlechter Stimmung sein	▸◂ (to) be in a good mood
whoever [huː'evə]	wer (auch) immer, wen/wem (auch) immer	Well, it's your birthday party, you can invite ~ you like.

wherever, whenever, whoever, whatever

Wherever you go, I'll come with you.	**Wo auch immer** du hingehst, ...
Visit me **whenever** you like.	..., **wann immer** du willst.
I won't open the door, **whoever** you are.	..., **wer immer** Sie **auch** sind.
Whoever told you that was wrong.	**Wer immer** dir das **auch** erzählt hat, hatte Unrecht.
I'll help you **whatever** happens.	..., **was immer auch** geschieht.

guest [gest]	Gast	The prince invited 200 ~*s* to his birthday party.
suspect ['sʌspekt]	*Verdächtige(r)*	
°sound engineer ['saʊnd_endʒɪˌnɪə]	Toningenieur/in, Tontechniker/in	
tape [teɪp]	(Ton-)Band	
incident ['ɪnsɪdənt]	*Zwischenfall, Vorkommnis*	
(to) **take a break**	eine Pause machen	You've worked for four hours, you should ~ *a break*.

German 'machen'

Schularbeiten **machen**	(to) **do** homework	einen Spaziergang **machen**	(to) **go for** a walk
Einkäufe **machen**	(to) **do** the shopping	eine Radtour **machen**	(to) **go on** a bike tour
eine Pause **machen**	(to) **take** a break	einen Ausflug **machen**	(to) **go on** a trip
Fotos **machen**	(to) **take** photos	Urlaub **machen**	(to) **go/be** on holiday
		ein Picknick **machen**	(to) **have** a picnic

scream [skriːm]	Schrei	verb: '(to) scream' – noun: *'scream'* 
(to) **lie** [laɪ], **lay** [leɪ], **lain** [leɪn]	liegen	(to) lie / liegen ⚠ -ing form: *lying*: Clothes *were lying* all over the floor.
clock [klɒk]	(Wand-, Stand-, Turm-) Uhr	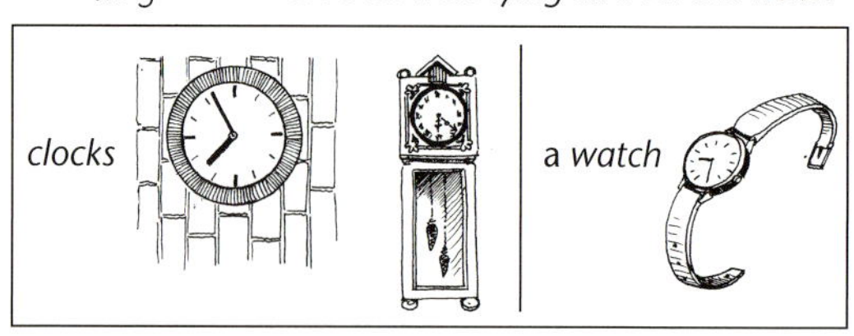
°saboteur [ˌsæbə'tɜː]	Saboteur/in	
witness ['wɪtnəs]	Zeuge, Zeugin	
suspect ['sʌspekt]	Verdächtige(r)	

p.88	*copy* ['kɒpi]	*Kopie*	
	column ['kɒləm]	*Spalte*	
	so far [səʊ 'fɑː]	*bis hierher, bis jetzt*	
	strong [strɒŋ]	stark	
	(to) **lift** [lɪft]	(an-, hoch)heben	
	store room ['stɔː ruːm]	Lagerraum	
	chaos ['keɪɒs]	Chaos	⚠ Aussprache: *chaos* ['keɪɒs]
p.89	(to) **break loose** [luːs]	sich losreißen, sich lösen	We tied the dog to a tree, but it *broke* ~ and ran away. ⚠ *loose* [luːs] is an adjective (= *locker, lose*) *(to) lose* [luːz] is a verb (= *verlieren*)
	(to) **take a step towards** sb.	einen Schritt auf jn. zugehen	
	(to) crash [kræʃ]	krachen	
	centimetre ['sentɪmiːtə]	Zentimeter	There are 100 ~*s* in a metre.
	(to) **lead** [liːd], **led** [led], **led**	führen, leiten	This road ~*s* to the next village. You ~ and we'll follow.

Keywords from the UK Mag

[p.94]	the UK (the United Kingdom) [ˌjuːˈkeɪ, juˌnaɪtɪd ˈkɪŋdəm]	das Vereinigte Königreich *(Großbritannien und Nordirland)*
	not … any more [ˌeni ˈmɔː]	nicht mehr; kein(e, n) … mehr
[p.95]	That's not what friends are about.	*etwa:* Unter Freunden stelle ich mir aber etwas anderes vor!
[p.96]	nightmare [ˈnaɪtmeə]	Albtraum
	(to) start arguing [ˈɑːgjuːɪŋ]	anfangen zu streiten
	advantage [ədˈvɑːntɪdʒ]	Vorteil
	disadvantage [ˌdɪsədˈvɑːntɪdʒ]	Nachteil
	tie [taɪ]	Krawatte
	(to) grow [grəʊ], grew [gruː], grown [grəʊn]	wachsen, groß werden
	(to) fit (-tt-) [fɪt]	passen
[p.97]	fairy [ˈfeəri]	Fee
	(to) tie [taɪ]	(an)binden
	slate [sleɪt]	Schieferplatte, -tafel
	(to) complain [kəmˈpleɪn]	sich beschweren
	harp [hɑːp]	Harfe
[p.98]	woodwind [ˈwʊdwɪnd]	Holzblasinstrument; Holzbläser
	recorder [rɪˈkɔːdə]	Blockflöte
	brass [brɑːs]	Blechbläser
	true [truː]	wahr
	century [ˈsentʃəri]	Jahrhundert
[p.99]	a taste of … [teɪst]	eine Kostprobe von …, ein Vorgeschmack auf …
	a word of warning [ˈwɔːnɪŋ]	ein Wort der Warnung
	See for yourself! [jəˈself]	*etwa:* Überzeug dich selbst!
	'The Auld Enemy' [ˌɔːld_ˈenəmi]	„Der alte Feind"
[p.100]	(to) grow up [ˌgrəʊ_ˈʌp], grew [gruː], grown [grəʊn]	aufwachsen, groß werden
	elsewhere [ˌelsˈweə]	woanders
	Hogmanay [ˈhɒgməneɪ]	Silvester *(in Schottland)*
	Auld Lang Syne [ˌɔːld læŋ ˈsaɪn]	*etwa:* Die gute, alte Zeit
	neighbour [ˈneɪbə]	Nachbar/in
	coal [kəʊl]	Kohle
	recipe [ˈresəpi]	Rezept
	flour [ˈflaʊə]	Mehl
	sugar [ˈʃʊgə]	Zucker
	salt [sɔːlt]	Salz
[p.101]	ceilidh [ˈkeɪli]	*lockeres Beisammensein mit Musik und Tanz (besonders in Schottland und Irland)*
	(to) fight [faɪt], fought [fɔːt], fought	kämpfen
	battle [ˈbætl]	Schlacht
	(to) escape [ɪˈskeɪp]	fliehen; entkommen
	(to) travel (-ll-) [ˈtrævl]	reisen
	servant [ˈsɜːvənt]	Diener/in
[p.102]	prime minister [ˌpraɪm ˈmɪnɪstə]	Premierminister/in; Ministerpräsident/in
	stage [steɪdʒ]	Bühne
	What's on in …?	Was ist los in …? Was gibt es in …?
[p.103]	maze [meɪz]	Irrgarten, Labyrinth
	(to) enjoy sth. [ɪnˈdʒɔɪ]	etwas genießen, an etwas Spaß haben
	reef [riːf]	Riff
	living corals [ˌlɪvɪŋ ˈkɒrəlz]	lebende Korallen
	You'll have to go there yourself. [jəˈself, *betont:* jɔːˈself]	Du musst selbst hingehen. / Du wirst selbst hingehen müssen.
[p.104]	coloured [ˈkʌləd]	farbig
	curly [ˈkɜːli]	kraus; gelockt
	poetry competition [ˈpəʊətri]	Gedichtwettbewerb
	(to) print [prɪnt]	(ab)drucken
	strong [strɒŋ]	stark
[p.105]	(to) adapt [əˈdæpt]	anpassen, adaptieren, bearbeiten
	You've got the nerve … [nɜːv]	Du hast den Nerv, …
	(to) grow up [ˌgrəʊ_ˈʌp], grew [gruː], grown [grəʊn]	aufwachsen, groß werden
	sick [sɪk]	krank
	out of work	arbeitslos
	(to) set sb. free, set, set [ˌset ˈfriː]	jn. freilassen, jn. erlösen
	I'm afraid … [əˈfreɪd]	leider …; ich fürchte …
[p.106]	Land ho! [lænd ˈhəʊ]	Land in Sicht!
	delighted [dɪˈlaɪtɪd]	hocherfreut
	shawl [ʃɔːl]	Umhängetuch
	(to) hurry sb. [ˈhʌri]	jn. antreiben
	Pilgrim [ˈpɪlgrɪm]	Pilger/in
[p.107]	(to) be sick [sɪk]	sich übergeben
	bucket [ˈbʌkɪt]	Eimer
	beam [biːm]	Balken
	cracked [krækt]	gerissen, angebrochen
	(to) smash [smæʃ]	zerschmettern

	printing press ['prɪntɪŋ pres]	Druckerpresse
	crazy ['kreɪzi]	verrückt
	screw [skruː]	Schraube
[p.108]	oar [ɔː]	Ruder, Riemen
	(to) lift [lɪft]	(an)heben
	(to) wave [weɪv]	winken
	(to) dig (-gg-) [dɪg], dug [dʌg], dug	graben
	(to) plant [plɑːnt]	pflanzen
	corn [kɔːn]	Mais; Getreide, Korn
[p.109]	Thanksgiving [ˌθæŋks'gɪvɪŋ]	Erntedankfest
	(to) hurry ['hʌri]	sich beeilen
	(to) hesitate ['hezɪteɪt]	zögern

DICTIONARY Alphabetical list of words

Das *dictionary* enthält den Wortschatz der Bände 1 bis 3.

° – Wörter, die mit einem kleinen Kringel (°) markiert sind, gehören nicht zum Lernwortschatz.
* – Unregelmäßige Verben sind mit einem Stern (*) gekennzeichnet (vgl. *List of irregular verbs*, S. 191–192).

Abkürzungen

jm. = jemandem	sb. = somebody/someone	*Part. Perf. = Partizip Perfekt*	*pl = plural*
jn. = jemanden	sth. = something	*si. past = simple past (form)*	*no pl = no plural* (kein Plural)

A

a, an [ə, ən] ein, eine
able ['eɪbl]: **be able to do sth.** etwas tun können; fähig sein, etwas zu tun
about [ə'baʊt] **1.** ungefähr; **2.** über; wegen • **It's about Mrs McCann.** Es ist wegen Mrs McCann. • **That was special about the family.** Das war außergewöhnlich an der Familie. • **a question about your book** eine Frage über dein Buch / zu deinem Buch **What's the letter about?** Wovon handelt der Brief? **this book is about** dieses Buch handelt von • **out and about** unterwegs, auf Achse **dream/hear/know about** träumen/hören/wissen von **What about ...?** Wie wärs mit ...? • **What about Jenny?** Was ist mit Jenny? / Und Jenny? • °**What do you like about them?** Was magst du an ihnen?
above [ə'bʌv] **1.** *(prep)* über, oberhalb (von); **2.** *(adv)* oben
abroad [ə'brɔːd] im/ins Ausland
accident ['æksɪdənt] Unfall
acid rain [ˌæsɪd 'reɪn] saurer Regen
across [ə'krɒs] **1.** (quer) über, durch; **2.** hinüber, herüber
act [ækt] spielen, schauspielern
activity [æk'tɪvəti] Aktivität, Tätigkeit
actor ['æktə] Schauspieler **actress** ['æktrəs] Schauspielerin
add [æd] addieren, hinzufügen, ergänzen
address [ə'dres] Adresse, Anschrift
°admiral ['ædmərəl] Admiral
adopt [ə'dɒpt] adoptieren, die Patenschaft übernehmen für
adventure [əd'ventʃə] Abenteuer
advertisement [əd'vɜːtɪsmənt] Anzeige, Inserat; Werbespot
aerobics [eə'rəʊbɪks] Aerobic
Afro-Caribbean [ˌæfrəʊ kærə'biːən] Afro-Karibe/Afro-Karibin *(Schwarze/r karibischer Herkunft)*
after ['ɑːftə] **1.** *(prep)* nach *(zeitlich)* • **after that** danach **look after sb.** sich um jn. kümmern; auf jn. aufpassen **run after sb.** hinter jm. herrennen **2.** *(conj)* nachdem
afternoon [ˌɑːftə'nuːn] Nachmittag • **Good afternoon.** Guten Tag. *(nachmittags)* **in the afternoon(s)** am Nachmittag, nachmittags **this afternoon** heute Nachmittag
again [ə'gen] wieder, noch einmal • °**again and again** immer wieder
against [ə'genst] gegen
agent ['eɪdʒənt] Agent/in
ago [ə'gəʊ]: **a long time ago** vor langer Zeit • **a minute ago** vor einer Minute
agree [ə'griː] sich einigen **agree with sb.** mit jm. übereinstimmen; jm. zustimmen
ahead [ə'hed]: **be ahead (of sb.)** führen, in Führung liegen (vor jm.); jm. voraus sein
air [eə] Luft
album ['ælbəm] Album
alcohol ['ælkəhɒl] Alkohol
alive [ə'laɪv]: **be alive** leben, am Leben sein
all [ɔːl] alle; alles • **all the kids** alle Kinder • **all day/morning/summer** den ganzen Tag/Morgen/Sommer (lang) **all the time/money/food** die ganze Zeit (lang)/das ganze Geld/Essen • **all alone** ganz allein • **all over the world** auf der ganzen Welt, überall auf der Welt • **all right** gut, in Ordnung, okay
allowed [ə'laʊd]: **be allowed to do sth.** etwas tun dürfen
almost ['ɔːlməʊst] fast, beinahe
alone [ə'ləʊn] allein
along [ə'lɒŋ] weiter-, vorwärts **along the cliffs** die Klippen entlang
alphabet ['ælfəbet] Alphabet
already [ɔːl'redi] schon, bereits
also ['ɔːlsəʊ] auch
alternative *(n; adj)* [ɔːl'tɜːnətɪv] Alternative; Alternativ-
always ['ɔːlweɪz] immer
am [ˌeɪ_'em]: **8 am** 8 Uhr morgens *(zwischen 0 und 12 Uhr)*
ambulance ['æmbjələns] Krankenwagen
American *(adj; n)* [ə'merɪkən] amerikanisch; Amerikaner/in
an [ən] ein, eine
and [ənd, *betont:* ænd] und °**and so on** und so weiter
angry (with) *(adj)* ['æŋgri] böse, zornig, wütend (auf) **angrily** *(adv)* ['æŋgrəli] zornig, wütend
animal ['ænɪml] Tier
anonymous [ə'nɒnɪməs] anonym
anorak ['ænəræk] Anorak
another [ə'nʌðə] ein anderer/anderes, eine andere; noch ein/e • **one another** einander, sich (gegenseitig)
answer ['ɑːnsə] **1.** antworten; beantworten • **answer the phone** ans Telefon gehen **2.** Antwort
Antarctic [æn'tɑːktɪk]: **the Antarctic** die Antarktis
anticlockwise [ˌænti'klɒkwaɪz] entgegen dem Uhrzeigersinn
any ['eni]: **not ... any** kein(e) **not ... any more** nicht mehr; kein(e, n) ... mehr • **any?** (irgend)welche?
anybody ['enibɒdi]: **not ... anybody** niemand • **anybody?** (irgend)jemand?
anyone ['eniwʌn]: **not ... anyone** niemand • **anyone?** (irgend)jemand?
anything ['eniθɪŋ]: **not ... anything** nichts • **anything?** (irgend)etwas?
anyway ['eniweɪ] jedenfalls, wie dem auch sei; außerdem, und überhaupt

appear ['ə'pɪə] erscheinen, auftauchen
apple ['æpl] Apfel
April ['eɪprəl] April
°**arcade** [ɑ:'keɪd] Arkade, Passage *(mit Geschäften, Spielhallen usw.)*
area ['eəriə] Bereich; Gebiet, Gegend
arm [ɑ:m] Arm
around [ə'raʊnd] um ... herum; in ... umher • **around Ashton** in Ashton umher, durch Ashton • **Look around (you).** Sieh dich um. • **run/stand around** herumrennen/ herumstehen • °**walk around** herumlaufen (in)
arrange [ə'reɪndʒ] (an)ordnen **arrangement** [ə'reɪndʒmənt] Vereinbarung, Abmachung
arrive [ə'raɪv] ankommen, eintreffen
°**arrow** ['ærəʊ] Pfeil
art [ɑ:t] Kunst
article ['ɑ:tɪkl] (Zeitungs-) Artikel
as [əz, *betont:* æz] **1.** *(conj)* als, während • **as you know** wie du weißt • **as if** als ob **2.** *(prep)* **as a shop assistant** als Verkäufer/in • **as long as** so lang wie
ask [ɑ:sk] fragen • **ask questions** Fragen stellen • °**ask for** fragen nach • **ask sb. for sth.** jn. um etwas bitten °**ask sb. for directions** jn. um eine Wegbeschreibung bitten; jn. nach dem Weg fragen
Assembly [ə'sembli] Schulversammlung • **assembly hall** [ə'sembli hɔ:l] Aula
assistant [ə'sɪstənt] Assistent/ Assistentin; Verkäufer/in
astronaut ['æstrənɔ:t] Astronaut/in
at [ət, *betont:* æt] an, bei • **at first** zuerst, anfangs, zu Anfang • **at home** zu Hause, daheim • **at Kingsway High School** an/auf der Kingsway High School • **at last** schließlich, endlich • **at night** in der Nacht, nachts • **at once** sofort, (so)gleich • **at school** in der Schule • **at sea** auf See **at six** um sechs • °**at the bottom of the page** am Fuß der Seite • **at the door** an der Tür • **at the front** vorn **at the moment** im Moment, gerade, zurzeit • **at the restaurant** im Restaurant **at the same time** zur gleichen Zeit • **at the weekend** am Wochenende • **at weekends** an Wochenenden • **at work** bei der Arbeit, am Arbeitsplatz
ate [et, eɪt] *si. past von „eat"*
athlete ['æθli:t] (Leicht-)Athlet/ (Leicht-)Athletin, Sportlerin **athletics** [æθ'letɪks] Leichtathletik
atlas ['ætləs] Atlas
attraction [ə'trækʃn] Attraktion
au pair [,əʊ 'peə] Aupair(-mädchen, -junge)
August ['ɔ:gəst] August
aunt [ɑ:nt] Tante
automatic *(adj)* [,ɔ:tə'mætɪk] automatisch • **automatically** *(adv)* automatisch
autumn ['ɔ:təm] Herbst
avenue ['ævənju:] Allee, Boulevard
°**aviary** ['eɪviəri] Vogelhaus
away [ə'weɪ] weg, fort

B

back [bæk] **1.** zurück • **turn back** umkehren, kehrtmachen • **back at the farm** daheim auf der Farm **2.** Rücken • **at the back (of)** hinten, am hinteren Ende (von)
bacon ['beɪkən] Schinkenspeck
bad [bæd] schlecht, schlimm **be bad at sth.** schlecht in etwas sein; etwas schlecht können
badminton ['bædmɪntən] Badminton, Federball
bag [bæg] Tasche, Beutel, Tüte
ball [bɔ:l] Ball
banana [bə'nɑ:nə] Banane
Bangladeshi [,bæŋglə'deʃi] Bangale/Bangalin *(jd. aus Bangladesch)*
bank [bæŋk] **1.** Bank, Sparkasse **bottle bank** Altglascontainer **2.** (Fluss-)Ufer
bar chart ['bɑ: tʃɑ:t] Balkendiagramm
barbecue ['bɑ:bɪkju:] Grillparty
basket ['bɑ:skɪt] Korb
basketball ['bɑ:skɪtbɔ:l] Basketball
bath [bɑ:θ] Bad • **have a bath** ein Bad nehmen, baden *(in der Wanne)*
bathroom ['bɑ:θru:m] Badezimmer
°**bazaar** [bə'zɑ:] Basar
be* [bi, *betont:* bi:] sein • **Be careful.** Sei vorsichtig. • **be in trouble** in Schwierigkeiten sein; Ärger kriegen • **be late** zu spät sein/kommen • **be late for school** zu spät zur Schule kommen • **be on holiday** in Urlaub sein; Ferien haben/machen • **be out** weg sein, nicht da sein • **be right 1.** Recht haben; **2.** richtig sein **be wrong 1.** sich irren, Unrecht haben; **2.** nicht in Ordnung sein, nicht stimmen
beach [bi:tʃ] Strand • **on the beach** am Strand
beat* [bi:t] besiegen; schlagen
beat [bi:t] *si. past von „beat"*
beaten ['bi:tn] *Part. Perf. von „beat"*
beautiful ['bju:tɪfl] (wunder-) schön
became [bɪ'keɪm] *si. past von „become"*
because [bɪ'kɒz] weil **because of** wegen
become* [bɪ'kʌm] werden
become [bɪ'kʌm] *Part. Perf. von „become"*
bed [bed] Bett
bedroom ['bedru:m] Schlafzimmer
been [bi:n, bɪn] *Part. Perf. von „be"* • **I've been to ... .** Ich war (schon mal) in ... . / Ich bin (schon) in ... gewesen.
beer [bɪə] Bier
before [bɪ'fɔ:] **1.** *(prep)* vor *(zeitlich)*; **2.** *(conj)* bevor; **3.** *(adv)* vorher; vorher schon mal
began [bɪ'gæn] *si. past von „begin"*
begin* **(-nn-)** [bɪ'gɪn] beginnen, anfangen (mit) **beginning** [bɪ'gɪnɪŋ] Anfang, Beginn
begun [bɪ'gʌn] *Part. Perf. von „begin"*
behind [bɪ'haɪnd] hinter
believe (in) [bɪ'li:v] glauben (an)
°**belong** [bɪ'lɒŋ] gehören; dazugehören
below [bɪ'ləʊ] **1.** *(prep)* unter, unterhalb (von); **2.** *(adv)* unten
bench [bentʃ] Bank *(zum Sitzen)*
best [best]: **(the) best** (der/ die/das) beste ...; am besten **like sth. best** etwas am liebsten mögen
better ['betə] besser • **like sth. better** etwas lieber mögen
between [bɪ'twi:n] zwischen
beyond [bɪ'jɒnd] über ... hinaus, jenseits (von)
bicycle ['baɪsɪkl] Fahrrad
big (-gg-) [bɪg] groß
bike [baɪk] Fahrrad • **ride a bike** Rad fahren • **bike ride** Radfahrt, Radtour
bikini [bɪ'ki:ni] Bikini
bill [bɪl] Rechnung
bin [bɪn] Papierkorb, Mülleimer
biology [baɪ'ɒlədʒi] Biologie
bird [bɜ:d] Vogel
biro ['baɪrəʊ] Kugelschreiber
birth [bɜ:θ] Geburt • **date of birth** Geburtsdatum • **place of birth** Geburtsort

birthday ['bɜːθdeɪ] Geburtstag **Happy birthday!** Herzlichen Glückwunsch zum Geburtstag! • **It's my birthday next week.** Ich habe nächste Woche Geburtstag. • **When's your birthday?** Wann hast du Geburtstag?

bit [bɪt]: **a bit** ein bisschen, etwas

black [blæk] schwarz

°**bleep** [bliːp] piepen, piepsen

blew [bluː] *si. past von „blow"*

°**blindfold** ['blaɪndfəʊld] die Augen verbinden

blond [blɒnd] blond

blood [blʌd] Blut

blouse [blaʊz] Bluse

blow* [bləʊ] wehen, blasen

blown [bləʊn] *Part. Perf. von „blow"*

blue [bluː] blau

blush [blʌʃ] rot werden, erröten

board [bɔːd] **1.** Brett; (Wand-)Tafel • **notice board** Anschlagtafel, schwarzes Brett °**2.** Spielbrett; **3. on board (the ship)** an Bord (des Schiffes) • **go on board** an Bord gehen

boat [bəʊt] Boot, Schiff

body ['bɒdi] Körper

bomb [bɒm] Bombe

bone [bəʊn] Knochen

book [bʊk] Buch • **exercise book** Übungs-, Schulheft

bookshelf ['bʊkʃelf], *pl* **bookshelves** ['-ʃelvz] Bücherregal

boring ['bɔːrɪŋ] langweilig

born [bɔːn]: **be born** geboren sein/werden

boss [bɒs] *(infml)* Boss, Chef/in

both [bəʊθ] beide, beides **both of you** alle beide; ihr beide

bottle ['bɒtl] Flasche • **a bottle of ...** eine Flasche ... **bottle bank** Altglascontainer

°**bottom** ['bɒtəm]: **at the bottom of the page** am Fuß der Seite

bought [bɔːt] **1.** *si. past von „buy"*; **2.** *Part. Perf. von „buy"*

boutique [buː'tiːk] Boutique

box [bɒks] Kasten, Kiste **a box of chocolates** eine Schachtel Pralinen **(tele)phone box** Telefonzelle

boy [bɔɪ] Junge

boyfriend ['bɔɪfrend] (fester) Freund

°**brackets** ['brækɪts] Klammern

brave [breɪv] tapfer, mutig

bread *(no pl)* [bred] Brot

break [breɪk] Pause • **take a break** eine Pause machen

break* [breɪk] (zer)brechen; kaputtmachen; kaputtgehen **break loose** sich losreißen, sich lösen

breakfast ['brekfəst] Frühstück **for breakfast** zum Frühstück **have breakfast** frühstücken

bridge [brɪdʒ] Brücke

bright [braɪt] leuchtend, hell

brilliant ['brɪliənt] toll, glänzend, großartig

bring* [brɪŋ] (mit-, her)bringen

British ['brɪtɪʃ] britisch • **He's/She's British.** Er ist Brite. / Sie ist Britin.

brochure ['brəʊʃə] Prospekt, Broschüre

broke [brəʊk] *si. past von „break"*

broken ['brəʊkən] **1.** *Part. Perf. von „break"*; **2.** *(adj)* gebrochen; zerbrochen

brother ['brʌðə] Bruder

brought [brɔːt] **1.** *si. past von „bring"*; **2.** *Part. Perf. von „bring"*

brown [braʊn] braun

brush [brʌʃ] **1.** (Haar-)Bürste; **2.** bürsten • **brush your teeth** sich die Zähne putzen

budgie ['bʌdʒi] Wellensittich

°**buffet** ['bʊfeɪ] Büfett

build* [bɪld] bauen • **builder** ['bɪldə] Bauarbeiter/in

building ['bɪldɪŋ] Gebäude

built [bɪlt] **1.** *si. past von „build"*; **2.** *Part. Perf. von „build"*

bus [bʌs] Bus • **on the bus** im Bus • **bus stop** Bushaltestelle

business ['bɪznəs] Unternehmen, Geschäft(e)

°**busker** ['bʌskə] Straßenmusikant/in

busy ['bɪzi] beschäftigt; belebt, verkehrsreich, hektisch

but [bət, *betont:* bʌt] aber

butter ['bʌtə] Butter

buy* [baɪ] kaufen

by [baɪ] **1.** von; **2.** an, neben; (nahe) bei; **3. by bike/car/...** mit dem Rad/Auto/...; **4. by 31st May** bis spätestens 31. Mai

Bye bye! [baɪ 'baɪ] Tschüs!

C

cable ['keɪbl] Kabel

café ['kæfeɪ] (kleines) Restaurant, Imbissstube; Café

cage [keɪdʒ] Käfig

cake [keɪk] Kuchen, Torte

calendar ['kælɪndə] Kalender

call [kɔːl] **1.** nennen; rufen; anrufen • **What do you call this?** Wie nennt man dies? **2.** Ruf, Anruf

camcorder ['kæmkɔːdə] Camcorder *(Videokamera mit eingebauter Abspielfunktion)*

came [keɪm] *si. past von „come"*

camera ['kæmərə] Kamera, Fotoapparat

camp [kæmp] (Trainings-, Zelt-)Lager

camp-site ['kæmpsaɪt] Campingplatz, Zeltplatz

can [kæn] Dose, Büchse

can [kən, *betont:* kæn] **1.** können; **2.** dürfen • **You can't ...** [kɑːnt] **(= You cannot ...)** ['kænɒt] Du kannst nicht ... / Du darfst nicht ...

canal [kə'næl] Kanal

candle ['kændl] Kerze

canteen [kæn'tiːn] Kantine, Schulmensa

capital ['kæpɪtl] Hauptstadt

captain ['kæptɪn] Kapitän/in

car [kɑː] Auto

card [kɑːd] Karte

°**cardboard** ['kɑːdbɔːd] Pappe, Karton

care [keə]: **I don't care.** Das ist mir egal.

careful *(adj)* ['keəfl] **1.** vorsichtig; **2.** sorgfältig • **carefully** *(adv)* ['keəfəli] **1.** vorsichtig; **2.** sorgfältig

carpenter ['kɑːpəntə] Zimmermann

carry ['kæri] tragen; befördern

carton ['kɑːtn] Karton, (Milch-, Saft-)Packung

cassette [kə'set] Cassette

castle ['kɑːsl] Burg, Schloss

cat [kæt] Katze, Kater

catch* [kætʃ] fangen; erwischen • **catch sb.'s arm** jn. am Arm packen/fassen **catch a train/bus** einen Zug/Bus nehmen, erreichen

cathedral [kə'θiːdrəl] Kathedrale, Dom

caught [kɔːt] **1.** *si. past von „catch"*; **2.** *Part. Perf. von „catch"*

cause [kɔːz] verursachen

CD [ˌsiː'diː] CD • **CD player** CD-Spieler

celebration [ˌselɪ'breɪʃn] (Gedenk-)Feier

cello ['tʃeləʊ] Cello

centimetre ['sentɪmiːtə] Zentimeter

centre ['sentə] Zentrum; Mitte

ceremony ['serəməni] Zeremonie; Feier(lichkeit)

°**certain** ['sɜːtn]: **a certain person** eine bestimmte Person

chair [tʃeə] Stuhl

champion ['tʃæmpiən] Wettkampfsieger/in, Champion, Meister/in • **championship** ['tʃæmpiənʃɪp] Meisterschaft

chance [tʃɑːns] Chance

change [tʃeɪndʒ] **1.** ändern **change into** (ver)ändern, umwandeln in; sich verändern in, werden zu • **change (trains)** umsteigen **2.** *(Geld)* wechseln, umtauschen; **3.** *(Kleidung)* wechseln;

sich umziehen; **4.** (Ver-)Änderung, Wechsel
°Changing of the Guard [gɑ:d] Wachablösung *(vor dem Buckingham Palace)*
channel ['tʃænl] Kanal • **the Channel** der Ärmelkanal
chaos ['keɪɒs] Chaos
°charity bazaar ['tʃærəti] Wohltätigkeitsbasar
chart [tʃɑ:t] Tabelle, Diagramm **bar chart** Balkendiagramm
chase sb. (away) [tʃeɪs] jn. (weg)jagen
cheap [tʃi:p] billig, preiswert
cheating ['tʃi:tɪŋ]: **That's cheating!** Das ist gemogelt/geschummelt! Du mogelst/schummelst!
check [tʃek] (über)prüfen, kontrollieren • °**checkpoint** ['tʃekpɔɪnt] Kontrollpunkt
cheer [tʃɪə] jubeln, Beifall klatschen
cheese [tʃi:z] Käse
chemistry ['kemɪstri] Chemie
chess [tʃes] Schach
chicken ['tʃɪkɪn] Huhn; (Brat-)Hähnchen
child [tʃaɪld], *pl* **children** ['tʃɪldrən] Kind • **childhood** ['tʃaɪldhʊd] Kindheit
Chinese *(adj; n)* [ˌtʃaɪ'ni:z] chinesisch; Chinesisch; Chinese/Chinesin
chips *(pl)* [tʃɪps] Pommes frites
chocolate ['tʃɒklət] **1.** Schokolade; **2.** Praline • **a box of chocolates** eine Schachtel Pralinen
choice [tʃɔɪs] (Aus-)Wahl
choir ['kwaɪə] Chor
choose* [tʃu:z] aussuchen, (aus)wählen
chose [tʃəʊz] *si. past von „choose"*
chosen ['tʃəʊzn] *Part. Perf. von „choose"*
Christmas ['krɪsməs] Weihnachten
church [tʃɜ:tʃ] Kirche
circus ['sɜ:kəs] (runder) Platz *(in einer Stadt)*
city ['sɪti] Stadt, Großstadt
class [klɑ:s] Klasse, Kurs °**classmate** ['klɑ:smeɪt] Klassenkamerad/in, Mitschüler/in **classroom** Klassenzimmer **classroom phrases** [ˌklɑ:sru:m 'freɪzɪz] *Redewendungen für das Klassenzimmer; Unterrichtssprache*
classical ['klæsɪkl] klassisch
clause [klɔ:z] (Teil-, Glied-)Satz **main clause** [ˌmeɪn 'klɔ:z] Hauptsatz
clean [kli:n] **1.** sauber; **2.** sauber machen
clear [klɪə] klar, deutlich
clever ['klevə] schlau, klug
°click [klɪk] (an-, hin)klicken
cliff [klɪf] Klippe
climb [klaɪm] klettern; hinaufklettern (auf)
cloakroom ['kləʊkru:m] Garderobe
clock [klɒk] (Wand-, Stand-, Turm-)Uhr • **clockwise** ['klɒkwaɪz] im Uhrzeigersinn
close [kləʊz] schließen, zumachen
clothes *(pl)* [kləʊðz, kləʊz] Kleidung, „Klamotten"
cloudy ['klaʊdi] bewölkt, wolkig
clown [klaʊn] Clown
club [klʌb] Klub; Verein
clue [klu:] Hinweis, Anhaltspunkt
°clunk [klʌŋk] dumpfes Geräusch
coach [kəʊtʃ] **1.** Reisebus; **2.** Trainer/in
coast [kəʊst] Küste • **on the coast** an der Küste
coat [kəʊt] Mantel
code [kəʊd] (Geheim-)Kode
coffee ['kɒfi] Kaffee
cola ['kəʊlə] Cola
cold [kəʊld] kalt • **be/feel cold** frieren • **I was/felt cold.** Mir war kalt.
°collage ['kɒlɑ:ʒ] Collage
collect [kə'lekt] (ein)sammeln **collection** [kə'lekʃn] Sammlung; *(das)* Sammeln
colour ['kʌlə] **1.** Farbe; °**2.** bunt anmalen • **What colour is it?** Welche Farbe hat es (er, sie)?
column ['kɒləm] **1.** Säule; °**2.** Spalte
°combination [ˌkɒmbɪ'neɪʃn] Kombination, Verbindung
come* [kʌm] kommen **Come here.** Komm her. **come (in) third** als Dritter durchs Ziel kommen, einlaufen; Dritter werden • **Come on.** Los, komm(t). / Na, komm(t). • **come round** vorbeischauen, vorbeikommen
come [kʌm] *Part. Perf. von „come"*
comic ['kɒmɪk] Comic-Heft
common ['kɒmən]: **have sth. in common** etwas miteinander gemein haben
compare [kəm'peə] vergleichen
compass ['kʌmpəs] Kompass
competition [ˌkɒmpə'tɪʃn] Wettbewerb, Wettkampf
complete [kəm'pli:t] vervollständigen, ergänzen
complex ['kɒmpleks] (Gebäude-)Komplex
computer [kəm'pju:tə] Computer, Rechner • °**computer nerd** [nɜ:d] *(infml) etwa:* Computerfreak
context ['kɒntekst] Zusammenhang, Kontext
°continue [kən'tɪnju:] weitermachen • °**Continue to collect words.** Sammle weiter Wörter.
control [kən'trəʊl] Kontrolle; *hier:* Kontrollzentrum °**controls** *(pl)* Schalttafel, Steuerpult
conversation [ˌkɒnvə'seɪʃn] Gespräch, Unterhaltung
cook [kʊk] **1.** kochen, zubereiten; **2.** Koch, Köchin
cooker ['kʊkə] Herd
cool [ku:l] cool, scharf, stark
copy ['kɒpi] **1.** übertragen, kopieren, abschreiben; °**2.** Kopie
cornflakes ['kɔ:nfleɪks] Cornflakes
Cornish ['kɔ:nɪʃ] kornisch *(aus Cornwall, zu Cornwall gehörig)*
correct [kə'rekt] **1.** verbessern, korrigieren; **2.** korrekt, richtig **correction** [kə'rekʃn] Korrektur, Berichtigung
corridor ['kɒrɪdɔ:] Gang, Korridor
cost* [kɒst] **1.** kosten; **2.** Kosten
cost [kɒst] **1.** *si. past von „cost";* **2.** *Part. Perf. von „cost"*
costume ['kɒstju:m] Kostüm, Verkleidung
cottage ['kɒtɪdʒ] (kleines) Landhaus, Häuschen
°couch potato [ˌkaʊtʃ pə'teɪtəʊ] *(infml)* „Dauerglotzer" *(wörtlich:* Sofakartoffel)
could [kəd, *betont:* kʊd] **1.** könnte(n); **2.** konnte(n)
count [kaʊnt] zählen
country ['kʌntri] Land • **in the country** auf dem Land
county ['kaʊnti] Grafschaft, Verwaltungsbezirk
course: **of course** [əv 'kɔ:s] natürlich, selbstverständlich
cousin ['kʌzn] Cousin/Cousine
cow [kaʊ] Kuh • **cowboy** Cowboy
crash [kræʃ] **1.** Krach, Krachen; Zusammenstoß; **2.** krachen **crash (into)** zusammenstoßen (mit), hineinfahren (in) °**3.** abstürzen *(Computer)*
cricket ['krɪkɪt] Kricket
crisps [krɪsps] Kartoffelchips
°Crown Jewels *(pl)* [ˌkraʊn 'dʒu:əlz] Kronjuwelen
cry [kraɪ] weinen; schreien
culture ['kʌltʃə] Kultur
cup [kʌp] Tasse • **a cup of tea** eine Tasse Tee
cupboard ['kʌbəd] Schrank
curry ['kʌri] *scharfes, mit Curry gewürztes Gericht*
customer ['kʌstəmə] Kunde, Kundin
cut* [kʌt] **1.** (-tt-) (aus)schneiden • **cut out** ausschneiden

2. **short cut** ['ʃɔ:t kʌt] Abkürzung

cut [kʌt] **1.** *si. past von „cut"*; **2.** *Part. Perf. von „cut"*

cycle ['saɪkl] Rad fahren
cycling ['saɪklɪŋ] *(das)* Radfahren • **cycle track** ['saɪkl træk] Radweg

D

dad [dæd] Vati, Papa; Vater

dance [dɑ:ns] **1.** tanzen; **2.** Tanz

danger ['deɪndʒə] Gefahr
dangerous ['deɪndʒərəs] gefährlich

dark [dɑ:k] dunkel; dunkelhaarig • **darkness** ['dɑ:knəs] Dunkelheit

date [deɪt] Datum • **What's the date?** Welches Datum haben wir? • **date of birth** Geburtsdatum

daughter ['dɔ:tə] Tochter

day [deɪ] Tag • **the next day** der nächste Tag; am nächsten Tag • **What day is 1st January?** Was für ein Tag ist der 1. Januar?

dead [ded] tot

dear [dɪə] Liebling, Schatz; mein Lieber / meine Liebe **Dear Katrin and Julia** Liebe Katrin, liebe Julia • **Dear Sir or Madam** Sehr geehrte Damen und Herren

December [dɪ'sembə] Dezember

decide (on) [dɪ'saɪd] sich entscheiden (für); beschließen
decision [dɪ'sɪʒn] Entscheidung

deep [di:p] tief

definitely ['defɪnətli] sicherlich, ganz bestimmt

°**dent** [dent] Delle, Beule

department store [dɪ'pɑ:tmənt stɔ:] Kaufhaus

describe sth. (to sb.) [dɪ'skraɪb] (jm.) etwas beschreiben
description [dɪ'skrɪpʃn] Beschreibung

design [dɪ'zaɪn] **1.** entwerfen, konstruieren; **2.** Entwurf; Design, Gestaltung, Konstruktion • **Design and Technology** Design und Technologie/ Technik *(engl. Schulfach)*

desk [desk] Schreibtisch, Schülertisch

destroy [dɪ'strɔɪ] zerstören, vernichten

detail ['di:teɪl] Detail, Einzelheit

°**dialogue** ['daɪəlɒg] Dialog

diary ['daɪəri] Tagebuch; Terminkalender

°**dictate** [dɪk'teɪt] diktieren
°**dictation** [dɪk'teɪʃn] Diktat

dictionary ['dɪkʃənri] Wörterbuch, *(alphabetisches)* Wörterverzeichnis

did [dɪd] *si. past von „do"*
I didn't go away. Ich bin nicht weggefahren.

die (of) [daɪ] sterben (an)

difference ['dɪfrəns] Unterschied • **different** ['dɪfrənt] verschieden, unterschiedlich; anders; andere(r, s) • **in different ways** auf verschiedene Weise(n)

difficult ['dɪfɪkəlt] schwierig, schwer

dining-room ['daɪnɪŋru:m] Esszimmer

dinner ['dɪnə] Abendessen, Abendbrot • **for dinner** zum Abendbrot • **have dinner** Abendbrot essen

directions *(pl)* [də'rekʃnz] Anweisung(en) • °**ask sb. for directions** jn. um eine Wegbeschreibung bitten; jn. nach dem Weg fragen

director [də'rektə] Regisseur/in

directory [də'rektəri] Inhaltsverzeichnis *(Computer)*

dirty ['dɜ:ti] schmutzig

disabled [dɪs'eɪbld] (körper-) behindert

disappear [ˌdɪsə'pɪə] verschwinden

disc jockey ['dɪsk dʒɒki] Diskjockey

disco ['dɪskəʊ] Disko

discover [dɪ'skʌvə] entdecken; herausfinden, feststellen
discovery [dɪ'skʌvəri] Entdeckung

discuss [dɪ'skʌs] besprechen, diskutieren über

dishes *(pl)* ['dɪʃɪz] Geschirr
wash the dishes / do the dishes das Geschirr abwaschen

°**Divide your group in two.** [dɪ'vaɪd] Teilt eure Gruppe in zwei Hälften auf.

divorced [dɪ'vɔ:st] geschieden

DJ [ˌdi:'dʒeɪ], **disc jockey** ['dɪsk dʒɒki] Diskjockey

do* [du:] tun, machen • **Don't do that.** Tu das nicht. / Lass das. • **do homework** Schularbeiten/die Hausaufgabe(n) machen • **do jobs** Arbeiten/ Aufträge erledigen • **do sport(s)** Sport treiben • **do the dishes** das Geschirr abwaschen • **do the shopping** Einkäufe machen/erledigen, einkaufen

dock [dɒk] Dock, Anlegestelle

doctor ['dɒktə] Arzt, Ärztin

dog [dɒg] Hund

dolphin ['dɒlfɪn] Delphin

°**dome** [dəʊm] Kuppel, Gewölbe

done [dʌn] *Part. Perf. von „do"*

door [dɔ:] Tür • **at the door** an der Tür

down [daʊn] **1.** hinunter, herunter, nach unten
down the tree den Baum hinunter
2. unten • **down south** unten im Süden

downstairs [ˌdaʊn'steəz] nach unten; unten

drama ['drɑ:mə] Drama, Schauspiel

drank [dræŋk] *si. past von „drink"*

draw* [drɔ:] zeichnen

drawn [drɔ:n] *Part. Perf. von „draw"*

dream [dri:m] **1.** Traum
dream house Traumhaus
2. dream (about) träumen (von)

dress [dres] Kleid

dressed [ˌget 'drest]: **get dressed** sich anziehen

drew [dru:] *si. past von „draw"*

drink* [drɪŋk] **1.** trinken; **2.** Getränk

drive* [draɪv] *(ein Auto, einen Bus usw.)* fahren • **driver** ['draɪvə] Fahrer/in

driven ['drɪvn] *Part. Perf. von „drive"*

drop (-pp-) [drɒp] fallen lassen

drove [drəʊv] *si. past von „drive"*

drum [drʌm] Trommel; Schlagzeug • **play the drums** Schlagzeug spielen

drunk [drʌŋk] *Part. Perf. von „drink"*

dry [draɪ] trocken

E

each [i:tʃ] jeder, jede, jedes (einzelne) • **each of them** jede/r Einzelne von ihnen
each other [i:tʃ_'ʌðə] einander, sich (gegenseitig)
°**with five things each** mit je fünf Dingen

ear [ɪə] Ohr

early ['ɜ:li] früh; zu früh

east [i:st] östlich; (nach) Osten **to the east** im Osten • **an eastbound train** ['i:stbaʊnd] ein Zug Richtung Osten

easy ['i:zi] leicht, einfach

eat* [i:t] essen

eaten ['i:tn] *Part. Perf. von „eat"*

°**ebony** ['ebəni] Ebenholz

°**edge** [edʒ] Rand, Kante

education [ˌedʒu'keɪʃn] (Schul-, Aus-)Bildung; Erziehung

egg [eg] Ei

either ['aɪðə, 'i:ðə]: **not (…) either** auch nicht; auch kein

electric [ɪ'lektrɪk] elektrisch
electrician [ɪˌlek'trɪʃn] Elektriker/in

electronic [ɪˌlek'trɒnɪk] elektronisch
elephant ['elɪfənt] Elefant
else [els]: **anyone/anything else** sonst (noch) jemand / sonst (noch) etwas • **everyone else** alle anderen • **no one else** niemand anderes, sonst niemand • **someone/something else** (noch) jemand anderes / (noch) etwas anderes • **who/what/where/why/… else?** wer/was/wo/warum/… sonst (noch)?
°**e-mail** ['i:meɪl] E-Mail, elektronische Post
embarrassed [ɪm'bærəst] verlegen
emergency [i'mɜ:dʒənsi] Notfall
empty ['empti] leer
end [end] Ende, Schluss • **at the end** am Ende, am Schluss
ending ['endɪŋ] Endung; Ende, Schluss • **happy ending** Happy End
energy ['enədʒi] Energie
solar energy [ˌsəʊlər'enədʒi] Sonnenenergie, Solarenergie
engine ['endʒɪn] Motor, Maschine
engineer [ˌendʒɪ'nɪə] Ingenieur/in, Techniker/in
England ['ɪŋglənd] England
English ['ɪŋglɪʃ] englisch; Englisch • **He's/She's English.** Er ist Engländer. / Sie ist Engländerin. • **in English** auf Englisch • **What's this in English?** Wie heißt das auf Englisch?
enjoy sth. [ɪn'dʒɔɪ] etwas genießen, an etwas Spaß haben, etwas gern haben/tun
Enjoy yourself! Viel Spaß! / Amüsier dich gut!
enough [ɪ'nʌf] genug
entrance ['entrəns] Eingang
environment [ɪn'vaɪrənmənt] Umwelt, Umgebung
environment-friendly umweltfreundlich
equipment *(no pl)* [ɪ'kwɪpmənt] Ausrüstung
escape (from sb./sth.) [ɪ'skeɪp] fliehen (vor jm. / aus etwas); entkommen
ethnic ['eθnɪk] ethnisch, Volks-
euro (€) ['jʊərəʊ] Euro
Europe ['jʊərəp] Europa
even ['i:vn] sogar, selbst
even better/worse/taller (sogar) noch besser/schlechter/größer • **even if** selbst wenn, auch wenn
evening ['i:vnɪŋ] Abend
Good evening. Guten Abend.
in the evening(s) am Abend, abends • **this evening** heute Abend
event [ɪ'vent] Veranstaltung; Ereignis
ever ['evə] je, jemals, schon mal
every ['evri] jede, jeder, jedes
everybody ['evribɒdi] jeder, alle
everyday *(adj)* ['evrideɪ] Alltags-; alltäglich
everyone ['evriwʌn] jeder, alle
everyone else alle anderen
everything ['evriθɪŋ] alles
everywhere ['evriweə] überall(hin)
exact *(adj)* [ɪg'zækt] genau
exactly *(adv)* [ɪg'zæktli] genau
example [ɪg'zɑ:mpl] Beispiel
for example zum Beispiel
°**excerpt** ['eksɜ:pt] Auszug, Ausschnitt
°**exchange rate** [ɪks'tʃeɪndʒ reɪt] Wechselkurs
excited (about) [ɪk'saɪtɪd] aufgeregt (wegen, über) • **exciting** [ɪk'saɪtɪŋ] aufregend, spannend
°**excuse** [ɪk'skju:s] Ausrede, Entschuldigung
Excuse me. [ɪk'skju:z] Entschuldigung. / Entschuldigen Sie.
exercise ['eksəsaɪz] Übung
exercise book Übungsheft, Schulheft
exhibition [ˌeksɪ'bɪʃn] Ausstellung
expensive [ɪk'spensɪv] teuer
experiment [ɪk'sperɪmənt] 1. Experiment; °2. **experiment with** experimentieren mit, ausprobieren
explain sth. to sb. [ɪk'spleɪn] jm. etwas erklären, erläutern
explanation [ˌeksplə'neɪʃn] Erklärung
expression [ɪk'spreʃn] Ausdruck
°**extract** ['ekstrækt] Auszug
eye [aɪ] Auge

F

face [feɪs] Gesicht
°**fact** [fækt] Tatsache, Fakt
fact [fækt]: **in fact** eigentlich, genau gesagt; in Wirklichkeit
factory ['fæktri] Fabrik
faithfully ['feɪθfəli]: **Yours faithfully** Mit freundlichen Grüßen / Hochachtungsvoll
fall* [fɔ:l] (hin)fallen
fallen ['fɔ:lən] *Part. Perf. von „fall"*
°**false friends** [fɔ:ls] falsche Freunde
family ['fæməli] Familie
family name Familienname, Nachname
famous (for) ['feɪməs] berühmt (für, wegen)
fan [fæn] Fan
°**fancy-dress party** ['fænsi] Kostümfest
fantastic [fæn'tæstɪk] fantastisch, toll
far [fɑ:] weit (entfernt)
farm [fɑ:m] Bauernhof, Farm
farther ['fɑ:ðə] weiter (entfernt)
farthest ['fɑ:ðɪst] am weitesten (entfernt)
fashion ['fæʃn] Mode
fast [fɑ:st] schnell • **fast food** Fast Food *(in Schnellrestaurants angebotenes Essen)*
fat **(-tt-)** [fæt] dick, fett
father ['fɑ:ðə] Vater
fault [fɔ:lt] Schuld; Fehler
favourite ['feɪvərɪt] Favorit/in; Lieblings-
February ['februəri] Februar
fed [fed] **1.** *si. past von „feed";* **2.** *Part. Perf. von „feed"*
fed up [ˌfed_'ʌp]: **get fed up (with sth.)** etwas satt haben/bekommen; die Nase voll haben (von etwas)
feed* [fi:d] füttern • **feeding times** Fütterungszeiten
feel* [fi:l] fühlen; sich fühlen
I felt cold/hot. Mir war kalt/heiß. • **That feels great.** Das ist ein tolles Gefühl. • **feel sorry for sb.** jn. bedauern
feeling ['fi:lɪŋ] Gefühl
feet [fi:t] *pl von „foot"*
fell [fel] *si. past von „fall"*
felt [felt] **1.** *si. past von „feel";* **2.** *Part. Perf. von „feel"*
felt-tip ['feltɪp] Filzstift
ferry ['feri] Fähre
festival ['festɪvl] Festival, Festspiele
fetch (from) [fetʃ] holen, abholen (von)
few [fju:]: **a few** ein paar, einige (wenige)
field [fi:ld] Feld, Wiese, Weide
in the field auf dem Feld, der Wiese, der Weide
figure ['fɪgə] Gestalt, Figur
fill in [ˌfɪl_'ɪn] **1.** einsetzen; **2.** ausfüllen
film [fɪlm] **1.** filmen; **2.** Film
finally ['faɪnəli] schließlich, endlich
find* [faɪnd] finden; suchen
find out herausfinden
fine [faɪn] gut, fein, schön
I'm fine. Mir gehts gut. / Es geht mir gut.
finger ['fɪŋgə] Finger
finish ['fɪnɪʃ] **1.** beenden, zu Ende machen; enden
finished fertig, vollendet
°**2.** Ziel; Finish
fire ['faɪə] Feuer, Brand • **fire brigade** ['faɪə brɪˌgeɪd] Feuerwehr • **firework** ['faɪəwɜ:k] Feuerwerkskörper • **fireworks** ['faɪəwɜ:ks] *(pl)* Feuerwerk
first [fɜ:st] **1.** erste(r, s) • **first floor** erster Stock

2. zuerst, als Erstes, erstens **at first** zuerst, anfangs, zu Anfang • **firstly, …** erstens …

fish, *pl* **fish** [fɪʃ] Fisch • **fish finger** Fischstäbchen

fisherman ['fɪʃəmən], *pl* **fishermen** ['fɪʃəmən] Fischer

fishing village Fischerdorf

fit **(-tt-)** [fɪt] passen

fit **(-tt-)** [fɪt] fit, in Form

fitness ['fɪtnəs] Fitness

fix [fɪks] reparieren, in Ordnung bringen

flash [flæʃ] aufleuchten, blinken

flat [flæt] Wohnung

flew [fluː] *si. past von „fly"*

floor [flɔː] **1.** Fußboden; **2.** Stock(werk) • **first floor** erster Stock • **ground floor** Erdgeschoss • °**floor manager** Aufnahmeleiter/in

flown [fləʊn] *Part. Perf. von „fly"*

fly* [flaɪ] fliegen

focus on words / on grammar ['fəʊkəs] *etwa:* Blickpunkt „Wörter"/„Grammatik"

°**fold (over)** [fəʊld] falten, umknicken

folk [fəʊk] Folk(musik)

follow ['fɒləʊ] folgen; verfolgen • **the following expressions** die folgenden Ausdrücke

food [fuːd] Essen; Lebensmittel; Futter • **fast food** Fast Food *(in Schnellrestaurants angebotenes Essen)*

foot [fʊt], *pl* **feet** [fiːt] Fuß **on foot** zu Fuß

football ['fʊtbɔːl] Fußball

for [fə, *betont:* fɔː] für • **for breakfast/lunch/dinner** zum Frühstück/Mittagessen/Abendbrot • **for example** zum Beispiel • **for the first time** zum ersten Mal • **for an hour** eine Stunde lang **for hours** stundenlang • **for 400 years** 400 Jahre (lang)

forest ['fɒrɪst] Wald

forget* **(-tt-)** [fə'get] vergessen

forgot [fə'gɒt] *si. past von „forget"*

forgotten [fə'gɒtn] *Part. Perf. von „forget"*

fork [fɔːk] Gabel

form [fɔːm] **1.** *(englische)* (Schul-)Klasse; **2.** Formular, Vordruck; **3.** Form • **top form** Höchstform

°**fortune-teller** ['fɔːtʃuːn telə] Wahrsager/in

forward(s) ['fɔːwəd(z)] vorwärts, nach vorn

found [faʊnd] **1.** *si. past von „find"*; **2.** *Part. Perf. von „find"*

°**freak** [friːk] Freak, Fanatiker/in

free [friː] frei; kostenlos • **free time** Freizeit, freie Zeit

free time activities Freizeitaktivitäten

French [frentʃ] französisch; Französisch

Friday ['fraɪdeɪ, 'fraɪdi] Freitag

fridge [frɪdʒ] Kühlschrank

friend [frend] Freund/in

friendly ['frendli] freundlich, nett • **friendliness** ['frendlɪnəs] Freundlichkeit

frightened ['fraɪtnd]: **be frightened (of)** Angst haben (vor), sich fürchten (vor)

from [frəm, *betont:* frɒm] aus; von • **I'm from …** Ich bin aus … / Ich komme aus … **Where are you from?** Wo kommst du her? • **from Monday to Friday** von Montag bis Freitag

front [frʌnt]: **at the front** vorn **in front of** vor • **front door** Wohnungstür, Haustür

fruit [fruːt] Obst, Früchte; Frucht

full (of) [fʊl] voll (mit/von)

fun [fʌn]: **have fun** Spaß haben, sich amüsieren • **Have fun!** Viel Spaß! • **Shopping is (great) fun.** Einkaufen macht (viel/großen) Spaß.

funny ['fʌni] witzig, komisch

future ['fjuːtʃə] Zukunft

G

gadget ['gædʒɪt] Gerät, Apparat

°**gallery** ['gæləri] Regie(raum)

game [geɪm] Spiel

garage ['gærɪdʒ] Garage

garden ['gɑːdn] Garten

garlic ['gɑːlɪk] Knoblauch

gate [geɪt] Tor, Pforte

gave [geɪv] *si. past von „give"*

Geography [dʒi'ɒgrəfi] Geographie, Erdkunde

German *(adj; n)* ['dʒɜːmən] **1.** deutsch; Deutsch; **2.** Deutsche(r)

Germany ['dʒɜːməni] Deutschland

get* **(-tt-)** [get] **1.** bekommen, kriegen; **2.** holen, besorgen; **3.** gelangen, (hin)kommen **Get back!** (Geh/Tritt) Zurück! **get dressed** sich anziehen **get fed up (with sth.)** etwas satt haben/bekommen; die Nase voll haben (von etwas) **get in** einsteigen • **get in(to) a car/taxi** in ein Auto/Taxi einsteigen • **get out of a car/taxi** aus einem Auto/Taxi aussteigen • **get off** aussteigen • **get off a bus/train/bike** aus einem Bus/Zug aussteigen; von einem Fahrrad absteigen • **get on a bus/train/bike** in einen Bus/Zug einsteigen; auf ein Fahrrad aufsteigen • **get ready** sich fertig machen, sich bereitmachen • **get through** durchkommen, Verbindung bekommen *(am Telefon)* • **get up** aufstehen

ghost [gəʊst] Geist, Gespenst

giant ['dʒaɪənt] riesig, gigantisch

gift [gɪft] Geschenk, Gabe

giraffe [dʒə'rɑːf] Giraffe

girl [gɜːl] Mädchen

girlfriend ['gɜːlfrend] (feste) Freundin

give* [gɪv] geben • °**Give the paper to the next person.** Gib das Papier an die nächste Person weiter. • **give sth. up** etwas aufgeben

given ['gɪvn] *Part. Perf. von „give"*

glad **(-dd-)** [glæd]: **be glad** froh sein, sich freuen

glass [glɑːs] Glas

glue [gluː] Klebstoff

go* [gəʊ] **1.** gehen; fahren; **2.** (hin)gehören, (hin)kommen; **3. go black/hard/…** schwarz/hart/… werden • **Let's go.** Auf gehts! • **I must go now!** *(Briefschluss)* Ich muss jetzt Schluss machen! • **go for a walk** einen Spaziergang machen • **go climbing/sailing/swimming** klettern/segeln/schwimmen gehen • **go shopping/go to the shops** einkaufen gehen • **go a long way** viel erreichen, viel bewirken • °**go for the try** *etwa:* versuchen Punkte zu erzielen **go on** **1.** fortfahren, weiterreden; °**2.** weitermachen; °**3.** im Gange sein, vorgehen; **4.** angehen *(Licht)* • **go on a trip** einen Ausflug / eine Reise machen • **go on board** an Bord gehen • **go on holiday** in Urlaub fahren • **go out** **1.** ausgehen; **2.** ausfahren, auslaufen • **go under** untergehen • **go up** steigen, in die Höhe gehen • **go with** **1.** passen zu; °**2.** einhergehen mit, gehören zu • **I'm going to phone.** Ich werde anrufen. / Ich habe vor anzurufen.

goal [gəʊl] Tor *(im Sport)* °**goal-line** Torlinie • °**goal-post** Torpfosten

God, god [gɒd] Gott • **Thank God!** [gɒd] Gott sei Dank!

gold [gəʊld] Gold • **golden** ['gəʊldən] golden

goldfish, *pl* **goldfish** ['gəʊldfɪʃ] Goldfisch

golf [gɒlf] Golf

gone [gɒn] *Part. Perf. von „go"*

good [gʊd] gut • **Good morning/afternoon/evening/night.** Guten Morgen/Tag/Abend/Gute Nacht. **Good luck.** Viel Glück. **Goodbye.** [ˌgʊd'baɪ] Auf Wiedersehen. • **be good at sth.** gut in etwas sein; etwas gut können • **That's no good.** Das geht nicht.
got [gɒt] **1.** *si. past von „get"*; **2.** *Part. Perf. von „get"*
have got* haben, besitzen
°**graffiti** *(pl)* [grə'fi:ti] Graffiti, Wandkritzeleien
grand- ['græn-]: **grandfather** Großvater • **grandma** Oma **grandmother** Großmutter **grandpa** Opa • **grandparents** Großeltern
grape [greɪp] Weintraube
gravy ['greɪvi] (Braten-)Soße
great [greɪt] **1.** großartig, toll **That feels great.** Das ist ein tolles Gefühl.
2. groß, beträchtlich;
3. bedeutend, berühmt
green [gri:n] grün
grew [gru:] *si. past von „grow"*
grey [greɪ] grau
groan [grəʊn] stöhnen, ächzen
ground [graʊnd] (Erd-)Boden **ground floor** Erdgeschoss
group [gru:p] Gruppe • **a group of girls** eine Gruppe (von) Mädchen • **in groups of four** in Vierergruppen
grow* [grəʊ] wachsen • **grow up** aufwachsen; erwachsen werden
grown [grəʊn] *Part. Perf. von „grow"*
guess [ges] raten, erraten
guest [gest] Gast
guide [gaɪd] **1.** führen, lenken, leiten; **2.** (Fremden-)Führer/in, Reiseleiter/in • **guidebook** Reiseführer
guitar [gɪ'tɑ:] Gitarre • **play the guitar** Gitarre spielen
gun [gʌn] Schusswaffe
gym [dʒɪm] Sport-, Turnhalle

H

had [hæd] **1.** *si. past von „have got" und „have"*; **2.** *Part. Perf. von „have got" und „have"*
hair *(no pl)* [heə] Haar, Haare
half [hɑ:f], *pl* **halves** [hɑ:vz] Hälfte • **a year and a half** eineinhalb Jahre, anderthalb Jahre • **the first half** die erste Hälfte/Halbzeit • **half-time** [ˌhɑ:f'taɪm] Halbzeitpause **half a mile** eine halbe Meile **half past eight** halb neun (8.30/20.30)
ham [hæm] Schinken
hamburger ['hæmbɜ:gə] Hamburger
hamster ['hæmstə] Hamster
hand [hænd] Hand • **handbag** Handtasche
hang* [hæŋ] hängen, aufhängen • **hang out** *(infml)* sich herumtreiben, rumhängen
happen (to) ['hæpən] *(jm.)* geschehen, passieren • **What's happening?** Was ist los? / Was geht hier vor?
happy ['hæpi] glücklich, froh **Happy birthday!** Herzlichen Glückwunsch zum Geburtstag! • **happy ending** Happy End • **happiness** ['hæpɪnəs] Glück
harbour ['hɑ:bə] Hafen
hard [hɑ:d] **1.** *(adj)* hart; schwierig, schwer; **2.** *(adv)* heftig, kräftig, sehr • **think hard** scharf/angestrengt nachdenken • **try hard** sich sehr bemühen, sich anstrengen
has [həz, *betont:* hæz]: **he/she/it has got** er/sie/es hat, besitzt
hat [hæt] Hut
hate [heɪt] hassen, gar nicht mögen • **hate shopping** gar nicht gern einkaufen gehen
have* [hæv] haben • **have breakfast/lunch/dinner** frühstücken/Mittag essen/Abendbrot essen • **have a cola/a hamburger** eine Cola trinken / einen Hamburger essen • **have a bath** ein Bad nehmen, *(in der Wanne)* baden **have a shower** (sich) duschen **have a party** eine Party veranstalten, feiern • **have fun** Spaß haben, sich amüsieren **Have a nice weekend.** Schönes Wochenende! • **have sth. in common** etwas miteinander gemein haben
have got* haben, besitzen **have got to do sth.** etwas tun müssen
have* to do sth. ['hæf tə, 'hæv tə] etwas tun müssen
he [hi, *betont:* hi:] er
head [hed] Kopf
headteacher [ˌhed'ti:tʃə] Schulleiter/in
healthy ['helθɪ] gesund
hear* [hɪə] hören
heard [hɜ:d] **1.** *si. past von „hear"*; **2.** *Part. Perf. von „hear"*
heat [hi:t] Hitze • **in this heat** bei dieser Hitze
heavy ['hevi] schwer *(von Gewicht)*
held [held] **1.** *si. past von „hold"*; **2.** *Part. Perf. von „hold"*
helicopter ['helɪkɒptə] Hubschrauber, Helikopter
Hello. [hə'ləʊ] Hallo. / Guten Tag.
helmet ['helmɪt] Helm
help [help] **1.** helfen • **May I help you?** Sie wünschen? **Help yourself.** Greif zu! / Bediene dich!
2. Hilfe
her [hə, *betont:* hɜ:] **1.** ihr, ihre; **2.** sie; ihr
here [hɪə] hier; hierher • **Here you are.** Bitte sehr. / Hier bitte.
hero ['hɪərəʊ], *pl* **heroes** ['hɪərəʊz] Held, Heldin; Idol
hers [hɜ:z] ihre(r, s)
herself [hə'self, *betont:* hɜ:'self] sich (selbst)
°**Highland Games** [ˌhaɪlənd 'geɪmz] *Festival mit Musik und Sportwettkämpfen im schottischen Hochland*
hill [hɪl] Hügel, Berg
him [hɪm] ihn; ihm
himself [hɪm'self] sich (selbst)
his [hɪz] **1.** sein/e; **2.** seine(r, s)
history ['hɪstri] Geschichte
hit [hɪt] Hit
hit* sb./sth. **(-tt-)** [hɪt] jn./etwas schlagen, treffen; gegen etwas stoßen
hit [hɪt] **1.** *si. past von „hit"*; **2.** *Part. Perf. von „hit"*
hobby ['hɒbi] Hobby
hockey ['hɒki] Hockey
hold* [həʊld] (fest)halten **Hold on!** Festhalten! Halt dich fest! • °**hold sth. up** etwas hochhalten, hochheben
hole [həʊl] Loch
holiday(s) ['hɒlədeɪ(z), 'hɒlədi(z)] Ferien, Urlaub **be/go on holiday** in Urlaub sein/fahren; Ferien haben/machen • **holidaymaker** Urlauber/in
°**hologram** ['hɒləgræm] Hologramm *(mithilfe eines Lasers erzeugtes dreidimensionales Bild)*
home [həʊm] **1.** Heim, Zuhause; **2.** nach Hause • **at home** zu Hause, daheim **We're home.** Wir sind (wieder) zu Hause. • **homeless** obdachlos • **homelessness** Obdachlosigkeit • **home page** *erste Seite eines Angebots im World Wide Web* **homework** *(no pl)* Hausaufgabe(n) • **do homework** Schularbeiten/die Hausaufgabe(n) machen
hook [hʊk]: **off the hook** ausgehängt, nicht aufgelegt *(Telefon)*
hope [həʊp] **1.** hoffen; **2.** Hoffnung
horrible ['hɒrəbl] scheußlich, grauenhaft
horror story ['hɒrə] Horrorgeschichte

horse [hɔːs] Pferd
hospital ['hɒspɪtl] Krankenhaus
hot (-tt-) [hɒt] heiß • **I was/felt hot.** Mir war heiß. • **hot dog** ['hɒt dɒg] Hot dog
hotel [həʊ'tel] Hotel • **stay at a hotel** in einem Hotel übernachten
hour ['aʊə] Stunde • **for hours** stundenlang
house [haʊs] Haus
how [haʊ] wie • **How are you?** Wie geht es dir/euch/Ihnen? • **how many?** wie viele? • **how much?** wie viel? **How much is ...?** Was/Wie viel kostet ...? • **how to do sth.** wie man etwas tun kann/soll • °**How do you know?** Woher weißt du das?
hung [hʌŋ] **1.** *si. past von „hang"*; **2.** *Part. Perf. von „hang"*
hungry ['hʌŋgri]: **be hungry** hungrig sein, Hunger haben
hurricane ['hʌrɪkən] Hurrikan, Orkan
hurt* [hɜːt] verletzen; wehtun **She wasn't hurt.** Sie war/wurde nicht verletzt.
hurt [hɜːt] **1.** *si. past von „hurt"*; **2.** *Part. Perf. von „hurt"*
husband ['hʌzbənd] Ehemann

I

I [aɪ] ich • **I'm fine.** Mir gehts gut. / Es geht mir gut.
ice [aɪs] Eis • **ice-cream** [ˌaɪs'kriːm] (Speise-)Eis • **ice-hockey** ['aɪs hɒki] Eishockey **ice skating** ['aɪs skeɪtɪŋ] *(das)* Eislaufen
idea [aɪ'dɪə] **1.** Idee, Einfall; **2. idea (of)** Vorstellung (von)
if [ɪf] wenn, falls • **if-clause** Nebensatz mit „if", „if"-Satz **as if** als ob • **even if** selbst wenn, auch wenn
ill [ɪl] krank • **illness** Krankheit
°**illustrate** ['ɪləstreɪt] illustrieren, mit Bildern/Zeichnungen versehen
imagine sth. [ɪ'mædʒɪn] sich etwas vorstellen • **imagination** [ɪˌmædʒɪ'neɪʃn] Vorstellungskraft, Fantasie
important [ɪm'pɔːtnt] wichtig
in [ɪn] in • **in there** dort drinnen • **in 1645** (im Jahre) 1645 • **in English** auf Englisch • **in fact** eigentlich, genau gesagt; in Wirklichkeit **in front of** vor • **in November** im November • **in the country** auf dem Land • **in the field** auf dem Feld/der Wiese/der Weide • **in the morning(s)/afternoon(s)/evening(s)** am Morgen, morgens / am Nachmittag, nachmittags / am Abend, abends **in the photo/picture** auf dem Foto/Bild • **in the sky** am Himmel • **in the street** auf der Straße • **in the world** auf der Welt • **go/come in** hineingehen/hereinkommen **work in television** beim Fernsehen arbeiten
°**incident** ['ɪnsɪdənt] Zwischenfall, Vorkommnis
include [ɪn'kluːd] (mit) einschließen, enthalten
Indian *(adj; n)* ['ɪndiən] **1.** indisch; **2.** Inder/in
indoor (activities) ['ɪndɔː] (Aktivitäten) im Haus
industry ['ɪndəstri] Industrie
information *(no pl)* [ˌɪnfə'meɪʃn] Information(en); Auskunft, Auskünfte
injury ['ɪndʒəri] Verletzung
inline skating ['ɪnlaɪn skeɪtɪŋ] *(das)* Inlineskaten
inside [ˌɪn'saɪd] **1.** *(adv)* drinnen; nach drinnen; **2.** *(prep)* innerhalb, im Innern (von); in (... hinein)
instruction [ɪn'strʌkʃn] Anweisung, Anleitung
instrument ['ɪnstrəmənt] Instrument
intelligent [ɪn'telɪdʒənt] klug, intelligent
interactive [ˌɪntər'æktɪv] interaktiv
interested ['ɪntrəstɪd]: **be interested (in)** interessiert sein (an), sich interessieren (für) **interesting** ['ɪntrəstɪŋ] interessant
international [ˌɪntə'næʃnəl] international
Internet ['ɪntənet] Internet **on the Internet** im Internet
°**interpret** [ɪn'tɜːprɪt] dolmetschen • °**interpreting** *(das)* Dolmetschen
interview ['ɪntəvjuː] **1.** Interview; **2.** befragen, interviewen
into ['ɪntə, *betont:* 'ɪntuː] in (... hinein)
invent [ɪn'vent] erfinden • **invention** [ɪn'venʃn] Erfindung **inventor** [ɪn'ventə] Erfinder/in
invite [ɪn'vaɪt] *(Gäste)* einladen **invitation** [ˌɪnvɪ'teɪʃn] Einladung
°**irregular** [ɪ'regjələ] unregelmäßig
island ['aɪlənd] Insel
issue ['ɪʃuː] (Streit-)Frage, Thema, Angelegenheit
it [ɪt] es *(bei Sachen und Tieren auch:* er, sie) • **its** [ɪts] sein, seine *(bei Sachen und Tieren auch:* ihr, ihre) • **It's me – Sita.** Ich bin es – Sita. • **It's my turn.** Ich bin dran. / Ich bin an der Reihe.
itself [ɪt'self] sich (selbst)
°**ivory** ['aɪvəri] Elfenbein

J

jacket ['dʒækɪt] Jacke; Jackett, Sakko
January ['dʒænjuəri] Januar
jar [dʒɑː] Glas, Topf
jazz [dʒæz] Jazz
jeans *(pl)* [dʒiːnz] Jeans
job [dʒɒb] Beruf, Arbeit, Job; Aufgabe • **do jobs** Arbeiten/Aufträge erledigen
jogging ['dʒɒgɪŋ] *(das)* Joggen, Jogging
join [dʒɔɪn] beitreten, eintreten in *(einen Verein usw.)*
°**joke** [dʒəʊk] Witz
journey ['dʒɜːni] Reise, Fahrt, Weg
judo ['dʒuːdəʊ] Judo
juice [dʒuːs] Saft
July [dʒu'laɪ] Juli
jump [dʒʌmp] springen
June [dʒuːn] Juni
junior ['dʒuːniə] Junioren-, Jugend-
just [dʒʌst] **1.** nur, bloß • **I'm just looking.** Ich sehe mich nur um. • **Just a moment!** Einen Moment mal (eben)! **just after/before 10.30** kurz nach/vor 10.30 **2.** einfach; **3.** gerade (eben), soeben • **just then** genau in dem Moment; gerade dann **4. just as tired (as you are)** genauso müde (wie du) • **just like** genau wie

K

keep* [kiːp] (be)halten • **keep sb./sth. away (from)** jn./etwas fern halten (von)
kept [kept] **1.** *si. past von „keep"*; **2.** *Part. Perf. von „keep"*
ketchup ['ketʃəp] Ketschup
keyboard ['kiːbɔːd] Tastatur
kick [kɪk] treten
kid [kɪd] Kind, Jugendliche(r)
kill [kɪl] töten
kilo ['kiːləʊ] Kilo(gramm) **2 kilos of meat** 2 Kilo Fleisch
kilometre ['kɪləmiːtə] Kilometer
kind [kaɪnd] freundlich, nett, gütig • **kindness** ['kaɪndnəs] Freundlichkeit, Liebenswürdigkeit
kind (of) [kaɪnd] Art, Sorte **What kind of ...?** Was für ein/e ...?
kindergarten ['kɪndəgɑːtn] Kindergarten; Vorschule
king [kɪŋ] König

kitchen ['kɪtʃɪn] Küche
kite [kaɪt] Drachen
knew [nju:] *si. past von „know"*
knife [naɪf], *pl* **knives** [naɪvz] Messer
knock [nɒk] klopfen, anklopfen
know* [nəʊ] **1.** wissen • **I don't know.** Ich weiß (es) nicht. °**How do you know?** Woher weißt du das? **2.** kennen
known [nəʊn] *Part. Perf. von „know"*
Kung Fu [ˌkʌŋ 'fu:] Kung-Fu

L

°**label** ['leɪbl] beschriften, etikettieren
°**ladder** ['lædə] *(die)* Leiter
lady ['leɪdi] Dame
lain [leɪn] *Part. Perf. von „lie"*
lake [leɪk] (Binnen-)See
land [lænd] **1.** (Fest-)Land; Grund und Boden; **2.** landen
language ['læŋgwɪdʒ] Sprache
large [lɑ:dʒ] groß, umfangreich
laser ['leɪzə] Laser
last [lɑ:st]: **last year** letztes Jahr, im letzten Jahr • **at last** schließlich, endlich
late [leɪt] spät; zu spät • **be late** zu spät sein/kommen **I'm late for school.** Ich komme zu spät zur Schule. **sleep late** lange schlafen **later** später
laugh [lɑ:f] lachen • **laugh at** lachen über; auslachen
lay [leɪ] *si. past von „lie"*
lazy ['leɪzi] faul, träge
lead* [li:d] führen, leiten
°**league** [li:g] Liga
learn [lɜ:n] lernen • **learn about** etwas erfahren über/von, etwas herausfinden über
leave* [li:v] **1.** (zurück)lassen, hinterlassen; verlassen • **leave a message** eine Nachricht hinterlassen • **leave school** von der Schule abgehen °**leave sth. out** etwas auslassen, etwas weglassen **2.** weggehen, abfahren
led [led] **1.** *si. past von „lead"*; **2.** *Part. Perf. von „lead"*
left [left] **1.** *si. past von „leave"*; **2.** *Part. Perf. von „leave"*
left [left] nach links; linke(r, s) **on the left** links, auf der linken Seite • **on your left** auf deiner Linken, links von dir
leg [leg] Bein
lemonade [ˌlemə'neɪd] Limonade
less [les] weniger
lesson ['lesn] Unterrichtsstunde • **lessons** *(pl)* Unterricht
let* sb. do sth. **(-tt-)** [let] jm. erlauben, etwas zu tun; jn. etwas tun lassen • **Let's swap.** Lass uns tauschen. / Tauschen wir. • **Let's go.** Auf gehts!
let [let] **1.** *si. past von „let"*; **2.** *Part. Perf. von „let"*
letter ['letə] **1.** Buchstabe; **2. letter (to)** Brief (an)
lettuce ['letɪs] (Kopf-)Salat
librarian [laɪ'breəriən] Bibliothekar/in • **library** ['laɪbrəri] Bibliothek, Bücherei
lie* [laɪ] liegen
life [laɪf], *pl* **lives** [laɪvz] (das) Leben • °**life-size** lebensgroß
lift [lɪft] (an-, hoch)heben
light* [laɪt] anzünden
light [laɪt] Licht, Lampe **traffic lights** *(pl)* ['træfɪk laɪts] Verkehrsampel
like [laɪk] wie • **just like** genau wie • **What's ... like?** Wie ist ...? • **Start like this: ...** Fang so an: ... • **like that** so
like [laɪk] mögen, gern haben °**What do you like about them?** Was magst du an ihnen? • **like sth. better/best** etwas lieber/am liebsten mögen • **like shopping** gern einkaufen gehen • **I'd like to go.** (= **I would like to go.**) Ich würde gern/möchte gehen. • **What would you like to do?** Was würdest/möchtest du gern machen?
line [laɪn] **1.** Zeile; **2.** Linie; U-Bahn-Linie; **3.** Reihe; **4.** (Telefon-)Leitung; °**5.** Leine, Schnur
link [lɪŋk] Verbindung **linking word** Bindewort
lion ['laɪən] Löwe
list [lɪst] **1.** auflisten, aufzählen; **2.** Liste
listen ['lɪsn] zuhören; horchen **listen for sth.** auf etwas horchen, auf etwas achten **listen to sb./sth.** jm. zuhören / sich etwas anhören **listener** ['lɪsnə] Zuhörer/in
lit [lɪt] **1.** *si. past von „light"*; **2.** *Part. Perf. von „light"*
litre ['li:tə] Liter • **2 litres of milk** 2 Liter Milch
little ['lɪtl] klein, jung • **a little** ein bisschen, ein wenig
live [lɪv] leben, wohnen °**What things can you live without?** Auf welche Dinge kannst du verzichten?
lives [laɪvz] *pl von „life"*
living-room ['lɪvɪŋru:m] Wohnzimmer
load [ləʊd] (auf-, ein)laden; beladen
local ['ləʊkl] örtlich, Lokal-; am/vom Ort
°**loch** [lɒx, lɒk] See *(schottisch)*
°**lock** [lɒk] Schleuse
lock [lɒk] abschließen • **locked** [lɒkt] abgeschlossen
Londoner ['lʌndənə] Londoner/Londonerin
lonely ['ləʊnli] einsam • **loneliness** ['ləʊnlɪnəs] Einsamkeit
long [lɒŋ] lang
look [lʊk] **1.** schauen, sehen **I'm just looking.** Ich sehe mich nur um. • **look at** anschauen, ansehen • **Look at the board.** Sieh an die Tafel. **look after sb.** sich um jn. kümmern, auf jn. aufpassen **look for** suchen **2.** aussehen • **Does this shirt look good on me?** Steht mir dieses Hemd?
loose [lu:s] locker, lose **break loose** sich losreißen, sich lösen
°**Lord** [lɔ:d] Lord *(engl. Adelstitel)* • °**Lord Mayor** [lɔ:d 'meə] *etwa:* Oberbürgermeister/in
lose* [lu:z] verlieren • **loser** ['lu:zə] Verlierer/in
lost [lɒst] **1.** *si. past von „lose"*; **2.** *Part. Perf. von „lose"*
lot: **lots (of)/a lot (of)** ['lɒts_əv, ə 'lɒt_əv] eine Menge, viel/e
loud [laʊd] laut
love [lʌv] **1.** lieben, sehr mögen **love shopping** sehr gern einkaufen gehen **2.** Liebe • **Love, ...** Viele liebe Grüße (von) ...
love [lʌv] null *(Tennis)*
lovely ['lʌvli] schön, herrlich, hübsch
lower ['ləʊə] herablassen, hinablassen
luck [lʌk]: **Good luck.** Viel Glück. • **You're lucky.** Du hast Glück. / Du bist gut dran. **Lucky you!** Du Glückspilz! **lucky day** Glückstag
lunch [lʌntʃ] Mittagessen **for lunch** zum Mittagessen **have lunch** Mittag essen **at lunch-time** mittags, zur Mittagszeit

M

machine [mə'ʃi:n] Maschine, Gerät
Madam ['mædəm]: **Dear Sir or Madam** Sehr geehrte Damen und Herren
made [meɪd] **1.** *si. past von „make"*; **2.** *Part. Perf. von „make"*
magazine [ˌmægə'zi:n] Zeitschrift
main [meɪn] Haupt- • **main clause** [ˌmeɪn 'klɔ:z] Hauptsatz

make* [meɪk] machen, bilden, bauen; zubereiten • **make notes** sich Notizen machen **make sb. do sth.** jn. dazu bringen, etwas zu tun; jn. zwingen etwas zu tun °**make sth. into sth.** etwas zu etwas machen • °**make sth. up** sich etwas ausdenken, etwas erfinden
make-up ['meɪkʌp] Make-up
man [mæn], *pl* **men** [men] Mann
many ['meni] viele • **how many?** wie viele?
map [mæp] Landkarte, Stadtplan
March [mɑːtʃ] März
mark [mɑːk] **1.** (Zeugnis-) Note, Zensur; **2.** Abdruck, Spur
market ['mɑːkɪt] Markt
marmalade ['mɑːməleɪd] (Orangen-)Marmelade
married ['mærid] verheiratet
mask [mɑːsk] Maske
match [mætʃ] **1.** Spiel, Wettkampf; **2.** Streichholz; **3.** zuordnen • °**Match the texts to the pictures.** Ordne die Texte den Bildern zu.
material [mə'tɪəriəl] Material, Stoff
Maths *(no pl)* [mæθs] Mathematik
May [meɪ] Mai
may [meɪ] dürfen • **May I help you?** Sie wünschen?
may [meɪ]: **He may be tired.** Vielleicht ist er müde. / Er könnte (vielleicht) müde sein.
maybe ['meɪbi] vielleicht
mayday ['meɪdeɪ] SOS-Ruf, Maydaysignal
mayor [meə] Bürgermeister/in °**Lord Mayor** [lɔːd 'meə] *etwa:* Oberbürgermeister/in
maze [meɪz] Irrgarten, Labyrinth
me [mi, *betont:* miː] mir; mich **It's me – Sita.** Ich bin es – Sita.
meal [miːl] Mahlzeit, Essen
mean* [miːn] **1.** meinen (= sagen wollen); **2.** bedeuten **mean something to sb.** jm. etwas bedeuten • **The name means nothing to me.** Der Name sagt mir nichts. / Ich kenne den Namen nicht. **meaning** ['miːnɪŋ] Bedeutung
meant [ment] **1.** *si. past von „mean"*; **2.** *Part. Perf. von „mean"*
meanwhile ['miːnwaɪl] inzwischen, währenddessen
meat [miːt] Fleisch
°**medical certificate** [ˌmedɪkl sə'tɪfɪkət] (ärztliches) Attest, Gesundheitszeugnis
meet* [miːt] sich treffen; *jn.* treffen • **Nice to meet you.** Freut mich, euch (dich/ Sie) kennen zu lernen. **meeting** ['miːtɪŋ] Treffen; Versammlung; Besprechung
mega ['megə] mega-; Mega-
°**member** ['membə] Mitglied
men [men] *pl von „man"*
°**menu** ['menjuː] Speisekarte
message ['mesɪdʒ] Botschaft, Nachricht • **leave a message** eine Nachricht hinterlassen **Can I take a message?** Kann ich (ihr/ihm) etwas ausrichten?
met [met] **1.** *si. past von „meet"*; **2.** *Part. Perf. von „meet"*
metal ['metl] Metall
metre ['miːtə] Meter
mice [maɪs] *pl von „mouse"*
microchip ['maɪkrəʊtʃɪp] Mikrochip
microwave ['maɪkrəweɪv] Mikrowelle, Mikrowellengerät
midday [ˌmɪd'deɪ] Mittags-; Mittagszeit
°**Midlands** ['mɪdləndz]: **the Midlands** Mittelengland
midnight ['mɪdnaɪt] Mitternacht
might [maɪt] könnte(n) vielleicht • **You might be right.** Du könntest Recht haben. / Vielleicht hast du Recht.
mile [maɪl] Meile *(= ca. 1,6 km)*
milk [mɪlk] Milch • **milk shake** ['mɪlk ʃeɪk] Milk-Shake
million ['mɪljən] Million
°**mime** [maɪm] vorspielen, pantomimisch darstellen • **mime group** Pantomimengruppe
°**Mind the spelling.** [maɪnd] Gib Acht auf die Schreibung.
mine [maɪn] meine(r, s)
mineral water ['mɪnərəl wɔːtə] Mineralwasser
°**mini-submarine** ['mɪni sʌbməˌriːn] Mini-U-Boot
minority [maɪ'nɒrəti] Minderheit
minute ['mɪnɪt] Minute
mirror ['mɪrə] Spiegel
miserable ['mɪzrəbl] unglücklich, elend; erbärmlich, armselig
Miss Hunt [ˌmɪs 'hʌnt] Fräulein/ Frau Hunt *(Anrede für unverheiratete Frauen)*
miss [mɪs] vermissen; verpassen, verfehlen • °**missing** fehlend • °**be missing** fehlen
mist [mɪst] Dunst, (feiner) Nebel
mistake [mɪ'steɪk] Fehler, Irrtum
mobile (phone) ['məʊbaɪl] Mobiltelefon, Handy
model ['mɒdl] **1.** **(-ll-)** nachbilden, modellieren; **2.** Modell, Modell-
modern ['mɒdn] modern
moment ['məʊmənt]: **at the moment** im Moment, gerade, zurzeit • **Just a moment!** Einen Moment mal (eben)!
Monday ['mʌndeɪ, 'mʌndi] Montag
money ['mʌni] Geld
monkey ['mʌŋki] Affe
monster ['mɒnstə] Monster, Ungeheuer
month [mʌnθ] Monat
mood [muːd] Laune, Stimmung • **be in a bad/good mood** schlechte Laune haben, in schlechter Stimmung sein / gute Laune haben, in guter Stimmung sein
more [mɔː] mehr, weitere **one more** noch ein(e), ein(e) weitere(r, s) • **not … any more** nicht mehr; kein(e, n) … mehr • **more important (than)** wichtiger (als)
morning ['mɔːnɪŋ] Morgen, Vormittag • **Good morning.** Guten Morgen. / Guten Tag. *(vormittags)* • **in the morning(s)** am Morgen, morgens **this morning** heute Morgen
most [məʊst] (der/die/das) meiste …; am meisten • **most kids/cars/…** die meisten Kinder/Autos/… • **(the) most important** (der/die/das) wichtigste …; am wichtigsten
mother ['mʌðə] Mutter
motor ['məʊtə] Motor **motorbike** ['məʊtəbaɪk] Motorrad
mountain ['maʊntən] Berg
mouse [maʊs], *pl* **mice** [maɪs] Maus
mouth [maʊθ] Mund
move [muːv] **1.** (sich) bewegen °**Move your counter.** Zieh deinen Spielstein. **2.** (um)ziehen • **move in** einziehen
Mr Snow ['mɪstə] Herr Snow
Mrs Snow ['mɪsɪz] Frau Snow *(Anrede für verheiratete Frauen)*
much [mʌtʃ] viel • **how much?** wie viel? • **How much is/are …?** Was kostet/kosten …? / Wie viel kostet/kosten …?
mud [mʌd] Schlamm, Matsch **muddy** schlammig, matschig
mum [mʌm] Mutti, Mama; Mutter
museum [mju'zɪəm] Museum
music ['mjuːzɪk] Musik
must [məst, *betont:* mʌst] müssen • **I must go now!** *(Briefschluss)* Ich muss jetzt Schluss machen! • **mustn't** ['mʌsnt] **(= must not)** nicht dürfen

my [maɪ] mein, meine
myself [maɪ'self] mir/mich (selbst)
mystery ['mɪstri] Geheimnis, Rätsel

N

name [neɪm] Name • **My name is ... .** Mein Name ist ... . / Ich heiße ... . • **What's your name?** Wie heißt du?
narrow ['nærəʊ] schmal, eng
nation ['neɪʃn] Nation, Volk **national** ['næʃnəl] national, National- • **nationality** [,næʃə'næləti] Staatsangehörigkeit, Nationalität
near (to) [nɪə] in der Nähe von, nahe (bei)
neck [nek] Hals
need [ni:d] brauchen, benötigen • **You needn't go.** Du brauchst nicht zu gehen. / Du musst nicht gehen.
neighbour ['neɪbə] Nachbar/in
nervous ['nɜ:vəs] nervös, aufgeregt
net [net] **1.** Netz; **2.** *kurz für „Internet"* • **network** ['netwɜ:k] (Wörter-)Netz, „Wörterspinne"
never ['nevə] nie, niemals
new [nju:] neu • **New Year** [,nju: 'jɪə] Neujahr • °**New Year's Eve** [,nju: jɪəz_'i:v] Silvester
news *(no pl)* [nju:z] Nachricht(en) • **newspaper** ['nju:speɪpə] Zeitung
next [nekst] **1.** nächste(r, s) *(zeitlich; Reihenfolge)* • **next Monday** (am) nächsten Montag • **next week** in der nächsten Woche, nächste Woche • **the next day** der nächste Tag; am nächsten Tag **Next, please.** Der Nächste / Die Nächste, bitte. **2.** als Nächstes
next to neben
nice [naɪs] schön, nett • **Nice to meet you.** Freut mich, euch (dich/Sie) kennen zu lernen.
nickname ['nɪkneɪm] Spitzname
night [naɪt] Nacht, (später) Abend • **at night** in der Nacht, nachts • **Good night.** Gute Nacht.
nil [nɪl] null • **one nil to Kingsway** eins zu null für Kingsway
no [nəʊ] **1.** nein; **2.** kein, keine **no one** niemand • **no one else** niemand anderes, sonst niemand • **That's no good.** Das geht nicht.
nobody ['nəʊbədi] niemand
noise [nɔɪz] Geräusch; Lärm **noisy** ['nɔɪzi] laut, lärmend
nominate ['nɒmɪneɪt] nominieren, vorschlagen
none [nʌn] keine(r, s)
normal ['nɔ:ml] gewöhnlich, normal
north [nɔ:θ] nördlich; (nach) Norden • **north-east** [,nɔ:θ'i:st] nordöstlich; (nach) Nordosten • **north-west** [,nɔ:θ'west] nordwestlich; (nach) Nordwesten • **to the north** im Norden • **a northbound train** ['nɔ:θbaʊnd] ein Zug Richtung Norden
nose [nəʊz] Nase
not [nɒt] nicht • **I'm not from Chester.** Ich bin nicht aus Chester. • **I'm not German.** Ich bin kein Deutscher / keine Deutsche. • **not ... any more** nicht mehr; kein(e, n) ... mehr **not (...) either** ['aɪðə, 'i:ðə] auch nicht; auch kein • **not (...) yet** noch nicht
note [nəʊt]: **make notes** sich Notizen machen • °**take notes** sich Notizen machen
nothing ['nʌθɪŋ] nichts
notice ['nəʊtɪs] bemerken
notice board ['nəʊtɪs bɔ:d] Anschlagtafel, schwarzes Brett
nought [nɔ:t] null
November [nəʊ'vembə] November
now [naʊ] nun, jetzt • **Now what?** Was nun?
number ['nʌmbə] Zahl, Ziffer **a small number of children** eine kleine Anzahl Kinder/von Kindern
nurse [nɜ:s] Krankenschwester, Krankenpfleger

O

o'clock [ə'klɒk]: **six o'clock** sechs Uhr
October [ɒk'təʊbə] Oktober
Odd word out [,ɒd wɜ:d_'aʊt] *etwa:* Das unpassende Wort raus
of [əv, *betont:* ɒv] von • **a picture of Chester** ein Bild von Chester • **a group of girls** eine Gruppe (von) Mädchen • **a small number of children** eine kleine Anzahl Kinder/von Kindern • **in groups of four** in Vierergruppen • **one of you** eine/r von euch • **both of you** alle beide; ihr beide • **the name of the street** der Name der Straße • **2 kilos of meat** 2 Kilo Fleisch • **2 litres of milk** 2 Liter Milch • **a piece of** ein Stück • **lots of/a lot of** eine Menge, viel/e • **think of** halten von, denken über
of course [əv 'kɔ:s] natürlich, selbstverständlich
off [ɒf] aus; von (... herunter/hinunter) • **off the hook** ausgehängt, nicht aufgelegt *(Telefon)* • °**off-road** [,ɒf 'rəʊd] abseits der Straßen **take off** ausziehen • **turn off the light** das Licht ausschalten
°**offer** ['ɒfə] anbieten
office ['ɒfɪs] Büro • **post office** Postamt
officer ['ɒfɪsə] Offizier/in • **police officer** Polizeibeamte(r)/Polizeibeamtin, Polizist/in
often ['ɒfn] oft
oil [ɔɪl] Öl • **oil rig** ['ɔɪl rɪg] (Öl-)Bohrinsel
old [əʊld] alt • **13-year-old** 13-jährige(r, s)
oldie ['əʊldi] Oldie
°**Olympic Games** [ə,lɪmpɪk 'geɪmz] Olympische Spiele
on [ɒn] auf • **on foot** zu Fuß **report/show/film on** Reportage/Show/Film über • **on and on** immer weiter • **on board the ship** an Bord des Schiffes • **on the beach** am Strand • **on the bus/train/plane** im Bus/Zug/Flugzeug **on the floor** auf dem Fußboden • **on the Internet** im Internet • **on the left** links, auf der linken Seite • **on the phone** am Telefon • **on TV/on the radio** im Fernsehen/im Radio • **on the right** rechts, auf der rechten Seite **on the River Elbe** an der Elbe **on the show** in der Show **on 12th January** am 12. Januar • **on Monday** am Montag • **on Mondays** montags, jeden Montag **on-screen** am Bildschirm **straight on** geradeaus weiter **turn on the light** das Licht einschalten
on top (of sth.) [ɒn 'tɒp] oben, obendrauf (auf etwas)
°**once** [wʌns] einmal
once: **at once** [ət 'wʌns] sofort, (so)gleich
one [wʌn]: **one more** noch ein(e), ein(e) weitere(r, s) **one of you** eine/r von euch **one morning/day** eines Morgens/Tages • **the first one** der/die/das erste • **the best ones** die besten • **no one** niemand • **one another** einander, sich (gegenseitig)
onion ['ʌnjən] Zwiebel
only ['əʊnli] nur, bloß; erst **the only boy/girl** der einzige Junge / das einzige Mädchen

onto ['ɒntə, *betont:* 'ɒntuː] auf (… hinauf)

open ['əʊpən] **1.** öffnen, aufmachen; sich öffnen; **2.** offen, geöffnet

opposite ['ɒpəzɪt] gegenüber (von)

or [ɔː] oder

orange ['ɒrɪndʒ] Apfelsine, Orange • **orange juice** Orangensaft

orchestra ['ɔːkɪstrə] Orchester

order ['ɔːdə] bestellen

order ['ɔːdə] Reihenfolge; (An-)Ordnung

ordinary ['ɔːdnəri] gewöhnlich, normal

organizer ['ɔːgənaɪzə] Organisator/in

°**orienteering** [ˌɔːriən'tɪərɪŋ] Orientierungslauf, -rennen

other ['ʌðə] andere • **the other** der/die/das andere, die anderen • **each other** einander, sich (gegenseitig)

our ['aʊə] unser, unsere

ours ['aʊəz] unsere(r, s)

ourselves [aʊə'selvz] uns (selbst)

out [aʊt] hinaus, heraus; draußen • **out there** dort draußen • **be out** weg sein, nicht da sein • **out and about** unterwegs, auf Achse • **out of** … aus … (heraus/hinaus) °**out of cardboard** aus Karton/Pappe

outdoor (activities) ['aʊtdɔː] (Aktivitäten) im Freien

outfit ['aʊtfɪt] Kleider, Kleidung

outside [ˌaʊt'saɪd] **1.** *(adv)* draußen; nach draußen **outside lights/walls/toilet** ['aʊtsaɪd] Außenbeleuchtung/Außenwände/Außentoilette **2.** *(prep)* außerhalb (von); aus (… heraus)

oval ['əʊvl] oval

over ['əʊvə] über, oberhalb von; mehr als • **all over the world** auf der ganzen Welt, überall auf der Welt • **over there** dort drüben, da drüben **be over** vorbei sein, zu Ende sein

overtake* [ˌəʊvə'teɪk] überholen

overtaken [ˌəʊvə'teɪkən] *Part. Perf. von „overtake"*

overtook [ˌəʊvə'tʊk] *si. past von „overtake"*

own [əʊn]: **your own room** dein/Ihr/euer eigenes Zimmer

P

pack [pæk] packen, einpacken

packet ['pækɪt] Paket, Päckchen; Packung, Tüte

page [peɪdʒ] (Buch-, Heft-)Seite • **on page 25** auf Seite 25 • **Open your books at page 5.** Schlagt Seite 5 auf.

paid [peɪd] **1.** *si. past von „pay"*; **2.** *Part. Perf. von „pay"*

pain [peɪn] Schmerz(en)

°**pair** [peə] Paar

Pakistani [ˌpɑːkɪ'stɑːni] Pakistani, Pakistaner/in

palace ['pæləs] Palast, Schloss

panic ['pænɪk] Panik

paper ['peɪpə] Papier

parade [pə'reɪd] Parade, Umzug

parents ['peərənts] Eltern

park [pɑːk] Park

parliament ['pɑːləmənt] Parlament • **the Houses of Parliament** *das Parlamentsgebäude in London*

part [pɑːt] Teil

partner ['pɑːtnə] Partner/in

party ['pɑːti] Party • **have a party** eine Party veranstalten, feiern

pass [pɑːs] vergehen, vorübergehen (Zeit)

passenger ['pæsɪndʒə] Passagier/in, Fahrgast

past [pɑːst] **1.** Vergangenheit; **2.** vorbei an, vorüber an; **3. half past eight** halb neun (8.30/20.30) • **quarter past eight** Viertel nach acht (8.15/20.15)

path [pɑːθ] Pfad, Weg

°**pause** [pɔːz] (Sprech-)Pause

pavement ['peɪvmənt] Gehweg, Fußweg

pay* (for) [peɪ] bezahlen

PE [ˌpiː‿'iː] **(Physical Education** [ˌfɪzɪkəl‿edʒu'keɪʃn]**)** Turnen, Sport(unterricht) *(in der Regel in der Halle)*

pea [piː] Erbse

peanut ['piːnʌt] Erdnuss

pen [pen] Füller

pence (p) *(pl)* [pens, piː] Pence

pencil ['pensl] Bleistift

pencil-case ['penslkeɪs] Federmäppchen

penguin ['peŋgwɪn] Pinguin

°**penicillin** [ˌpenɪ'sɪlɪn] Penizillin

penny ['peni] *kleinste britische Münze*

people *(pl)* ['piːpl] Leute, Menschen

per cent (%) [pə'sent] Prozent

perfect ['pɜːfɪkt] perfekt, einwandfrei, vollkommen; ideal

perhaps [pə'hæps, præps] vielleicht

person ['pɜːsn] Person

persuade sb. (to do sth.) [pə'sweɪd] jn. überzeugen (etwas zu tun)

pet [pet] Haustier

phone [fəʊn] **1.** anrufen; **2.** Telefon • **answer the phone** ans Telefon gehen • **on the phone** am Telefon • **phone box** Telefonzelle • **phone number** Telefonnummer

photo ['fəʊtəʊ] Foto • **in the photo** auf dem Foto • **take photos** Fotos machen, fotografieren

°**phrases** ['freɪzɪz] Ausdrücke

Physical Education [ˌfɪzɪkəl‿edʒu'keɪʃn] Turnen, Sport(unterricht) *(meist in der Halle)*

physics *(no pl)* ['fɪzɪks] Physik

piano [pi'ænəʊ] Klavier • **play the piano** Klavier spielen

°**pickpocket** ['pɪkpɒkɪt] Taschendieb/in

picnic ['pɪknɪk] Picknick

picture ['pɪktʃə] Bild • **a picture of Chester** ein Bild von Chester • **in the picture** auf dem Bild

piece [piːs]: **a piece of** ein Stück

pig [pɪg] Schwein

pink [pɪŋk] rosa, pinkfarben

pipe [paɪp] (Tabaks-)Pfeife °**Put that in your pipe and smoke it.** *(infml) etwa:* Lass dir das gesagt sein. / Schreib dir das hinter die Ohren.

pizza ['piːtsə] Pizza • **pizzeria** [ˌpiːtsə'riːə] Pizzeria

place [pleɪs] Ort, Platz, Stelle **place of birth** Geburtsort **take third place** den dritten Platz belegen

plan [plæn] **1. (-nn-)** planen **plan to do sth.** planen etwas zu tun **2.** Plan

plane [pleɪn] Flugzeug

plastic ['plæstɪk] Plastik, Kunststoff

plate [pleɪt] Teller

platform ['plætfɔːm] Bahnsteig, Gleis

play [pleɪ] **1.** spielen • **play the drums/the guitar** Schlagzeug/Gitarre spielen • **play a trick on sb.** jm. einen Streich spielen • **player** Spieler/in **2.** Theaterstück

please [pliːz] bitte *(in Fragen und Aufforderungen)*

pleased [pliːzd]: **be pleased (with)** zufrieden sein (mit), sich freuen (über)

plug [plʌg] Stecker

pm [ˌpiː‿'em]: **8 pm** 8 Uhr nachmittags/abends *(zwischen 12 und 24 Uhr)*

pocket ['pɒkɪt] Tasche *(an einem Kleidungsstück)* **pocket money** Taschengeld

poem ['pəʊɪm] Gedicht

point [pɔɪnt] **1.** Punkt; **2. point (at, to)** zeigen, deuten (auf) • **point sth. at sb.** etwas auf jn. richten

police *(pl)* [pə'li:s] Polizei
police officer Polizeibeamte(r)/Polizeibeamtin, Polizist/in • **police station** Polizeiwache, Polizeirevier
pollute [pə'lu:t] *(die Umwelt)* verschmutzen • **pollution** [pə'lu:ʃn] (Umwelt-)Verschmutzung
pony ['pəʊni] Pony
poor [pɔ:, pʊə] arm • **poor Trundle** der arme Trundle
pop [pɒp] Pop(musik)
popcorn ['pɒpkɔ:n] Popcorn
popular (with) ['pɒpjələ] beliebt (bei)
population [ˌpɒpju'leɪʃn] Bevölkerung, Einwohner(zahl)
°**porthole** ['pɔ:thəʊl] Seitenfenster, Bullauge
°**possible** ['pɒsəbl] möglich
post [pəʊst] Post(sendungen)
post office Postamt • **postbox** Briefkasten • **postcard** Postkarte • °**postman** Briefträger, Postbote
poster ['pəʊstə] Poster
potato [pə'teɪtəʊ], *pl* **potatoes** [pə'teɪtəʊz] Kartoffel
pound (£) [paʊnd] Pfund *(britische Währung)*
power ['paʊə] Strom, Energie
power station ['paʊə ˌsteɪʃn] Kraftwerk, Elektrizitätswerk
practice *(no pl)* ['præktɪs] Praxis, Übung(en)
°**practise** ['præktɪs] üben, trainieren
present ['preznt] **1.** Geschenk; **2.** Gegenwart
present sth. (to sb.) [prɪ'zent] (jm.) etwas präsentieren, zeigen, vorstellen • **presentation** [ˌprezn'teɪʃn] Präsentation, Darbietung, Vorstellung
presenter [prɪ'zentə] Moderator/in
pretty ['prɪti] hübsch
price [praɪs] (Kauf-)Preis
prince [prɪns] Prinz • **princess** [ˌprɪn'ses] Prinzessin
prison ['prɪzn] Gefängnis
prisoner ['prɪznə] Gefangene, Gefangener
prize [praɪz] Preis, Gewinn
problem ['prɒbləm] Problem
professor [prə'fesə] Professor/in
programme ['prəʊgræm] Programm, (Radio-, Fernseh-) Sendung
project ['prɒdʒekt] Projekt
°**pronunciation** [prəˌnʌnsi'eɪʃn] Aussprache
proof *(no pl)* [pru:f] Beweis(e), Nachweis(e)
proud (of sb./sth.) [praʊd] stolz (auf jn./etwas)
pull [pʊl] ziehen
pullover ['pʊləʊvə] Pullover
°**punctuation** [ˌpʌŋktʃu'eɪʃn] Zeichensetzung
°**Punjabi** [pʌn'dʒɑ:bi] Pandschabi *(im Pandschab – einer Gegend in Nordpakistan und Nordindien – gesprochene Sprache)*
pupil ['pju:pl] Schüler/in
push [pʊʃ] schieben, stoßen, drücken
put* **(-tt-)** [pʊt] legen, stellen, *(etwas wohin)* tun • °**Put that in your pipe and smoke it.** *(infml) etwa:* Lass dir das gesagt sein. / Schreib dir das hinter die Ohren. • **put down** hinstellen, hinlegen • °**put in** einsetzen • **put sth. on** etwas anziehen *(Kleidung)*
put [pʊt] **1.** *si. past von „put“;* **2.** *Part. Perf. von „put“*
puzzle ['pʌzl] Rätsel

Q

quarter past eight [ˌkwɔ:tə pɑ:st‿'eɪt] Viertel nach acht (8.15/20.15) • **quarter to nine** [ˌkwɔ:tə tə 'naɪn] Viertel vor neun (8.45/20.45)
queen [kwi:n] Königin
question ['kwestʃn] Frage
ask questions Fragen stellen
questionnaire [ˌkwestʃə'neə] Fragebogen
quick *(adj)* [kwɪk] schnell
quickly *(adv)* ['kwɪkli] schnell
quiet ['kwaɪət] ruhig, leise, still
quite [kwaɪt] ziemlich, ganz
quiz [kwɪz] Quiz, Ratespiel

R

rabbit ['ræbɪt] Kaninchen
race [reɪs] Rennen, (Wett-)Lauf
racing ['reɪsɪŋ] Rennsport
racism ['reɪsɪzəm] Rassismus
racist ['reɪsɪst] **1.** rassistisch; **2.** Rassist/in
radar ['reɪdɑ:] Radar
radio ['reɪdiəʊ] **1.** Radio • **on the radio** im Radio
2. Funk; Funkgerät
railway ['reɪlweɪ] Eisenbahn
rain [reɪn] **1.** regnen; **2.** Regen
rainy regnerisch
ran [ræn] *si. past von „run“*
rang [ræŋ] *si. past von „ring“*
rap [ræp] Rap *(rhythmischer Sprechgesang)*
rattle ['rætl] rütteln; klappern
RE [ˌɑ:r‿'i:] **(Religious Education)** [rɪˌlɪdʒəs‿edʒu'keɪʃn] Religion(sunterricht)
reach [ri:tʃ] erreichen
read* [ri:d] lesen • °**read out** vorlesen • **read sth. to sb.** jm. etwas vorlesen • **reader** Leser/in
read [red] **1.** *si. past von „read“;* **2.** *Part. Perf. von „read“*
ready ['redi] bereit, fertig
get ready sich fertig machen, sich bereitmachen
real [rɪəl] echt, wirklich
really ['rɪəli] wirklich
record [rɪ'kɔ:d] aufnehmen, aufzeichnen *(auf Band)*
recycle [ˌri:'saɪkl] wieder verwerten, wieder aufbereiten
recycling [ˌri:'saɪklɪŋ] Wiederverwertung, Wiederaufbereitung
red **(-dd-)** [red] rot
reggae ['regeɪ] Reggae
rehearsal [rɪ'hɜ:sl] Probe *(Theater, Film)*
relax [rɪ'læks] (sich) entspannen, sich ausruhen
Religious Education [rɪˌlɪdʒəs‿edʒu'keɪʃn] Religion(sunterricht)
remark [rɪ'mɑ:k] Bemerkung
remember sth. [rɪ'membə] sich an etwas erinnern; an etwas denken, sich etwas merken
°**repeat** [rɪ'pi:t] wiederholen
report [rɪ'pɔ:t] **1.** berichten, melden; **2. report (on)** Bericht, Reportage (über)
reporter Reporter/in
rescue ['reskju:] retten; befreien
°**rest** [rest] Rest
restaurant ['restrɒnt] Restaurant • **at the restaurant** im Restaurant
°**result** [rɪ'zʌlt] Ergebnis
retell* [ˌri:'tel] nacherzählen
retold [ˌri:'təʊld] *Part. Perf. von „retell“*
retold [ˌri:'təʊld] *si. past von „retell“*
return [rɪ'tɜ:n] **1.** zurückkehren; zurücksenden, -bringen; **2.** Rückkehr, Wiederkehr
revision [rɪ'vɪʒn] Wiederholung *(des Lernstoffs)*
revolution [ˌrevə'lu:ʃn] Revolution
rhyme [raɪm] Reim
ridden ['rɪdn] *Part. Perf. von „ride“*
ride* [raɪd] **1.** reiten; **2. ride a bike** Rad fahren • **Let's ride our bikes to school.** Lass(t) uns mit dem Rad zur Schule fahren. • **riding** *(das)* Reiten, Reitsport
3. bike ride Radfahrt, Radtour
rig ['ɔɪl rɪg]: **oil rig** (Öl-)Bohrinsel
right [raɪt] **1.** richtig • **You're right.** Stimmt. / Du hast Recht. **Right, Debbie?** Nicht wahr, Debbie? • **all right** gut, in Ordnung, okay

2. nach rechts; rechte(r, s) **on the right** rechts, auf der rechten Seite • **on your right** auf deiner Rechten, rechts von dir
ring* [rɪŋ] klingeln, läuten; anrufen
rise* [raɪz] (an-, auf)steigen; aufgehen *(Sonne)*
risen ['rɪzn] *Part. Perf. von „rise"*
rival ['raɪvl] Rivale, Rivalin; Konkurrent/in
river ['rɪvə] Fluss • **on the River Elbe** an der Elbe
road [rəʊd] Straße, Landstraße **road sign** Verkehrszeichen
robot ['rəʊbɒt] Roboter
rock [rɒk] 1. Fels, Felsen; 2. Rock(musik)
rode [rəʊd] *si. past von „ride"*
role [rəʊl] Rolle • **role-play** Rollenspiel
roll over [ˌrəʊl_'əʊvə] sich (auf den Rücken) drehen, umkippen
room [ru:m] Zimmer, Raum
rope [rəʊp] Seil
rose [rəʊz] *si. past von „rise"*
round [raʊnd] 1. rund; 2. um … (herum) • **the wrong way round** verkehrt herum **come round** vorbeischauen, vorbeikommen
route [ru:t] Route, Strecke
rubber ['rʌbə] Radiergummi
rubbish ['rʌbɪʃ] 1. Abfall, Müll; 2. *(infml)* Quatsch, Blödsinn
rucksack ['rʌksæk] Rucksack
rude [ru:d] unhöflich, grob
rugby ['rʌgbi] Rugby
rule [ru:l] Regel, Vorschrift
ruler ['ru:lə] Lineal
run* (-nn-) [rʌn] laufen, rennen • **run after sb.** hinter jm. herrennen • **run around** umherrennen, herumrennen °**run for the try** *etwa:* versuchen Punkte zu erzielen **running** *(das)* Laufen
run [rʌn] *Part. Perf. von „run"*
rung [rʌŋ] *Part. Perf. von „ring"*

S

°sabotage ['sæbətɑ:ʒ] sabotieren • °**saboteur** [ˌsæbə'tɜ:] Saboteur/in
sad (-dd-) [sæd] traurig • **sadness** ['sædnəs] Traurigkeit
safe [seɪf] sicher, gefahrlos **safety** ['seɪfti] Sicherheit
said [sed] 1. *si. past von „say"*; 2. *Part. Perf. von „say"*
sail [seɪl] segeln • **sailor** ['seɪlə] Seemann, Matrose
salad ['sæləd] Salat *(als Gericht oder Beilage)*
salami [sə'lɑ:mi] Salami
same [seɪm]: **the same** der-/die-/dasselbe, dieselben
°samosa [sə'məʊsə] *dreieckige Teigtaschen mit würziger Gemüse- oder Fleischfüllung*
sanctuary ['sæŋktʃuəri] (Natur-, Tier-, Vogel-)Schutzgebiet
sandal ['sændl] Sandale
sandwich ['sænwɪdʒ] *(zusammengeklapptes)* belegtes Brot, Sandwich
sang [sæŋ] *si. past von „sing"*
sank [sæŋk] *si. past von „sink"*
°sari ['sɑ:ri] Sari *(besonders von indischen Frauen getragenes Kleidungsstück)*
sat [sæt] 1. *si. past von „sit"*; 2. *Part. Perf. von „sit"*
Saturday ['sætədeɪ, 'sætədi] Samstag, Sonnabend
sausage ['sɒsɪdʒ] (Brat-, Bock-) Würstchen, Wurst
save [seɪv] retten • **save sb. from sth.** jn. vor etwas retten **save the day** die Situation retten, der Retter sein *(in einer bestimmten Situation)*
saw [sɔ:] *si. past von „see"*
say* [seɪ] sagen • **you say** du sagst / man sagt
scan (-nn-) [skæn] 1. (ein-) scannen; 2. *(einen Text)* überfliegen *(um bestimmte Informationen zu finden)*
scared [skeəd]: **be scared (about; of)** Angst haben (wegen; vor)
scarf [skɑ:f], *pl* **scarves** [skɑ:vz] Schal
scary ['skeəri] unheimlich, gruselig
school [sku:l] Schule • **at school** in der Schule • **leave school** von der Schule abgehen • **school bag** Schultasche • **school subject** Schulfach
science ['saɪəns] (Natur-) Wissenschaft
scissors *(pl)* ['sɪzəz] *(eine)* Schere
score [skɔ:] Spielstand, (Spiel-) Ergebnis, Punktestand
Scotsman/Scotswoman ['skɒtsmən/'skɒtswʊmən] Schotte/Schottin
Scottish-American [ˌskɒtɪʃ_ə'merɪkən] Amerikaner/in schottischer Herkunft
scrapbook ['skræpbʊk] Sammelalbum
scream [skri:m] 1. schreien, kreischen; 2. Schrei
screen [skri:n] Bildschirm; Leinwand • **on-screen** [ˌɒn'skri:n] am Bildschirm
script [skrɪpt] Drehbuch
sea [si:] Meer, *(die)* See • **at sea** auf See
sea lion ['si: laɪən] Seelöwe
seal [si:l] Robbe, Seehund
search (for) [sɜ:tʃ] 1. suchen (nach), durchsuchen; 2. Suche (nach), Durchsuchung
second ['sekənd] 1. Sekunde; 2. zweite(r, s) • **secondly, …** zweitens … • **second-hand shop** Secondhandshop
°Secret Service [ˌsi:krət 'sɜ:vɪs] Geheimdienst
secretary ['sekrətri] Sekretär/in °**secretary general** [ˌsekrətri: 'dʒenrəl] Generalsekretär/in
section ['sekʃn] Abschnitt, Teil
see* [si:] 1. sehen • **see the sights** sich die Sehenswürdigkeiten ansehen • **See you.** Tschüs. / Bis bald. / Bis dann. **I see!** Ich verstehe! / Aha! / Ach so! • **you see** weißt du, nämlich • **wait and see** abwarten
2. besuchen, aufsuchen
seem (to be/do) [si:m] (zu sein/tun) scheinen
seen [si:n] *Part. Perf. von „see"*
sell* [sel] verkaufen
send* (to) [send] schicken, senden (an)
sent [sent] 1. *si. past von „send"*; 2. *Part. Perf. von „send"*
sentence ['sentəns] Satz
September [sep'tembə] September
service ['sɜ:vɪs] Dienst, Service
°set [set] Bühnenbild, Kulisse
set* sth. up (-tt-) [ˌset_'ʌp] etwas aufbauen, einrichten
set [set] 1. *si. past von „set"*; 2. *Part. Perf. von „set"*
shake* [ʃeɪk] zittern; schütteln
shaken ['ʃeɪkən] *Part. Perf. von „shake"*
she [ʃi, *betont:* ʃi:] sie
sheep, *pl* **sheep** [ʃi:p] Schaf
shelf [ʃelf], *pl* **shelves** [ʃelvz] Regal
shine* [ʃaɪn] scheinen; leuchten
ship [ʃɪp] Schiff
shirt [ʃɜ:t] (Ober-)Hemd
shocked [ʃɒkt] schockiert
shoe [ʃu:] Schuh
shone [ʃɒn] 1. *si. past von „shine"*; 2. *Part. Perf. von „shine"*
shook [ʃʊk] *si. past von „shake"*
shop [ʃɒp] 1. Laden, Geschäft; 2. (-pp-) einkaufen gehen **shopping** ['ʃɒpɪŋ] *(das)* Einkaufen; Einkäufe • **go to the shops/go shopping** einkaufen gehen • **do the shopping** einkaufen, Einkäufe machen/erledigen
shoplifter ['ʃɒplɪftə] Ladendieb/in
short [ʃɔ:t] 1. kurz; 2. klein *(Körpergröße)* • **short cut** ['ʃɔ:t kʌt] Abkürzung

shorts *(pl)* [ʃɔːts] Shorts, kurze Hose
should [ʃəd, *betont:* ʃʊd]: **it should be ...** es sollte ... sein
shout (at) [ʃaʊt] rufen, (an)schreien • **shout for help** um Hilfe rufen
show* [ʃəʊ] **1.** zeigen; **2.** Schau, Show; (Fernseh-, Radio-)Sendung • **on the show** in der Show/Sendung
shower ['ʃaʊə] Dusche; Regenschauer • **have a shower** (sich) duschen
shown [ʃəʊn] *Part. Perf. von „show"*
Shut up. [ˌʃʌt_'ʌp] Halt den Mund!
shy [ʃaɪ] scheu, zurückhaltend
side [saɪd] Seite
sights *(pl)* [saɪts] Sehenswürdigkeiten • **see the sights** sich die Sehenswürdigkeiten ansehen
sign [saɪn] Schild; Zeichen
road sign Verkehrszeichen
silly ['sɪli] albern, dumm
silliness ['sɪlinəs] Albernheit, Dummheit
sincerely [sɪn'sɪəli]: **Yours sincerely,** Mit freundlichen/herzlichen Grüßen
sing* [sɪŋ] singen • **singer** Sänger/in
sink* [sɪŋk] sinken, untergehen; versenken
Sir [sɜː]: **Dear Sir or Madam** Sehr geehrte Damen und Herren
sister ['sɪstə] Schwester
sit* **(-tt-)** [sɪt] sitzen; sich (hin)setzen • **Sit down.** Setz dich hin. / Setzt euch hin.
°**sitar** [sɪ'tɑː] Sitar *(indisches Saiteninstrument)*
situation [ˌsɪtʃu'eɪʃn] Situation
size [saɪz] Größe • **What size are you?** Welche Größe hast du / haben Sie?
ski-lift ['skiːlɪft] Skilift • **skier** ['skiːə] Skifahrer/in • **skiing** ['skiːɪŋ] *(das)* Skilaufen, Skisport
skill [skɪl] Fertigkeit, Fähigkeit
skirt [skɜːt] Rock
sky [skaɪ] Himmel • **in the sky** am Himmel
sleep* [sliːp] **1.** schlafen
sleep late lange schlafen
2. Schlaf
slept [slept] **1.** *si. past von „sleep"*; **2.** *Part. Perf. von „sleep"*
°**slogan** ['sləʊgən] Slogan, Werbespruch
slow [sləʊ] langsam
small [smɔːl] klein
smell [smel] riechen
smile [smaɪl] **1. smile (at sb.)** (jn. an)lächeln; **2.** Lächeln
smoke [sməʊk] rauchen
°**snack** [snæk] Snack, Imbiss
snake [sneɪk] Schlange
so [səʊ] **1.** deshalb, daher; also; **2.** so • **so lonely** so einsam
so soon so früh, so schnell
°**so far** bis hierher, bis jetzt
3. so (that) sodass, damit
Social Studies [ˌsəʊʃl 'stʌdiz] Gesellschaftslehre
sock [sɒk] Socke, Strumpf
sofa ['səʊfə] Sofa
solar ['səʊlə]: **solar energy** Sonnenenergie, Solarenergie
solar-powered mit Sonnenenergie betrieben
sold [səʊld] **1.** *si. past von „sell"*; **2.** *Part. Perf. von „sell"*
some [səm, *betont:* sʌm] einige, ein paar; etwas
somebody ['sʌmbədi] jemand
someone ['sʌmwʌn] jemand
someone else jemand anderes, sonst jemand
something ['sʌmθɪŋ] etwas
sometimes ['sʌmtaɪmz] manchmal
son [sʌn] Sohn
°**sonar** ['səʊnɑː] Sonar
song [sɒŋ] Lied
soon [suːn] bald • **so soon** so früh, so schnell • **sooner** eher, früher
sorry ['sɒri]: **Sorry. / I'm sorry.** Entschuldigung. / Tut mir Leid.
Sorry? Wie bitte? • **feel sorry for sb.** jn. bedauern
sort (of) [sɔːt] Art, Sorte
sound [saʊnd] **1.** klingen, sich *(gut/...)* anhören; **2.** Laut, Klang
°**sound engineer** ['saʊnd_endʒɪˌnɪə] Toningenieur/in, Tontechniker/in
south [saʊθ] südlich; (nach) Süden • **south-east** [ˌsaʊθ'iːst] südöstlich; (nach) Südosten • **south-west** [ˌsaʊθ'west] südwestlich; (nach) Südwesten • **to the south** im Süden • **a south-bound train** ['saʊθbaʊnd] ein Zug Richtung Süden
space [speɪs] (der) Weltraum; Raum, Platz
speak* [spiːk] sprechen
speaker Sprecher/in
special ['speʃl] **1.** besondere(r, s) • **be special** etwas Besonderes sein • **That was special about the family.** Das war außergewöhnlich an der Familie.
2. special (on) ['speʃl] Sonderprogramm, Sondersendung (über)
°**speech bubble** ['spiːtʃ bʌbl] Sprechblase
spell [spel] buchstabieren
spelling ['spelɪŋ] (Recht-)Schreibung, Schreibweise
spend* time/money (on) [spend] Zeit verbringen (mit) / Geld ausgeben (für)
spent [spent] **1.** *si. past von „spend"*; **2.** *Part. Perf. von „spend"*
spoke [spəʊk] *si. past von „speak"*
spoken ['spəʊkən] *Part. Perf. von „speak"*
spoon [spuːn] Löffel
sport [spɔːt] Sport, Sportart
do sport(s) Sport treiben
spot [spɒt]: **Spot the difference.** Entdecke den Unterschied.
spring [sprɪŋ] Frühling
square [skweə] Platz *(in einer Stadt)*
stadium ['steɪdiəm] Stadion
staff room ['stɑːf ruːm] Lehrerzimmer
stage [steɪdʒ] Bühne
stairs *(pl)* [steəz] Treppe; Treppenstufen
stall [stɔːl] Stand
stamp [stæmp] Briefmarke
stand* [stænd] stehen; sich (hin)stellen • **stand back (from)** zurücktreten (von); entfernt stehen (von)
star [stɑː] **1.** Stern; **2.** (Film-, Pop-)Star
start [stɑːt] anfangen, beginnen (mit) • **start a car** ein Auto anlassen, starten
°**statement** ['steɪtmənt] Aussage
station ['steɪʃn] **1.** Station; **2.** Bahnhof • **police station** Polizeiwache, Polizeirevier
power station Kraftwerk, Elektrizitätswerk
statue ['stætʃuː] Statue
stay [steɪ] bleiben; übernachten • **stay at a hotel** in einem Hotel übernachten
step [step] **1.** Stufe; **2.** Schritt
step by step Schritt für Schritt • **take a step towards sb.** einen Schritt auf jn. zugehen
stereo ['steriəʊ] Stereoanlage; Stereo
stick* [stɪk] kleben
sticker ['stɪkə] Sticker, Aufkleber
still [stɪl] **1.** (immer) noch; **2.** trotzdem, dennoch
stone [stəʊn] Stein
stood [stʊd] **1.** *si. past von „stand"*; **2.** *Part. Perf. von „stand"*
stop [stɒp] **1. (-pp-)** anhalten, stoppen; **2.** Halt; Haltestelle
bus stop Bushaltestelle
store room ['stɔː ruːm] Lagerraum
storm [stɔːm] Sturm; Gewitter
story ['stɔːri] Geschichte, Erzählung
straight on [streɪt_'ɒn] geradeaus weiter

stranger ['streɪndʒə] Unbekannte(r), Fremde(r)
street [striːt] Straße *(in einer Stadt)* • **in the street** auf der Straße
°**stress** [stres] Betonung °**stressed syllable** [ˌstrest 'sɪləbl] betonte Silbe
strict (with sb.) [strɪkt] streng (mit/zu jm.)
string [strɪŋ] Schnur, Bindfaden
strong [strɒŋ] stark
stuck [stʌk] 1. *si. past von „stick"*; 2. *Part. Perf. von „stick"*
studio ['stjuːdiəʊ] Studio
°**study** ['stʌdi] studieren, sorgfältig durchlesen
stuff [stʌf] *(infml)* Zeug, Kram
stupid ['stjuːpɪd] blöd, dämlich
subject ['sʌbdʒɪkt] (Unterrichts-)Fach
°**submarine** [ˌsʌbmə'riːn] U-Boot
suddenly ['sʌdnli] plötzlich, auf einmal
°**suggest** [sə'dʒest] vorschlagen
summer ['sʌmə] Sommer • **in (the) summer** im Sommer
sun [sʌn] Sonne • **sunny** sonnig
Sunday ['sʌndeɪ, 'sʌndi] Sonntag
sung [sʌŋ] *Part. Perf. von „sing"*
sunk [sʌŋk] *Part. Perf. von „sink"*
super ['suːpə] super, toll
supermarket ['suːpəmɑːkɪt] Supermarkt
suppose [sə'pəʊz] annehmen, vermuten
sure [ʃʊə, ʃɔː] sicher(lich) **Sure!** Sicher! / Natürlich! / Klar!
surfing ['sɜːfɪŋ] *(das)* Wellenreiten, Surfen • **go surfing** wellenreiten/surfen gehen
surprised (at) [sə'praɪzd] überrascht (über)
survey (of) ['sɜːveɪ] Umfrage, Untersuchung (über)
suspect ['sʌspekt] Verdächtige(r, s)
swam [swæm] *si. past von „swim"*
swap (-pp-) [swɒp] tauschen
sweatshirt ['swetʃɜːt] Sweatshirt
swim* **(-mm-)** [swɪm] schwimmen • **swimming-pool** ['swɪmɪŋpuːl] Swimmingpool, Schwimmbad • **swimming-trunks** *(pl)* ['swɪmɪŋtrʌŋks] Badehose • **swimsuit** ['swɪmsuːt] Badeanzug
swum [swʌm] *Part. Perf. von „swim"*
°**syllable** ['sɪləbl] Silbe
synthesizer ['sɪnθəsaɪzə] Synthesizer

T

table ['teɪbl] 1. Tisch • **table tennis** Tischtennis 2. Tabelle
°**tackle** ['tækl] angreifen, fassen
take* [teɪk] 1. nehmen; mitnehmen; (weg)bringen; 2. dauern, *(Zeit)* brauchen **take a break** eine Pause machen • **take a step towards sb.** einen Schritt auf jn. zugehen • **Can I take a message?** Kann ich (ihr/ihm) etwas ausrichten? • °**take notes** sich Notizen machen **take off** ausziehen *(Kleidung)* **take photos** Fotos machen, fotografieren • °**take the dog for a walk** mit dem Hund rausgehen • **take third place** den dritten Platz belegen °**take turns** sich abwechseln
taken ['teɪkən] *Part. Perf. von „take"*
talk (to) [tɔːk] reden (mit), sich unterhalten (mit)
tall [tɔːl] groß (gewachsen); hoch *(Bäume, Türme usw.)*
tape [teɪp] (Ton-)Band
tartan ['tɑːtn] Schottenstoff, Schottenmuster
taught [tɔːt] 1. *si. past von „teach"*; 2. *Part. Perf. von „teach"*
taxi ['tæksi] Taxi
tea [tiː] Tee
teach* [tiːtʃ] unterrichten, lehren • **teach sb. sth.** jm. etwas beibringen • **teacher** ['tiːtʃə] Lehrer/in
team [tiːm] Team, Mannschaft
technique [tek'niːk] (Arbeits-)Verfahren, Technik, Methode
technology [tek'nɒlədʒi] Technologie; Technik
teenager ['tiːneɪdʒə] Teenager, Jugendliche(r)
teeth [tiːθ] *pl von „tooth"*
telephone ['telɪfəʊn] Telefon **telephone box** Telefonzelle **telephone number** Telefonnummer
television ['telɪvɪʒn] Fernsehen; Fernsehgerät • **work in television** beim Fernsehen arbeiten
tell* **(about)** [tel] erzählen (von), berichten (über) **tell sb. the way (to)** jm. den Weg (zu/nach …) beschreiben
tennis ['tenɪs] Tennis
term [tɜːm] Trimester
terrible ['terəbl] schrecklich, furchtbar
test [test] 1. Test, Prüfung, Klassenarbeit; °2. testen, prüfen
text [tekst] Text

than [ðən]: **quicker than** schneller als
thank [θæŋk] danken • **Thank you.** Danke (schön). **thanks** danke • **Thanks a lot.** Danke vielmals. / Vielen Dank. • **thanks to Ben and Jenny** dank Ben und Jenny; wegen Ben und Jenny
that [ðət, *betont:* ðæt] 1. das (dort); jene(r, s) • **that afternoon/day/night** an jenem Nachmittag/Tag/in jener Nacht • **That's when we saw …** In dem Moment sahen wir … • **That's why …** Darum/ Deshalb … 2. dass • **so that** sodass, damit 3. der/die/das, die *(Relativpronomen)*
the [ðə] der, die, das; die **the 1980s** die Achtzigerjahre **the next day** der nächste Tag; am nächsten Tag • **the same** der-/die-/dasselbe, dieselben • **the two of them** die beiden; alle beide • **the wrong way round** verkehrt herum
theatre ['θɪətə] Theater
their [ðeə] ihr, ihre *(Plural)*
theirs [ðeəz] ihre(r, s)
them [ðəm, *betont:* ðem] sie; ihnen • **the two of them** die beiden; alle beide
themselves [ðəm'selvz] sich (selbst)
then [ðen] dann, danach **just then** genau in dem Moment; gerade dann
there [ðeə] da, dort; dahin, dorthin • **in there** dort drinnen • **out there** dort draußen • **over there** dort drüben, da drüben • **there are** es sind (vorhanden); es gibt • **there's** = **there is** es ist (vorhanden); es gibt
these [ðiːz] diese, die (hier)
they [ðeɪ] sie *(Plural)*
thief [θiːf], *pl* **thieves** [θiːvz] Dieb, Diebin
thin **(-nn-)** [θɪn] dünn
thing [θɪŋ] Ding, Sache
think* [θɪŋk] glauben, meinen, denken • **think (about)** nachdenken (über) • **think about/of** halten von, denken über • **think of** denken an, sich (aus)denken • **think hard** scharf/angestrengt nachdenken
third [θɜːd] dritte(r, s) **thirdly, …** drittens …
thirsty ['θɜːsti]: **be thirsty** durstig sein, Durst haben
this [ðɪs] diese(r, s); dies (hier) **this morning/afternoon/ evening** heute Morgen/

Nachmittag/Abend • **this way** 1. hier entlang; 2. so, auf diese Weise
those [ðəʊz] die (da), jene (dort)
thought [θɔ:t] 1. *si. past von „think"*; 2. *Part. Perf. von „think"*
threw [θru:] *si. past von „throw"*
through [θru:] durch
throw* [θrəʊ] werfen °**Throw the dice.** Würfle.
thrown [θrəʊn] *Part. Perf. von „throw"*
Thursday ['θɜ:zdeɪ, 'θɜ:zdi] Donnerstag
tick [tɪk] 1. mit einem Häkchen versehen, ankreuzen; °2. Häkchen
ticket ['tɪkɪt] 1. Eintrittskarte; 2. Fahrkarte, Fahrschein
tidy ['taɪdi] ordentlich, aufgeräumt • **tidy up** aufräumen
tie (to) [taɪ] (an)binden (an)
tiger ['taɪgə] Tiger
till [tɪl] bis
time [taɪm] 1. Zeit • **What time is it?** Wie spät ist es? **What time is the film?** Wann fängt der Film an? • **a long time ago** vor langer Zeit **all the time** immer, die ganze Zeit (lang) • **at the same time** zur gleichen Zeit • **free time** Freizeit, freie Zeit • **free time activities** Freizeitaktivitäten • **time phrase** Zeitangabe • **feeding times** Fütterungszeiten
2. **time(s)** Mal(e); -mal • **for the first time** zum ersten Mal **five times nought** fünf mal null
timetable ['taɪmteɪbl] 1. Stundenplan; 2. Fahrplan
tin [tɪn] Dose, Büchse
tired ['taɪəd] müde
title ['taɪtl] Titel; Überschrift
to [tə, *betont:* tu:] 1. zu, nach **I've been to Rügen.** Ich war (schon mal) in Rügen. / Ich bin (schon) in Rügen gewesen. **Welcome to ...** Willkommen in ... • **to the west/east/...** im Westen/Osten/... • **letter to** Brief an • **quarter to nine** Viertel vor neun (8.45/20.45) **3.50 to 5.30** 3 Uhr 50 bis 5 Uhr 30 • **from Monday to Friday** von Montag bis Freitag • **next to** neben **one nil to Kingsway** eins zu null für Kingsway • **listen to** *jm.* zuhören; sich *etwas* anhören • **talk to** reden mit, sich unterhalten mit
2. um zu
3. **try/plan/... to do sth.** versuchen/planen/... etwas zu tun • **He was the first ... to be ... .** Er war der erste ..., der ... war/wurde.
toast [təʊst] Toast(brot)
today [tə'deɪ] heute • **today's match** das heutige Spiel
together [tə'geðə] zusammen
toilet ['tɔɪlət] Toilette
told [təʊld] 1. *si. past von „tell"*; 2. *Part. Perf. von „tell"*
tomato [tə'mɑ:təʊ], *pl* **tomatoes** Tomate
tomorrow [tə'mɒrəʊ] morgen **tomorrow morning/afternoon/evening** morgen Vormittag/Nachmittag/Abend
tonight [tə'naɪt] heute Nacht, heute Abend
too [tu:] 1. auch • **I'm from Berlin, too.** Ich komme auch aus Berlin.
2. **too little** zu klein
took [tʊk] *si. past von „take"*
tool [tu:l] Werkzeug • **tool box** Werkzeugkasten
tooth [tu:θ], *pl* **teeth** [ti:θ] Zahn • **brush your teeth** sich die Zähne putzen
top [tɒp]: **on top (of sth.)** oben, obendrauf (auf etwas) °**at the top (of)** oben, am oberen Ende (von), an der Spitze (von) • °**on the top left** links oben • **top form** Höchstform
topic ['tɒpɪk] Thema, Themenbereich
tortoise ['tɔ:təs] Schildkröte
total *(n; adj)* ['təʊtl] 1. Gesamtbetrag, Summe; 2. Gesamt-
touch [tʌtʃ] berühren, anfassen
tour [tʊə] Tour, (Rund-)Reise
tourist ['tʊərɪst] Tourist/in
towards her [tə'wɔ:dz] auf sie zu, in ihre Richtung
tower ['taʊə] Turm
town [taʊn] Stadt • **town hall** [ˌtaʊn 'hɔ:l] Rathaus
toy [tɔɪ] Spielzeug
traffic ['træfɪk] Verkehr **traffic lights** *(pl)* ['træfɪk laɪts] Verkehrsampel
tragedy ['trædʒədi] Tragödie
train [treɪn] Zug
trainer ['treɪnə] Trainer/in
training ['treɪnɪŋ] Training, Ausbildung
tram [træm] Straßenbahn
°**translate** [træns'leɪt] übersetzen
transport *(no pl)* ['trænspɔ:t] Verkehrsmittel
travel (-ll-) ['trævl] reisen **travel agent** ['trævl‿eɪdʒənt] Reisebürokaufmann/-kauffrau; *hier auch:* Reisebüro
tree [tri:] Baum
trend [trend] (Mode-)Trend
trick [trɪk]: **play a trick on sb.** jm. einen Streich spielen
trip (to) [trɪp] Ausflug, Reise (nach, zu) • **go on a trip** einen Ausflug, eine Reise machen
trouble ['trʌbl]: **be in trouble** in Schwierigkeiten sein; Ärger kriegen • **trouble spot** *hier etwa:* Falle
trousers *(pl)* ['traʊzəz] (lange) Hose
true [tru:] wahr • **truth** [tru:θ] Wahrheit
try [traɪ] 1. versuchen, (aus-)probieren • **try hard** sich sehr bemühen, sich anstrengen • **try on** anprobieren *(Kleidung)* • **try to do sth. / try and do sth.** versuchen etwas zu tun
°2. „Versuch" *(Rugby: ähnlich einem Tor beim Fußball)* °**run/go for the try** *etwa:* versuchen Punkte zu erzielen
T-shirt ['ti:ʃɜ:t] T-Shirt
tube [tju:b]: **the tube** *(no pl)* *(infml)* die U-Bahn *(in London)* *(eigentlich:* Rohr, Röhre)
Tuesday ['tju:zdeɪ, 'tju:zdi] Dienstag
°**tune** [tju:n] Melodie
tunnel ['tʌnl] Tunnel
turn [tɜ:n]: 1. **turn (around)** sich umdrehen • **turn back** umkehren, kehrtmachen **turn right/left (into)** (nach) rechts/links abbiegen (in) **turn to sb.** sich jm. zuwenden; sich an jn. wenden
2. **turn on/off the light** das Licht ein-/ausschalten
3. **It's my turn (to write).** Ich bin an der Reihe (zu schreiben). • °**take turns** sich abwechseln
TV [ˌti:'vi:] Fernsehgerät; Fernsehen • **on TV** im Fernsehen • **watch TV** fernsehen
°**twice** [twaɪs] zweimal
twins [twɪnz] Zwillinge

U

umbrella [ʌm'brelə] Regenschirm
°**UN** [ju:‿'en] **(United Nations)** [juˌnaɪtɪd 'neɪʃnz] UN (Vereinte Nationen)
uncle ['ʌŋkl] Onkel
under ['ʌndə] unter • **go under** untergehen
underground ['ʌndəgraʊnd]: **the underground** *(no pl)* die U-Bahn
°**underline** [ˌʌndə'laɪn] unterstreichen • °**underlined** [ˌʌndə'laɪnd] unterstrichen
understand* [ˌʌndə'stænd] verstehen, begreifen

understood [ˌʌndəˈstʊd] **1.** *si. past von „understand"*; **2.** *Part. Perf. von „understand"*
underwater [ˌʌndəˈwɔːtə] unter Wasser; Unterwasser-
unfriendly [ˌʌnˈfrendli] unfreundlich
unhappy [ʌnˈhæpi] unglücklich
unhealthy [ʌnˈhelθɪ] ungesund
uniform [ˈjuːnɪfɔːm] Uniform
unimportant [ˌʌnɪmˈpɔːtnt] unwichtig
unit [ˈjuːnɪt] Kapitel, Lektion
°**United Nations** [juˌnaɪtɪd ˈneɪʃnz] Vereinte Nationen
university [ˌjuːnɪˈvɜːsəti] Universität, Hochschule
unkind [ˌʌnˈkaɪnd] unfreundlich
unpack [ˌʌnˈpæk] auspacken
unpopular [ʌnˈpɒpjələ] unbeliebt
unsafe [ʌnˈseɪf] unsicher, nicht sicher
untidy [ˌʌnˈtaɪdi] unordentlich, unaufgeräumt
until [ənˈtɪl] bis
up [ʌp] **1.** hinauf, herauf, nach oben • **up the tree** den Baum hinauf
2. oben
upset [ˌʌpˈset] aufgebracht, aufgeregt; betrübt
upside-down [ˌʌpsaɪd ˈdaʊn] verkehrt herum, auf dem Kopf
upstairs [ˌʌpˈsteəz] nach oben; oben
°**Urdu** [ˈʊəduː] Urdu *(in Pakistan und Indien gesprochene Sprache)*
us [əs, *betont:* ʌs] uns
use [juːz] gebrauchen, verwenden, benutzen
useful [ˈjuːsfl] nützlich
useless [ˈjuːsləs] nutzlos, zu nichts nütze
usually [ˈjuːʒuəli] meistens, gewöhnlich, normalerweise

V

valley [ˈvæli] Tal
van [væn] Lieferwagen, Transporter
vegetable [ˈvedʒtəbl] *(ein)* Gemüse
vegetarian [ˌvedʒəˈteəriən] Vegetarier/in
°**verse** [vɜːs] Vers
very [ˈveri] sehr
video [ˈvɪdiəʊ] Video • **video recorder** [ˈvɪdiəʊ rɪˌkɔːdə] Videorecorder
villa [ˈvɪlə] Villa, Ferienhaus
village [ˈvɪlɪdʒ] Dorf
violent [ˈvaɪələnt] gewalttätig, gewaltsam
virtual [ˈvɜːtʃuəl] virtuell *(nicht echt, aber echt erscheinend)*
visit [ˈvɪzɪt] **1.** besuchen; besichtigen; **2.** Besuch
vocabulary [vəˈkæbjələri] Vokabelverzeichnis, Wörterverzeichnis
voice [vɔɪs] Stimme
volleyball [ˈvɒlibɔːl] Volleyball
volunteer [ˌvɒlənˈtɪə] Freiwillige(r)

W

wait (for) [ˈweɪt fɔː] warten (auf) **wait and see** abwarten
waiter [ˈweɪtə] Kellner **waitress** [ˈweɪtrəs] Kellnerin
wake up* [ˌweɪk_ˈʌp] aufwachen; *jn.* (auf)wecken
walk [wɔːk] **1.** Spaziergang **go for a walk** einen Spaziergang machen • °**take the dog for a walk** mit dem Hund rausgehen
2. zu Fuß gehen; spazieren gehen • °**walk around** herumlaufen (in)
walkie-talkie [ˌwɔːki ˈtɔːki] Walkie-Talkie *(tragbares Funksprechgerät)*
walkman [ˈwɔːkmən] Walkman
wall [wɔːl] Wand; Mauer
°**wallpaper** [ˈwɔːlpeɪpə] Tapete
want [wɒnt] (haben) wollen **I want to go.** Ich will/möchte gehen. • **We want people to write lots of articles.** Wir möchten, dass die Leute viele Artikel schreiben.
wardrobe [ˈwɔːdrəʊb] Kleiderschrank
warm [wɔːm] warm
was [wəz, *betont:* wɒz]: **(I/he/she/it) was** *si. past von „be"*
wash [wɒʃ] waschen • **wash the dishes** das Geschirr abwaschen
watch [wɒtʃ] **1.** Armbanduhr; **2.** beobachten, sich *etwas* ansehen • **watch TV** fernsehen
water [ˈwɔːtə] Wasser
wave [weɪv] Welle
°**wavy lines** [ˌweɪvi ˈlaɪnz] Wellenlinien, Schlangenlinien
wax [wæks] Wachs
way [weɪ] **1.** Weg • **tell sb. the way (to …)** jm. den Weg (zu/nach …) beschreiben **Can you tell me the way to …?** Können Sie mir sagen, wie ich nach/zu … komme? **on my way (to)** unterwegs (nach/zu) • **go a long way** viel erreichen, viel bewirken
2. Richtung • **this way** hier entlang • **the wrong way** in die falsche Richtung • **the wrong way round** verkehrt herum
3. Art und Weise • **this way** so, auf diese Weise • **in different ways** auf verschiedene Weise(n) • °**different ways of reading** verschiedene Arten zu lesen
we [wi, *betont:* wiː] wir
wear* [weə] tragen, anhaben *(Kleidung)*
weather [ˈweðə] Wetter
website [ˈwebsaɪt] *alle Seiten eines Anbieters im World Wide Web*
Wednesday [ˈwenzdeɪ, ˈwenzdi] Mittwoch
week [wiːk] Woche • **next week** nächste Woche, in der nächsten Woche
weekend [ˌwiːkˈend] Wochenende • **at the weekend** am Wochenende • **at weekends** an Wochenenden • **Have a nice weekend.** Schönes Wochenende.
welcome [ˈwelkəm] **1.** willkommen • **Welcome to …** Willkommen in … • **You're welcome.** Bitte sehr. / Nichts zu danken. / Gern geschehen.
2. welcome sb. jn. willkommen heißen
well [wel] **1.** *(adj)* gesund; **2.** *(adv)* gut • **Well, …** Nun, …; Also, …
Welsh [welʃ] walisisch; Walisisch
went [went] *si. past von „go"*
were [wə, *betont:* wɜː]: **(we/you/they) were** *si. past von „be"*
west [west] westlich; (nach) Westen • **to the west** im Westen • **a westbound train** [ˈwestbaʊnd] ein Zug Richtung Westen
wet (-tt-) [wet] feucht, nass
what [wɒt] **1.** was; **2.** welche, welcher, welches? • **What kind of …?** Was für ein/e …? **Now what?** Was nun? **What about a calendar?** Wie wärs mit einem Kalender? **What about Jenny?** Was ist mit Jenny? / Und Jenny? **What are they talking about?** Worüber reden sie? **What is the letter about?** Wovon handelt der Brief? **What colour is it?** Welche Farbe hat es (er, sie)? • **What day is 1st January?** Was für ein Tag ist der 1. Januar? **What do you call this?** Wie nennt man dies? • **What's … like?** Wie ist …? • **What size are you?** Welche Größe hast du / haben Sie? • **What time is it?** Wie spät ist es? • **What time is the film?** Wann fängt der Film an? • **What's the date?** Welches Datum haben

wir? • **What's this in English?** Wie heißt das auf Englisch? • **What's your name?** Wie heißt du? / Wie heißen Sie?
whatever [wɒt'evə] was (auch) immer
wheelchair ['wi:ltʃeə] Rollstuhl
when [wen] **1.** wann • **When is it?** Wann fängt es an? **When's your birthday?** Wann hast du Geburtstag? **2.** wenn; **3.** als; nachdem **That's when we saw ...** In dem Moment sahen wir ...
whenever [wen'evə] wann (auch) immer
where [weə] wo; wohin **Where are you from?** Wo kommst du her?
wherever [weər'evə] wohin (auch) immer; wo (auch) immer
which [wɪtʃ] °**1. which group** welche Gruppe • **Which do you like best?** Welche(n, s) magst du am liebsten? **2.** der/die/das, die *(Relativpronomen)*
while [waɪl] während
whisper ['wɪspə] flüstern
white [waɪt] weiß
who [hu:] **1.** wer; **2.** wen/wem; **3.** der/die/das, die *(Relativpronomen)*
whoever [hu:'evə] wer (auch) immer, wen/wem (auch) immer
whole [həʊl] ganze(r, s), gesamte(r, s)
whose [hu:z] **1.** wessen **Whose are these (CDs)?** Wem gehören die (CDs) hier? **2.** deren, dessen *(Relativpronomen)*
why [waɪ] warum • **That's why ...** Darum/Deshalb ...
wife [waɪf], *pl* **wives** [waɪvz] Ehefrau
wild [waɪld] wild
will [wɪl]: **The world will be fantastic.** Die Welt wird fantastisch sein. • **You won't find many.** [wəʊnt] **(= You will not find many.)** Du wirst nicht viele finden.
win* [wɪn] **1. (-nn-)** gewinnen; **2.** Sieg • **winner** ['wɪnə] Gewinner/in, Sieger/in
wind [wɪnd] Wind • **windy** windig
window ['wɪndəʊ] Fenster
windsurfing ['wɪndsɜ:fɪŋ] *(das)* Windsurfen
winter ['wɪntə] Winter
wish [wɪʃ] **1.** wünschen; **2.** Wunsch
with [wɪð] mit (... zusammen), bei
without [wɪ'ðaʊt] ohne
witness ['wɪtnəs] Zeuge, Zeugin
wives [waɪvz] *pl von „wife"*
woke up [ˌwəʊk_'ʌp] *si. past von „wake up"*
woken up ['wəʊkən] *Part. Perf. von „wake up"*
woman ['wʊmən], *pl* **women** ['wɪmɪn] Frau
won [wʌn] **1.** *si. past von „win";* **2.** *Part. Perf. von „win"*
wonderful ['wʌndəfl] wunderbar
wood [wʊd] Holz
word [wɜ:d] Wort • °**word building** *etwa:* das „Bauen"/ Bilden von Wörtern • **word group** Wortgruppe • **word link** Wortverbindung °**word order** Wortstellung
wore [wɔ:] *si. past von „wear"*
work [wɜ:k] **1.** Arbeit • **at work** bei der Arbeit, am Arbeitsplatz **2.** arbeiten • **work on sth.** an etwas arbeiten **3.** funktionieren
world [wɜ:ld] Welt • **in the world** auf der Welt
worn [wɔ:n] *Part. Perf. von „wear"*
worried (about) ['wʌrid] beunruhigt (wegen), besorgt (wegen/um)
worry ['wʌri] **1.** Sorge, Kummer; **2. worry (about)** sich Sorgen machen (wegen, um) **worry sb.** jn. beunruhigen, jm. Sorgen machen
worse [wɜ:s] schlechter, schlimmer
worst [wɜ:st]: **(the) worst** (der/die/das) schlechteste, schlimmste ...; am schlechtesten, schlimmsten
would [wəd, *betont:* wʊd] würde, würdest, würden • **I'd like to go. (= I would like to go.)** Ich würde gern/möchte gehen. • **What would you like to do?** Was würdest/ möchtest du gern machen? **I would like my parents to buy me ... .** Ich möchte, dass meine Eltern mir ... kaufen.
write* (to) [raɪt] schreiben (an) **write on the board** an die Tafel schreiben • **write sth. down** etwas aufschreiben, notieren • **writer** Schreiber/in, Schriftsteller/in
written ['rɪtn] *Part. Perf. von „write"*
wrong [rɒŋ] falsch • **the wrong way round** verkehrt herum • **be wrong 1.** sich irren, Unrecht haben; **2.** nicht in Ordnung sein, nicht stimmen
wrote [rəʊt] *si. past von „write"*

Y

year [jɪə] Jahr; Jahrgangsstufe **a year and a half** eineinhalb Jahre, anderthalb Jahre **13-year-old** 13-jährige(r, s)
yellow ['jeləʊ] gelb
yes [jes] ja
yesterday ['jestədeɪ,-di] gestern
yet [jet]: **... yet?** ... schon ...? **not (...) yet** noch nicht
you [ju, *betont:* ju:] **1.** du; ihr; Sie; **2.** dich/dir; euch/euch; Sie/Ihnen; **3.** man • **You're welcome.** Bitte sehr. / Nichts zu danken. / Gern geschehen. **you see** weißt du; nämlich **How are you?** Wie geht es dir/euch/Ihnen? • **Thank you.** Danke (schön).
young [jʌŋ] jung
your [jɔ:] dein/deine; euer/ eure; Ihr/Ihre
yours [jɔ:z] deine(r, s); eure(r, s); Ihre(r, s) • **Yours,** dein(e)/ Ihr(e)/euer, eure *(Briefschluss)* **Yours faithfully** ['feɪθfəli] Mit freundlichen Grüßen / Hochachtungsvoll • **Yours sincerely,** Mit freundlichen/herzlichen Grüßen
yourself [jɔ'self, *betont:* jɔ:'self] dir/dich (selbst)
yourselves [jə'selvz, *betont:* jɔ:'selvz] euch (selbst)
°**youth hostel** ['ju:θ hɒstl] Jugendherberge
Yuck! [jʌk] Igitt! / Bäh!

Z

zebra ['zebrə] Zebra
zero ['zɪərəʊ] null
zoo [zu:] Zoo, Tierpark

Bildquellen

AA Photolibrary, Basingstoke (S. 25 links); Action Press, Hamburg (S. 21, Bild 6; S. 29); Anthony Verlag, Starnberg (S. 71, Bild 2); Anna Baker, York (S. 7 Mitte; S. 71, Bild 3, 6); Barnaby's Picture Library, London (S. 21, Bild 1; S. 38 rechts; S. 52 rechts; S. 117, Bild 4, Mitte;); Bavaria Bildagentur, Gauting (S. 19, Bild 3; S. 46, Bild 1, 2; S. 50 oben rechts; S. 71 Hintergrund; S. 71, Bild 4; S. 99 oben; S. 101 oben); Bavaria June, München (S. 40, Bild 4; S. 117, Bild 4, oben); Bavaria VCL, München (S. 40, Bild 2; S. 117, Bild 2, oben); John Birdsall, Nottingham (S. 51 unten; S. 60; S. 61); Bosch Pressebild, München (S. 35 oben links; S. 117, Bild 5, Mitte); Bradford Metropolitan City Council, Bradford (S. 62 rechts); Mike Brett Photography, Sale (S. 19, Bild 5; S. 21, Bild 2); Brian Brown Photography, Dover (S. 87); Britische Zentrale für Fremdenverkehr, Frankfurt am Main © BTA, (S. 53); Trevor Burrows Photography, Plymouth (S. 74); J. Allan Cash Photolibrary, London (S. 19, Bild 4, 6; S. 25 oben; S. 40, Bild 3, 5; S. 62 links; S. 117, Bild 3 oben, 5 oben; S. 59 Hintergrund; S. 97, rechts; S. 118, Bild 1); Anita Corbin, The Sunday Times, London (S. 37); Corbis-Bettmann, New York (S. 109); Crown Copyright, Historic Royal Palaces (S. 47, Bild 4; S. 102); Dartmoor National Park (S. 80); Karen Davies, Chester (S. 19, Bild 2); dpa, Frankfurt (S. 118, Bild 3); East Sussex Press, Crowborough (S. 46/47); The Edinburgh Photographic Library, Edinburgh (S. 38 links; S. 43; S. 44; S. 100/101); Omar El-Houni, London (S. 67); Angelika Fischer, Berlin (S. 8/9; S. 16; S. 32; S. 34/35; S. 86; S. 88); Format Photographers, London (S. 96 rechts); Fotex, Hamburg (S. 63, Mitte, rechts); John Fryer, Manchester (S. 94/95); HarperCollins Publishers, London (S. 68; S. 69); Tim Hetherington, London (S. 50 unten); IFA Bilderteam, Berlin (S. 40, Bild 1; S. 47, Bild 6; S.117, Bild 1, oben); Image Bank, Berlin (S. 21 Bild 5; S. 35 oben rechts, unten rechts; S. 71, Bild 1, 5; S. 117, Bild 2, Mitte); Impact (Geray Sweeney), London (S. 96 links); Ute Klaphake, London (S. 9 oben rechts; S. 52 oben); Fotoagentur Max Kohr, Berlin (S. 105); Bob Langrish, Bisley (S. 21, Bild 4); London Dungeon, London (S. 47, Bild 5; S. 118, Bild 6); London Regional Transport, London (S. 8 unten links; S. 48); Museum of Welsh Life, Cardiff (S. 97, links); Mike Macfarlane, Stanford in the Vale (S. 36 Mitte); Madame Tussaud's, London (S. 49); MOMI, London (S. 46, Bild 3; S. 118, Bild 4); Peter Newark's American Pictures, Bath (S. 106; S. 108); Okapia, Frankfurt/M. (S. 19, Bild 1); Clay Perry, The Sunday Times, London (S. 36 unten; S. 37; S. 117, Bild 1 Mitte, Bild 3 Mitte); Plimoth Plantation, Plymouth, MA (S. 107); Henrik Pohl, Berlin (S. 100/101 Shortbread); Redferns, London (S. 63 links; S. 98); River Dart Country Park Ltd., Ashburton (S. 113); Alasdair Smith, Aberdeen (S. 6 oben); Tim Smith, Bradford Festival (S. 59 links, Mitte, rechts); Sony, Köln-Ossendorf (S. 35 unten links); Sportsphoto Agency, Scarborough (S. 99 Mitte); Still Moving Picture Company, Edinburgh (S. 99 unten; S. 100 oben; S. 101 unten); Transglobe/TG Movie © Buena Vista International (S. 40, Bild 6; S. 117, Bild 6, oben); Wales Tourist Board, Cardiff (S. 25 unten rechts); Woodlands Country Park, Blackawton (S. 76); ZEFA, Hamburg (S. 21, Bild 3)
Umschlag: Mauritius, Berlin (Tower Bridge); Bavaria, Gauting (Bus)

Liedquellen

You've got a friend by Carole King. © 1971 by Colgmens–EMI Music Inc. USA.
D/A/CH/Osteuropäische Länder: EMI Music Publishing Germany GmbH, Hamburg
We are the Champions by Freddie Mercury. © by Queen Music Ltd.
D/A/CH/Osteuropäische Länder: EMI Music Publishing Germany GmbH, Hamburg
Maybe it's because I'm a Londoner by Hubert Gregg. © 1947 by Francis, Day & Hunter Ltd. London.
D/A/CH/Osteuropäische Länder: EMI Music Publishing Germany GmbH, Hamburg
We don't need another hero by Graham Lyle and Terry Britten. © by Myaxe Music Ltd./Good Single Ltd.
D/CH/GUS/Osteuropäische Länder: Neue Welt Musikverlag, München/Musikverlag Rondor GmbH, Hamburg
And you got the fucking nerve (To call me coloured) Music by Dennis-Pierre Sarratou, text by Thomas Carstanjen. © 1995 Neue Welt Musikverlag, München
Guns in the ghetto © EMI Virgin Music Inc.
D/A/CH/Osteuropäische Länder: EMI Virgin Music Publishing Germany GmbH, Hamburg

Textquellen

Seite 69: adapted from *Anita and Me* by Meera Syal. © 1996 Meera Syal. Reproduced by permission of the author c/o Rogers, Coleridge & White Ltd., 20 Powis Mews, London W11 1JN.
Out of the mouths of Babes by Kathryn Clarke. © The Telegraph plc, London, 1994

Nicht alle Copyrightinhaber konnten ermittelt werden; deren Urheberrechte werden hiermit vorsorglich und ausdrücklich anerkannt.

LIST OF NAMES

Girls / Women

Andrea ['ændriə, æn'dreɪə]
Angela ['ændʒələ]
Anita [ə'ni:tə]
Catherine ['kæθrɪn]
Diana [daɪ'ænə]
Doreen ['dɔ:ri:n]
Gwen [gwen]
Gwenllian ['gwenliən]
Juliet ['dʒu:liət]
Kathryn ['kæθrɪn]
Laura ['lɔ:rə]
Lisa ['li:sə]
Liz [li:z]
Maggie ['mægi]
Mandy ['mændi]
Marie [mə'ri:]
Mary ['meəri]
Meena ['mi:nə]
Megan ['megən]
Moira ['mɔɪrə]
Nazreen [næz'ri:n]
Ruth [ru:θ]
Selima [sə'li:mə]
Sheena ['ʃi:nə]
Susanna [su:'zænə]
Yasmin ['jæsmɪn]
Yvonne [ɪ'vɒn]
Zahida [zæ'hi:də]

Boys / Men

Aled ['æled]
Alex ['ælɪks]
Andrew ['ændru:]
Bert [bɜ:t]
Gareth ['gærəθ]
Gerry ['dʒeri]
Giles [dʒaɪlz]
Ian ['i:ən]
Jason ['dʒeɪsn]
Lee [li:]
Leroy ['li:rɔɪ, lə'rɔɪ]
Nathan ['neɪθən]
Rajiv [rɑ:'dʒi:v]
Robin ['rɒbɪn]
Rod [rɒd]
Romeo ['rəʊmiəʊ]
Ronald ['rɒnəld]
Rory ['rɔ:ri]
Stephen ['sti:vn]
Thomas ['tɒməs]
Tony ['təʊni]
William ['wɪljəm]
Winston ['wɪnstən]

Family names

Alsford ['ɔ:lsfəd]
Armstrong ['ɑ:mstrɒŋ]
Baird [beəd]
Barnes [bɑ:nz]
Bates [beɪts]
Burnett [bə'net]
Carver ['kɑ:və]
Chilton ['tʃɪltən]
Clarke [klɑ:k]
Evans ['evnz]
Gladstone ['glædstən]
Grant [grɑ:nt]
Hanson ['hænsn]
Hardy ['hɑ:di]
Herbert ['hɜ:bət]
Hopkins ['hɒpkɪnz]
Jenkins ['dʒeŋkɪnz]
Jessup ['dʒesəp]
Jones [dʒəʊnz]
Kumar [ku:'mɑ:]
Lal [lɑ:l]
Logan ['ləʊgən]
Maceba [mæ'si:bə]
Masters ['mɑ:stəz]
McGough [mə'gɒf]
McKenna [mə'kenə]
McKenzie [mə'kenzi]
McPherson [mək'fɜ:sn]
Mitchell ['mɪtʃəl]
O'Hear [əʊ'hɪə]
Owen ['əʊɪn]
Patel [pə'tel]
Picken ['pɪkn]
Porter ['pɔ:tə]
Rice [raɪs]
Roberts ['rɒbəts]
Ross [rɒs]
Rosser ['rɒsə]
Ruddock ['rʌdək]
Shaw [ʃɔ:]
Stewart ['stju:ət]
Tremaine [trɪ'meɪn]
Watson ['wɒtsn]
Wells [welz]
Winslow ['wɪnzləʊ]
Wong [wɒŋ]

Place names

Aberdeen [,æbə'di:n]
Acapulco [,ækə'pʊlkəʊ]
Anson Road [,ænsn 'rəʊd]
Ashburton [æʃ'bɜ:tn]
Atlanta [ət'læntə]
Aviemore ['ævimɔ:]
Baker Street ['beɪkə stri:t]
Bangor ['bæŋgə]
Bayswater ['beɪzwɔ:tə]
Birmingham ['bɜ:mɪŋəm]
Blackawton [blæk'ɔ:tən]
Bradford ['brædfəd]
Braemar [,breɪ'mɑ:]
Brecon Beacons National Park [,brekən 'bi:kənz ,næʃnəl 'pɑ:k]
Burghley Road [,bɜ:li 'rəʊd]
Camden ['kæmdən]
the Caribbean [,kærə'bi:ən]
Chiltern Edge School [,tʃɪltən_edʒ 'sku:l]
Cilcain [kɪl'keɪn]
Corris ['kɒrɪs]
Covent Garden [,kɒvnt 'gɑ:dn]
Culloden [kə'lɒdn]
Dart Country Park [,dɑ:t ,kʌntri 'pɑ:k]
Dartmoor ['dɑ:tmɔ:]
Dartmouth ['dɑ:tməθ]
Dean Street ['di:n stri:t]
Delhi ['deli]
Denbigh ['denbi]
Devon ['devn]
Downing Street ['daʊnɪŋ stri:t]
Euston Station [,ju:stən 'steɪʃn]
Fox Mire [,fɒks 'maɪə]
Frankfurt ['fræŋkfɜ:t]
Gerrard Street ['dʒerɑ:d stri:t]
Globe Theatre [,gləʊb 'θɪətə]
Great Mis Tor [,greɪt mɪs 'tɔ:]
Greenwich ['grenɪtʃ]
Hollywood ['hɒliwʊd]
Holne Park [,həʊln 'pɑ:k]
Inverness [,ɪnvə'nes]
Kentucky [ken'tʌki]
Lister Park [,lɪstə 'pɑ:k]
Loch Ness [lɒx 'nes]
Louisville ['lu:ivɪl]
Marylebone Road [,mærələbən 'rəʊd]
Monk Stone ['mʌŋk stəʊn]
Newton Abbot [,nju:tn_'æbət]
Norwich ['nɒrɪdʒ]
Notting Hill [,nɒtɪŋ 'hɪl]
Oamaru [əʊ'mɑ:ru:]
Paddington Station [,pædɪŋtən 'steɪʃn]
Plymouth ['plɪməθ]
Plymouth Hoe [,plɪməθ 'həʊ]
Portsmouth ['pɔ:tsməθ]
Princetown ['prɪnstaʊn]
Queensway ['kwi:nzweɪ]
Regent Street ['ri:dʒənt stri:t]
Shaftesbury Avenue [,ʃɑ:ftsbəri_'ævənju:]
Snowdonia [snəʊ'dəʊniə]
Sydney ['sɪdni]
Thames [temz]
Totnes ['tɒtnɪs]
Trinidad ['trɪnɪdæd]
Tufnell Park School [,tʌfnl ,pɑ:k 'sku:l]
Wardour Street ['wɔ:də: stri:t]
Waterlow Park [,wɔ:tələʊ 'pɑ:k]
Westminster Pier [,westmɪnstə 'pɪə]
Wolverhampton [,wʊlvə'hæmptən]

Other names

Alexander Fleming [ælɪg,zɑ:ndə 'flemɪŋ]
Alexander Graham Bell [ælɪg,zɑ:ndə ,greɪəm 'bel]
the All Saints [,ɔ:l 'seɪnts]
Anne Boleyn [,æn bə'lɪn]
Arsenal ['ɑ:snəl]
BBC [,bi: bi: 'si:], **British Broadcasting Corporation** [,brɪtɪʃ 'brɔ:dkɑ:stɪŋ kɔ:pə,reɪʃn]
Betty Burke [,beti 'bɜ:k]
Bonnie Prince Charlie [,bɒni prɪns 'tʃɑ:li]
Christopher Columbus [,krɪstəfə kə'lʌmbəs]
Flora Macdonald [,flɔ:rə mək'dɒnəld]
Henry VIII [,henri ði_'eɪtθ]
Hogmanay ['hɒgməneɪ]
Jackie Chan [,dʒæki 'kɑ:n]
James Thomson [,dʒeɪmz 'tɒmsən]
John Logie Baird [,dʒɒn ,ləʊgi 'beəd]
King Arthur [,kɪŋ_'ɑ:θə]
LaMont Humphrey [lə,mɒnt 'hʌmfri]
Lord Nelson [,lɔ:d 'nelsn]
Louis XVI (= Louis Seize) [,lu:i 'sez]
Madog ['mædɒg]
Marie-Antoinette [,mæri_æntwə'net]
Marie Tussaud [mə,ri: 'tu:səʊ]
Marilyn Monroe [,mærəlɪn mən'rəʊ]
Mayflower ['meɪflaʊə]
Meera Syal [,mɪərə saɪ'ɑ:l]
Mela ['meɪlə]
Moby Dick [,məʊbi 'dɪk]
Mohammed Ajeeb [məʊ,hæmɪd_ə'dʒi:b]
Paul McCartney [,pɔ:l mə'kɑ:tni]
Rowan Atkinson [,rəʊən_'ætkɪnsən]
Scoobidoo [,sku:bi'du:]
Sherlock Holmes [,ʃɜ:lɒk 'həʊmz]
Sir Christopher Wren [sə ,krɪstəfə 'ren]
Sir Francis Drake [sə ,frɑ:nsɪs 'dreɪk]
Sir James Watson-Watt [sə ,dʒeɪmz 'wɒtsn 'wɒt]
Squanto ['skwɒntəʊ]
Stephen King [,sti:vn 'kɪŋ]
William Shakespeare [,wɪljəm 'ʃeɪkspɪə]

COUNTRIES AND CONTINENTS (Länder und Kontinente)

Country/Continent	Person	People	Adjective
Africa ['æfrɪkə] *Afrika*	an African ['æfrɪkən]	the Africans	African
Albania [æl'beɪniə] *Albanien*	an Albanian [æl'beɪniən]	the Albanians	Albanian
America [ə'merɪkə] *Amerika*	an American [ə'merɪkən]	the Americans	American
Asia ['eɪʃə, 'eɪʒə] *Asien*	an Asian ['eɪʒn]	the Asians	Asian
Australia [ɒ'streɪliə] *Australien*	an Australian [ɒ'streɪliən]	the Australians	Australian
Austria ['ɒstriə] *Österreich*	an Austrian ['ɒstriən]	the Austrians	Austrian
Bangladesh [ˌbæŋglə'deʃ] *Bangladesch*	a Bangladeshi [ˌbæŋglə'deʃi]	the Bangladeshis	Bangladeshi
Belgium ['beldʒəm] *Belgien*	a Belgian ['beldʒən]	the Belgians	Belgian
Bosnia-Herzegovina [ˌbɒzniə ˌhɜːtsəgə'viːnə] *Bosnien-Herzegowina*	a Bosnian ['bɒzniən]	the Bosnians	Bosnian
Bulgaria [bʌl'geəriə] *Bulgarien*	a Bulgarian [bʌl'geəriən]	the Bulgarians	Bulgarian
(Great) Britain ['brɪtn] *Großbritannien*	a Briton ['brɪtn]	the British ['brɪtɪʃ]	British
China ['tʃaɪnə] *China*	a Chinese [ˌtʃaɪ'niːz]	the Chinese	Chinese
Croatia [krəʊ'eɪʃə] *Kroatien*	a Croatian [krəʊ'eɪʃən]	the Croatians	Croatian
the **Czech Republic** [ˌtʃek rɪ'pʌblɪk] *die Tschechische Republik*	a Czech [tʃek]	the Czechs	Czech
Denmark ['denmɑːk] *Dänemark*	a Dane [deɪn]	the Danes	Danish ['deɪnɪʃ]
England ['ɪŋglənd] *England*	an Englishman/-woman	the English ['ɪŋglɪʃ]	English
Europe ['jʊərəp] *Europa*	a European [ˌjʊərə'piːən]	the Europeans	European
Finland ['fɪnlənd] *Finnland*	a Finn [fɪn]	the Finns	Finnish ['fɪnɪʃ]
France [frɑːns] *Frankreich*	a Frenchman/-woman	the French [frentʃ]	French
Germany ['dʒɜːməni] *Deutschland*	a German ['dʒɜːmən]	the Germans	German
Greece [griːs] *Griechenland*	a Greek [griːk]	the Greeks	Greek
Hungary ['hʌŋgəri] *Ungarn*	a Hungarian [hʌŋ'geəriən]	the Hungarians	Hungarian
India ['ɪndiə] *Indien*	an Indian ['ɪndiən]	the Indians	Indian
Ireland ['aɪələnd] *Irland*	an Irishman/-woman	the Irish ['aɪrɪʃ]	Irish
Italy ['ɪtəli] *Italien*	an Italian [ɪ'tæliən]	the Italians	Italian
Jamaica [dʒə'meɪkə] *Jamaika*	a Jamaican [dʒə'meɪkən]	the Jamaicans	Jamaican
Japan [dʒə'pæn] *Japan*	a Japanese [ˌdʒæpə'niːz]	the Japanese	Japanese
the **Netherlands** ['neðələndz] *die Niederlande, Holland*	a Dutchman/-woman	the Dutch [dʌtʃ]	Dutch
New Zealand [ˌnjuː 'ziːlənd] *Neuseeland*	a New Zealander	the New Zealanders	New Zealand[1]
Norway ['nɔːweɪ] *Norwegen*	a Norwegian [nɔː'wiːdʒən]	the Norwegians	Norwegian
Pakistan [ˌpɑːkɪ'stɑːn] *Pakistan*	a Pakistani [ˌpɑːkɪ'stɑːni]	the Pakistanis	Pakistani
Poland ['pəʊlənd] *Polen*	a Pole [pəʊl]	the Poles	Polish ['pəʊlɪʃ]
Portugal ['pɔːtʃʊgl] *Portugal*	a Portuguese [ˌpɔːtʃu'giːz]	the Portuguese	Portuguese
Romania [ru'meɪniə] *Rumänien*	a Romanian [ru'meɪniən]	the Romanians	Romanian
Russia ['rʌʃə] *Russland*	a Russian ['rʌʃn]	the Russians	Russian
Scotland ['skɒtlənd] *Schottland*	a Scotsman/-woman, a Scot [skɒt]	the Scots, the Scottish	Scottish ['skɒtɪʃ]
Slovakia [sləʊ'vɑːkiə, sləʊ'vækiə] *die Slowakei*	a Slovak ['sləʊvæk]	the Slovaks	Slovak
Slovenia [sləʊ'viːniə] *Slowenien*	a Slovene ['sləʊviːn], a Slovenian [ɛləʊ'viːniən]	the Slovenes, the Slovenians	Slovenian, Slovene
Spain [speɪn] *Spanien*	a Spaniard ['spænɪəd]	the Spaniards	Spanish ['spænɪʃ]
Sweden ['swiːdn] *Schweden*	a Swede [swiːd]	the Swedes	Swedish ['swiːdɪʃ]
Switzerland ['swɪtsələnd] *die Schweiz*	a Swiss [swɪs]	the Swiss	Swiss
Turkey ['tɜːki] *die Türkei*	a Turk [tɜːk]	the Turks	Turkish ['tɜːkɪʃ]
the **United Kingdom** (the UK) [juˌnaɪtɪd 'kɪŋdəm, ˌjuː'keɪ] *das Vereinigte Königreich (Großbritannien und Nordirland)*	a Briton ['brɪtn]	the British ['brɪtɪʃ]	British
the **United States of America** (the USA) [juˌnaɪtɪd ˌsteɪts_əv_ə'merɪkə, ˌjuː_es_'eɪ] *die Vereinigten Staaten von Amerika*	an American [ə'merɪkən]	the Americans	American
Vietnam [ˌviːet'næm] *Vietnam*	a Vietnamese [viˌetnə'miːz]	the Vietnamese	Vietnamese
Wales [weɪlz] *Wales*	a Welshman/-woman	the Welsh [welʃ]	Welsh
Yugoslavia [juːgəʊ'slɑːviə] *Jugoslavien*	a Yugoslav ['juːgəʊslɑːv]	the Yugoslavs	Yugoslavian [juːgəʊ'slɑːviən]

[1] wird nur vor Nomen verwendet: *New Zealand sheep;* aber: *these sheep are from* New Zealand (nicht: *these sheep* ~~are New Zealand~~)

GRAMMATICAL TERMS (Grammatische Fachbegriffe)

			Summary-Abschnitt
adjective ['ædʒɪktɪv]	Adjektiv	*good, new, red, funny, boring*	
adverb ['ædvɜ:b]	Adverb	*always, badly, here, really, today*	
adverb of frequency ['fri:kwənsi]	Häufigkeitsadverb	*always, usually, often, sometimes, never*	
adverb of indefinite time [ɪn,defɪnət 'taɪm]	Adverb der unbestimmten Zeit	*already, always, before, ever, just, never, often, yet, not ... yet*	
adverb of manner ['mænə]	Adverb der Art und Weise	*badly, nicely, happily, terribly, electronically, fast, hard, well*	
article ['ɑ:tɪkl]	Artikel	*the, a/an*	
auxiliary [ɔ:g'zɪliəri]	Hilfsverb		
comparison [kəm'pærɪsn]	Steigerung; Vergleich	*tall – taller – tallest; boring – more boring – most boring* *easily – more easily – most easily*	
conditional sentence [kən,dɪʃənl 'sentəns]	Bedingungssatz	*If it rains, we won't see the mountains.*	**U2**: 2
conjunction [kən'dʒʌŋkʃn]	Konjunktion	*Let's play* ***when*** *you come home.* *Wash your hands* ***before*** *we eat.*	
contact clause ['kɒntækt klɔ:z]	Relativsatz ohne Relativpronomen	*That's the man* ***we met*** *last week.* *The bike* ***I got*** *is great.*	**U4**: 1
countable noun [,kaʊntəbl 'naʊn]	zählbares Nomen	*girl – girls, ruler – rulers*	**U4**: 2
defining relative clause [dɪ,faɪnɪŋ ,relətɪv 'klɔ:z]	bestimmender Relativsatz, notwendiger Relativsatz	*That's the girl* ***who helped me.*** *They invented a telephone* ***that really worked.***	**U3**: 1 / **U4**: 1
definite article [,defɪnət_'ɑ:tɪkl]	bestimmter Artikel	*the*	
future ['fju:tʃə]	Futur, Zukunft		
***going to*-future**	Futur mit *going to*	***I'm going to watch*** *TV tonight.* *Look at the clouds.* ***It's going to rain.***	**U7**: 1/2
***if*-clause** ['ɪf klɔ:z]	Nebensatz mit „if", „if"-Satz	***If it rains,*** *we won't see the mountains.*	**U2**: 2
imperative [ɪm'perətɪv]	Imperativ (Befehlsform)	***Open*** *your books.* ***Don't talk.***	
indefinite article [ɪn,defɪnət_'ɑ:tɪkl]	unbestimmter Artikel	*a/an*	
infinitive [ɪn'fɪnətɪv]	Infinitiv	*(to) open, (to) see, (to) hear*	**U5**: 2 / **U6**: 3
irregular verb [ɪ,regjələ 'vɜ:b]	unregelmäßiges Verb	*(to) go – went – gone*	
main clause [,meɪn 'klɔ:z]	Hauptsatz	*If it rains,* ***we won't see the mountains.***	**U2**: 2
modal auxiliary [,məʊdl_ɔ:g'zɪliəri]	modales Hilfsverb, Modalverb	*can, could, may, must, needn't, should, would*	
negative statement [,negətɪv 'steɪtmənt]	verneinter Aussagesatz	*I'm not ten. I haven't got a sister. I don't like pop songs.*	
noun [naʊn]	Nomen	*Nick, Debbie, girl, brother, time*	
object ['ɒbdʒɪkt]	Objekt	*Sita is cleaning* ***the kitchen.***	
object question	Objektfrage, Frage nach dem Objekt	*Who do they help? What did you eat?*	
past [pɑ:st]	Vergangenheit		
past participle [,pɑ:st 'pɑ:tɪsɪpl]	Partizip Perfekt	*climbed, saved, stopped, tidied, bought, fallen, gone, written*	
past perfect [,pɑ:st 'pɜ:fɪkt]	Plusquamperfekt, Vorvergangenheit	*Mike was late because he* ***had missed*** *the bus.*	**U6**: 4
past progressive [,pɑ:st prə'gresɪv]	Verlaufsform der Vergangenheit	*I* ***was washing*** *my hair at 8 o'clock yesterday evening.*	**U3**: 2
personal pronoun [,pɜ:snəl 'prəʊnaʊn]	Personalpronomen (persönliches Fürwort)	*I, you, he, she, it, we, they, me, him, her, us, them*	
plural ['plʊərəl]	Plural		
positive statement [,pɒzətɪv 'steɪtmənt]	bejahter Aussagesatz	*I'm ten. I've got a sister. I like pop songs.*	
possessive determiner [pə,zesɪv dɪ'tɜ:mɪnə]	Possessivbegleiter (besitzanzeigender Begleiter)	*my, your, his, her, its, our, their*	
possessive pronoun [pə,zesɪv 'prəʊnaʊn]	Possessivpronomen	*mine, yours, his, hers, ours, theirs*	

			Summary-Abschnitt
preposition [ˌprepəˈzɪʃn]	Präposition	*after, at, in, next to, on, to, under*	
present [ˈpreznt]	Präsens, Gegenwart		
present perfect [ˌpreznt ˈpɜːfɪkt]	*present perfect* (Perfekt)	*I've **packed** my bag. **Have** you **packed** yours? – Yes, I **have**.*	U1
present progressive [ˌpreznt prəˈgresɪv]	Verlaufsform der Gegenwart	*Debbie **is reading** a book. Nick **isn't reading**. He's **playing**. I'm **leaving** England tomorrow.*	U6: 2 / U7: 2
pronoun [ˈprəʊnaʊn]	Pronomen		
prop-word [ˈprɒpwɜːd]	Stützwort	*I've got three dogs, a black **one** and two brown **ones**.*	U2: 1
quantifier [ˈkwɒntɪfaɪə]	Mengenbezeichnung	*some, any; much, many, a little, a few*	U4: 2
question tag [ˈkwestʃən tæg]	Frageanhängsel	*Ann lives in Chester, **doesn't she?** But she isn't British, **is she?***	U6: 1
question word [ˈkwestʃən wɜːd]	Fragewort	*who?, what?, when?, where?, why?, how?*	
reflexive pronoun [rɪˌfleksɪv ˈprəʊnaʊn]	Reflexivpronomen	*myself, yourself, himself, herself, itself, ourselves, yourselves, themselves*	U5: 1
regular verb [ˌregjələ ˈvɜːb]	regelmäßiges Verb	*(to) help – helped – helped*	
relative clause [ˌrelətɪv ˈklɔːz]	Relativsatz	*That's the girl **who helped me**. They invented a telephone **that really worked**.*	U3: 1 / U4: 1
relative pronoun [ˌrelətɪv ˈprəʊnaʊn]	Relativpronomen	*who, that, which, whose*	U3: 1 / U4: 1
***s*-genitive** [ˈes ˌdʒenətɪv]	*s*-Genitiv	*Debbie**'s** brother; my teacher**'s** name*	
simple past [ˌsɪmpl ˈpɑːst]	einfache Form der Vergangenheit	*I **didn't go** to school yesterday. I **stayed** at home. **Did** you **go**?*	U1 / U6: 4
simple present [ˌsɪmpl ˈpreznt]	einfache Form der Gegenwart	*I **start** school at 8.45 every day. When **do** you **start** school? The next train to Leeds **leaves** in 10 minutes.*	U7: 2
singular [ˈsɪŋgjələ]	Singular		
sub-clause [ˈsʌbklɔːz], **subordinate clause** [səˌbɔːdɪnət ˈklɔːz]	Nebensatz	***If it rains**, we won't see the mountains. I can't come **because I'm ill**.*	
subject [ˈsʌbdʒɪkt]	Subjekt	***My dog** is black. **His name** is Tim.*	
subject question	Subjektfrage, Frage nach dem Subjekt	*Who helped you? What woke you up?*	
uncountable noun [ʌnˌkaʊntəbl ˈnaʊn]	nicht zählbares Nomen	*music, water, butter, money, homework, information*	U4: 2
verb [vɜːb]	Verb	*count, hear, open, rain, see*	
***will*-future**	Futur mit *will*	***I'll be** 13 next week. I'm thirsty. – **I'll make** you a cup of tea.*	U7: 1/3
word order [ˈwɜːd_ɔːdə]	Wortstellung		
yes/no question	Entscheidungsfrage	*Are you eleven? Have you got a sister?*	

LIST OF IRREGULAR VERBS

Infinitive	Simple past	Past participle	
(to) **be**	**was/were**	**been**	sein
(to) **beat**	**beat**	**beaten**	schlagen; besiegen
(to) **become**	**became**	**become**	werden
(to) **begin**	**began**	**begun**	beginnen, anfangen (mit)
(to) **blow**	**blew**	**blown**	wehen, blasen
(to) **break** [eɪ]	**broke**	**broken**	(zer)brechen; kaputtgehen
(to) **bring**	**brought**	**brought**	(mit-, her-)bringen
(to) **build**	**built**	**built**	bauen
(to) **buy**	**bought**	**bought**	kaufen
(to) **catch**	**caught**	**caught**	fangen; erwischen
(to) **choose** [uː]	**chose** [əʊ]	**chosen** [əʊ]	(aus)wählen, aussuchen
(to) **come**	**came**	**come**	kommen
(to) **cost**	**cost**	**cost**	kosten
(to) **cut**	**cut**	**cut**	(aus)schneiden
(to) **do**	**did**	**done** [ʌ]	tun, machen
(to) **draw**	**drew**	**drawn**	zeichnen
(to) **drink**	**drank**	**drunk**	trinken
(to) **drive** [aɪ]	**drove**	**driven** [ɪ]	*(ein Auto, einen Bus usw.)* fahren
(to) **eat**	**ate** [et, eɪt]	**eaten**	essen
(to) **fall**	**fell**	**fallen**	(hin)fallen
(to) **feed**	**fed**	**fed**	füttern
(to) **feel**	**felt**	**felt**	fühlen; sich fühlen
(to) **find**	**found**	**found**	finden
(to) **fly**	**flew**	**flown**	fliegen
(to) **forget**	**forgot**	**forgotten**	vergessen
(to) **get**	**got**	**got**	bekommen; holen, besorgen; gelangen, hinkommen
(to) **give**	**gave**	**given**	geben
(to) **go**	**went**	**gone** [ɒ]	gehen; fahren
(to) **grow**	**grew**	**grown**	wachsen
(to) **hang**	**hung**	**hung**	hängen, aufhängen
(to) **have (have got)**	**had**	**had**	haben
(to) **hear** [ɪə]	**heard** [ɜː]	**heard** [ɜː]	hören
(to) **hit**	**hit**	**hit**	schlagen, treffen
(to) **hold**	**held**	**held**	(fest)halten
(to) **hurt**	**hurt**	**hurt**	verletzen, wehtun
(to) **keep**	**kept**	**kept**	(be)halten
(to) **know** [nəʊ]	**knew** [njuː]	**known** [nəʊn]	wissen; kennen
(to) **lead**	**led**	**led**	führen, leiten
(to) **leave**	**left**	**left**	(zurück)lassen; verlassen; weggehen, abfahren
(to) **let**	**let**	**let**	(zu)lassen
(to) **lie** [aɪ]	**lay** [eɪ]	**lain** [eɪ]	liegen
(to) **light**	**lit**	**lit**	anzünden
(to) **lose** [uː]	**lost** [ɒ]	**lost** [ɒ]	verlieren
(to) **make**	**made**	**made**	machen
(to) **mean** [iː]	**meant** [e]	**meant** [e]	bedeuten; meinen, sagen wollen
(to) **meet**	**met**	**met**	(sich) treffen
(to) **overtake**	**overtook**	**overtaken**	überholen
(to) **pay**	**paid**	**paid**	bezahlen
(to) **put**	**put**	**put**	legen, stellen, *(wohin)* tun
(to) **read** [iː]	**read** [e]	**read** [e]	lesen
(to) **retell**	**retold**	**retold**	nacherzählen
(to) **ride**	**rode**	**ridden**	reiten; *(Rad)* fahren
(to) **ring**	**rang**	**rung**	klingeln, läuten; anrufen
(to) **rise**	**rose**	**risen**	(an-, auf)steigen; aufgehen *(Sonne)*
(to) **run**	**ran**	**run**	rennen, laufen
(to) **say** [eɪ]	**said** [e]	**said** [e]	sagen
(to) **see**	**saw**	**seen**	sehen; besuchen
(to) **sell**	**sold**	**sold**	verkaufen
(to) **send**	**sent**	**sent**	schicken, senden
(to) **set up**	**set up**	**set up**	aufbauen, einrichten

Infinitive	Simple past	Past participle	
(to) **shake**	**shook**	**shaken**	zittern; schütteln
(to) **shine**	**shone** [ɒ]	**shone** [ɒ]	scheinen; leuchten
(to) **show** [əʊ]	**showed** [əʊ]	**shown** [əʊ]	zeigen
(to) **sing**	**sang**	**sung**	singen
(to) **sink**	**sank**	**sunk**	sinken; versenken
(to) **sit**	**sat**	**sat**	sitzen; sich setzen
(to) **sleep**	**slept**	**slept**	schlafen
(to) **speak**	**spoke**	**spoken**	sprechen
(to) **spend**	**spent**	**spent**	*(Zeit)* verbringen; *(Geld)* ausgeben
(to) **stand**	**stood**	**stood**	stehen; sich (hin)stellen
(to) **stick**	**stuck**	**stuck**	kleben
(to) **swim**	**swam**	**swum**	schwimmen
(to) **take**	**took**	**taken**	(mit)nehmen; (weg)bringen
(to) **teach**	**taught**	**taught**	unterrichten, lehren
(to) **tell**	**told**	**told**	erzählen, berichten
(to) **think**	**thought**	**thought**	(nach)denken; glauben, meinen
(to) **throw**	**threw**	**thrown**	werfen
(to) **understand**	**understood**	**understood**	verstehen, begreifen
(to) **wake up**	**woke up**	**woken up**	aufwachen; (auf)wecken
(to) **wear** [eə]	**wore**	**worn**	tragen, anhaben
(to) **win**	**won** [ʌ]	**won** [ʌ]	gewinnen
(to) **write**	**wrote**	**written**	schreiben